ROUGH
MUSIC

ROUGH MUSIC

FOLK CUSTOMS, TRANSGRESSION AND ALTERNATIVE BRITAIN

Liz Williams

REAKTION BOOKS

Published by
REAKTION BOOKS LTD
Unit 32, Waterside
44–48 Wharf Road
London N1 7UX, UK
www.reaktionbooks.co.uk

First published 2025
Copyright © Liz Williams 2025

Printed and bound in Great Britain by Bell & Bain, Glasgow

A catalogue record for this book is available from the British Library

ISBN 978 1 83639 060 2

Contents

Introduction

Nothing says Christmas like opening your front door to find a man in a sheet wearing a horse's skull and demanding money. If this happened at your house and you weren't expecting it, it would be enough to give you a heart attack. Yet in parts of Wales, a century or so ago, this would be an entirely normal thing to happen at certain times of the year – for the grinning, shrouded visitor would be none other than the Mari Lwyd, the curious apparition that toured Welsh villages in the winter months, singing songs and snapping her skeletal jaws at the people she met. With the bearer beneath concealed by a sheet and the skull of a horse carried on top, with her mane of colourful streamers or her crown of holly and ivy, the Mari Lwyd seems to ride straight out of our pagan past: a midwinter spirit striding across the coldest months.

The Mari Lwyd is joined by many other odd figures following the wheel of the year and its festivals: the Obby Oss in Padstow, for instance, which gained notoriety in 2019 for accidentally striking nurse Laura Smallwood, who subsequently died of the resulting head injury. Jacks in the Green emerge from the cultural woodwork around May Day, accompanied by their leafy retinues of fools and bogies. In late autumn, children dress up as witches or zombies to celebrate Hallowe'en, and in many towns blazing barrels of tar are still driven through the streets prior to Bonfire Night firework displays. Across the country and throughout the year, health and safety regulations and basic sensible behaviour are valiantly defied: enormous cheeses are chased down near-vertical hills; annual town-centre football matches see scrums and skirmishes in English streets. Lengthy tug-of-war competitions spring up in front of ancient pubs, and Morris dancing, that love-it-or-hate-it activity, is familiar to everyone – or is it? Today, your local Morris side might be made up of young women in ravewear, if you're local to Stroud. Mumming and mummers are still going strong, along with occasional mystery plays in both their ancient and modern forms. Wassailing around Twelfth Night is undergoing a revival at farms in the southwest and elsewhere. And then there's worm charming, if you're down in Cornwall.

Many of these customs are beloved by both tourists and local communities, but what is it about them that makes them so durable? In our digital world of social media and big data, where children never seem to look up from their screens, what drives someone to join a Morris dancing side or don an enigmatic costume made out of an old table top, or walk through the streets on stilts, shrouded in greenery?

In this book, we're going to take a look at some of these customs, but with a twenty-first-century eye. We're going to consider what the enduring appeal of folk customs such as the Mari Lwyd and the Padstow Oss might be. We'll look at the history of the Bonfire Night revels and the origins of burning people in effigy, at street football matches and Morris dancing, at green men and skimmity rides. Where do these customs come from? Why did people celebrate them in the past, and what did they mean? Why do people participate in them now – and has their meaning changed?

Folklore is often seen as something timeless, a trigger for nostalgia and cosiness, a vision of twee Olde England, but we're going to face in this book some uncomfortable questions: about public shaming, threatening behaviour, coercion, bigotry and spite. For these aspects are part of those customs, part of their cultural context – not all customs, to be sure, and not the whole of them, for these matters are complex, but they do form a darker side that often gets swept under the cultural carpet, or written off as 'boys being boys' or 'traditional'. We'll visit more modern events in these pages, too: the gatherings at Stonehenge and their public fallout in the 1980s, their connections with the peace movement and the alternative fringe cultures of contemporary Britain. And, because this is such a big part of most people's lives today, we'll also be looking a little bit at social media.

We start with the Green Man and the Jacks in the Green that leap out of the woodwork around May Day. Where does the Green Man image come from, and how does it relate to guerrilla fighters and wild men?

Next, we consider the custom of the Mari Lwyd, which used to be common throughout the villages and communities of south Wales around Christmas and Twelfth Night. It's a Wassailing practice; that is, it follows the old practice of Wassail in which a band of people, sometimes accompanied by a figure in disguise, sing in exchange for food and drink. Recently, the custom of the Mari Lwyd has undergone a substantial revival, centred on the January celebrations in Chepstow but also undertaken in many other parts of Wales. We'll take a look at its origins, why it almost died out – and why it has been revived. The custom of the Mari Lwyd also seems linked to the annual south Welsh custom of the hunting of the wren – how are they connected, and how do they resemble other masked/guise customs? Wassailing itself is staging a comeback, too, and we're going to take a look at the history of this winter custom, both in the UK and, briefly, in the Americas. How transgressive are these practices, and how is this pattern of mock threat and demand licensed by the communities in which they appear?

Morris dancing is a familiar aspect of summer Bank Holiday celebrations. It is often seen as the classic folk custom, sometimes derided – like folk music – as rather naff. Where did it start, and how is it changing in response to more progressive social movements such as anti-racism and Black Lives Matter? Recently, Morris groups, known as 'sides', have appeared in the press mainly due to protests over the removal of blackface – but what is the actual origin of 'blacking up'? Is it connected to the Moors and to the history of Black Britain? How is it linked to the sweeps' parades of previous times? What about the cross-dressing version of Molly dancing? And how has Morris itself, in turn, been targeted by other legislation that might emerge from bigotry?

Throughout English history, the Devil appears in folk festivals and folklore in various guises. He carves huge gouges in the landscape, legend tells us, such as Devil's Dyke in Sussex. His alarming horned presence features in mystery plays and as comic relief in pageants, such as the demon Titivillus in the Wakefield or Towneley Mystery Plays, who comments satirically on human foibles. Is he the biblical Satan, however, or does he have different origins? We will take a look at the English devils, their role in plays and pageants, and their connections with other horned, masked figures in folklore.

From the mystery plays we move to one of the biggest festivals of the British year, and one of the most unique: Bonfire Night. We all know about gunpowder, treason and plot, and here we'll look at the ongoing history of lawlessness associated with 5 November and the many controversies that still surround its customs. We'll then take a look at fairs and festivals, and dive into the counterculture that has become an integral part of festivals since the 1960s, by visiting the infamous Battle of the Beanfield.

One of the weirdest English customs is surely the cheese rolling, which takes place every year at Cooper's Hill in Gloucestershire. We'll examine why it's so popular and, following on from this, we'll look at some of the many outbreaks of street football, some of them quite violent, which take place across the country at various times of the year. In addition, we visit the mock-Viking festival of Up Helly Aa in Shetland.

At Hallowe'en, there are often complaints about 'American' customs such as trick or treat – but are they really an import from the USA, or is there a home-grown version?

We'll also examine the old practice of charivari, or skimmity riding, and here we see a deviation from customs in which transgression is an emergent property (such as criminal behaviour at fairs) or a form of licensed expression (such as bonfire revels and street football). Charivari/skimmity riding is purely about shaming someone. 'Charivari' means 'a parade': a mock serenade using pots, ladles and pans rather than musical instruments. The word probably comes from Latin, deriving from ancient Greek, and the custom of the charivari is similarly an old one. It is also known as 'rough music', hence the title of this book, and it relates to public customs of humiliation and embarrassment, often centring around domestic violence. Men who beat their wives were subject to the charivari in the nineteenth century – but in earlier years the custom was directed at men who were considered to be henpecked. Thus the charivari is closely related to changing gender norms and to the violation of perceived societal order, and we will look at the laws around these issues as well as the gaps in those laws that allowed the charivari to occur – and that perhaps made it deemed to be a necessity. The charivari has died out in the twenty-first century – but has it really gone? Or has its spirit passed into the digital realm, to be incorporated into modern social media movements such as #MeToo?

Finally, we will make some predictions about the future of folk practice.

BEFORE WE BEGIN, we're going to take a quick look at what transgression and shame actually mean in this culture.

In the nineteenth century, for example, if you blacked your face to go Morris dancing, it is unlikely that this would generate censure from your neighbours, let alone from people who didn't know you. Nowadays, you'd be shamed across social media, because racism has come to the fore as a moral transgression, something for which it is acceptable to call people out. Centuries ago, mystery plays were attacked by some religious authorities because of the perceived blasphemy of a mortal man portraying Christ. This is something that would be unlikely to attract much criticism in modern Britain. When I was growing up in Gloucester in the 1970s, there was plenty of concern about the safety of the annual Cooper's Hill cheese-rolling competition, but if you mentioned the ethics of using a giant cheese, people would have thought you were mad (many still do!). In 2023, however, PETA implored the organizers to use a vegan cheese instead. Some customs are retained in their own proper season but change in their underlying nature, such as May Day, which has gradually become more counter-cultural since its revival in the twentieth century.

In our final chapter, I intend to take a look at the future of nostalgia, as well as a little bit about its history, but what we can say for certain is that there has never been a timeless, Platonic England in which Bonfire Night celebrations went merrily on with the full support of the local community, or in which town-wide football matches with a side-helping of violence took place and were welcomed by all. The customs at which we're going to look have always been developing and altering, right from the start. Like social morality, their only constant has been that of change and contention. Attempts to decry a sudden outbreak of 'wokeness' when applied to Morris dancing or Padstow's Oss or Bonfire Night therefore don't hold up to historical scrutiny: transgression runs right through them, like the pink letters in a stick of old-fashioned seaside rock, and so do public and private responses to that transgression. Folk customs have been well and truly dragged into the culture wars in the twenty-first century, but the fact is that they've never been outside this culture: they are embedded within it, and are therefore prone to its currents and tides, its ethical ebbs and flows.

The 'rough music' that we look at in this book, in the section on charivari, is primarily stigmatic. It's called 'rough' for a reason: this is not some example of sophisticated psychological treatment that seeks to reintegrate and rehabilitate the offender. It may be spontaneous or planned on the spur of the moment, or at best with little lead time, and quite often it isn't based on any sense of responsibility for the outcome, even if this might prove to be tragic, as in Hardy's famous account of a skimmity ride in *The Mayor of Casterbridge* in which the character of Lucetta dies. The kinds of customs here are purely to show someone, or several people, up.

Some of the practices used to enforce public shame gradually began to be regarded as humiliating, and thus eroding of public dignity. Flogging, branding and the pillory were all abolished by the mid-nineteenth century. But being shamed by one's peers, in the practices that we look at in this book, continued. In 1820s Bristol, blacklegs were tied to a mast and hauled around the city. Even as late as 1971, during the Northern Irish Troubles (1968–88), Catholic women who dated British soldiers ran the risk of being tied to streetlamps, having their hair cut off, and being tarred and feathered.

But publicly pointing out social transgressions these days carries risks. Accounts in the papers regarding road rage bears this out, and although the incidence of violent crime has actually been decreasing in recent years, paranoia and concern about becoming the victim of such a crime seems to be on the rise, fuelled in part by scare stories in the press. Shaming on social media seems safer – the 'keyboard warrior' phenomenon. But as we will see, the old charivari has not quite died out.

To break this down, throughout this book we will be looking at customs that are deliberately transgressive (such as Molly dancing); customs in which transgression is found as an emergent property (such as cheese rolling); customs that have been prone to transgressive behaviour but that are not in themselves transgressive (such as fairs); customs that have become transgressive, perhaps despite themselves, over time, because public morality has changed (such as blacking up in Morris dancing); customs that used to be transgressive, but that are no longer (such as those that flouted religious prohibitions in various forms of Christianity) or about which there was debate at the time (for example, Ronald Hutton cites William Kethe, an evangelist in Dorset who regarded dancing, drinking and blood sports as being wrong in themselves and tried to stop the church ales – not a locally popular move);[1] and customs which have been banned for an underlying reason, for example when May Day celebrations are banned ostensibly for licentious or violent behaviour, where the real concern is that they might provide cover for rebellion or dissent.

ONE

What Is Folklore?

Folklore is sometimes referred to as 'cultural DNA', and in an age that has become conscious of phenomena such as memes – ideas that spread from person to person and group to group – this is perhaps as good a way as any of looking at it. Folk customs may be seen as strands of practice: rarely unbroken, sometimes fraying, often transforming and changing, yet persisting down the ages to the present day. Some Victorian historians (James George Frazer, Margaret Murray, Jane Ellen Harrison and the members of the 'Cambridge School') and their academic descendants (Robert Graves) were enthusiastic supporters of what we might term the 'ancient roots' school of thought, in which the majority of folk customs in Britain (and elsewhere) are perceived as legacies of antique religions, featuring the death and resurrection of a fertility god. Modern readers may smile at the thought of Morris sides being the holdover of some tribal fertility dance, but these theories were widespread to the point of being mainstream for some time and did not really start to be seriously challenged until the late 1970s and '80s, when writers such as Roy Dommett and A. G. Barrand began to bring a more scholarly approach into the origins of these practices and questioned the prevailing orthodoxy.

People – particularly, I think, the British – like the idea of a timeline stretching back beyond the Romans; we are a nation that hangs onto its traditions and that still regards older as being better. We'll take a look at the roots of this in a little while. It's an attitude that may be changing as the digital age opens up new avenues of thought – but perhaps this preference for the old days, often manifesting as a benign or, conversely, a toxic nostalgia, hasn't quite gone yet. The enormous numbers of people who took time off work to file past the late queen's coffin in Westminster Hall might be an indication of that.

One American folklore website describes folklore as follows:

Every group with a sense of its own identity shares, as a central part of that identity, folk traditions – the things that people learn to do largely through oral communication and by example: believe (religious customs, creation myths, healing charms), do (dance, make music, sew clothing), know (how to build an irrigation dam, how to nurse an ailment, how to prepare barbecue), make (architecture, art, craft, music), and say (personal experience stories, riddles, song lyrics).

These ways of believing and knowing are circulated among small groups of people. Local knowledge often responds to, augments, and fills the gaps in between its own understanding and knowledge created by larger, more dominant, or mainstream groups. Folklore asserts group identity, challenges cultural norms, and provides examples for ways of living a good life. The word 'folklore' names an enormous and deeply significant dimension of culture.[1]

This definition of folklore is thus very wide, encompassing all manner of social customs and practices; note that transgression is baked into this definition in the comment relating to challenging cultural norms. Folklorist Alan Dundes spreads the net even more extensively:

> The term 'folk' can refer to any group of people whatsoever who share at least one common factor. It does not matter what the linking factor is – it could be a common occupation, language, or religion – but what is important is that a group formed for whatever reason will have some traditions which it calls its own. In theory a group must consist of at least two persons, but generally most groups consist of many individuals. A member of the group may not know all other members, but he will probably know the common core of traditions belonging to the group, traditions which help the group have a sense of group identity.[2]

This book is not going to examine the entire span of folklore as defined above. Although later on we are going to make passing mention of phenomena such as urban legends and digital trolling, we are primarily going to keep to a remit of examining physical customs: dancing, theatre, costuming, commemoration of death, sculpture and art. Since a part of our work here is an examination of shaming within folk custom, we're also going to look at manifestations of public shaming (starting with skimmity riding and associated practices, and ending with their digital descendants – call-out culture on social media, trolling and cancelling). We will spend more of our time examining transgressive elements that are not concerned with shame in some of these customs, too: from cross-dressing in mystery plays to rowdiness in annual street football matches, the use of blackface in bonfire processions and the flouting of health and safety regulations in customs such as the Cooper's Hill cheese-rolling competition.

Yet we will be looking at the non-transgressive aspects of these practices as well. I am reluctant to shoehorn transgression and shaming into every practice and custom; many of them do not have this function and, in addition, there is another side to many practices – that of social bonding, community spirit and, never to be forgotten, the aim of simply having a laugh. Those aims are arguably much more significant than the transgressive elements: most people do not join a Morris side with the aim of being drawn into a controversy about racism; most do not sign up for a bonfire society because they're anti-Catholic. In this book, therefore, we must remember that shame and transgression are a single strand of customs that perform a much wider social function.

A note: many of these customs overlap. My chapter divisions are therefore rough and not to be held up as set in stone. Mumming and Morris dancing often bear a relationship to one another, for example, and Morris dancing accompanies other customs such as the Mari Lwyd and the Padstow Oss. Guising occurs at Hallowe'en and Christmas, and at other times of the year. Green men can be part of mumming. Folk custom in Britain is an interwoven tapestry – perhaps a cliché, but a useful one in the context of the practices that we are going to look at now.

The Non-Ancient Origins of Ancient Origins

It is worth taking a look here at the claims of ancient origins that bedevil claims about folklore like a swarm of wasps: wherever there is a folk custom, you will find claims that it derives from ancient practices. Pretty much every custom or tradition in the UK has such a contention attached to it: that it comes from Phoenician sun worship (cheese rolling), old pagan gods (the Green Man) or fertility rites (Morris dancing and pretty much everything else). Why should this be the case? Are these customs genuinely ancient? If they are not, then where do these ideas stem from?

The origins of these claims lie in a succession of enthusiastic historians, both professional and amateur, from the seventeenth century onwards, but most specifically in the work of particular Victorian and Edwardian academics, writers and poets: James George Frazer, Laurence Gomme, Jane Ellen Harrison, Edward Burnett Tylor, Margaret Murray and, a little later on, Robert Graves. It also derives from a prevailing British attitude, still in evidence today, and which we have already mentioned above, that 'older is better'.

Anthropologist James Frazer published his most influential work, *The Golden Bough*, in 1890.[3] Interest in the theories that it promoted was considerable and it was reprinted in the early 1900s. Frazer was part of a developing movement of British interest in folklore, which had emerged from German Romanticism and the work of Wilhelm Mannhardt. Frazer believed that most ancient religions were actually fertility cults, and he used examples of the sacrifice of a 'sacred king' (Dionysus, Osiris, Adonis, Tammuz and Christ) as the basis for his claims. When *The Golden Bough* came out, it was seen as scandalous and verging on heresy, since Frazer connected Christ with other sacrificial kings. The book's impact on anthropology was ultimately less significant than its literary heritage. Frazer's work had a substantial subsequent influence on people such as W. B. Yeats, Arthur Machen, Dion Fortune, Aleister Crowley (who had a high regard for Frazer), Gerald Gardner, the founder of modern Wicca, and Robert Graves.

Frazer himself appears to have been an atheist, despite some interest in Neoplatonism. He came out of the radical Free Church of Scotland, and he sought to show, in *The Golden Bough*, that Christianity was just another form of superstition; the folk customs of Britain emerged from ancient pagan practices, Christianity is analogous to these and thus it cannot be considered as superior. So it's ironic that his work was seminal in inspiring what Hutton has described as the only religion that Britain has ever given the world, Wicca.

Unfortunately, Frazer did not anticipate quite how appealing this idea was to prove. Rather than putting people off Christianity because it was just another old superstition, he succeeded in making those old superstitions more attractive. I suspect he underestimated how much people actually like folk customs.

Frazer was not alone in his linkage of folk customs to ancient religious practices. There were other academics who latched onto these concepts, too. Jane Ellen Harrison, who read Classics at Newnham College, Cambridge, in the mid-1870s, was the Mary Beard of her day: 1,600 people came to one of her talks in Glasgow. She was a vibrant, rather charismatic personality. An atheist, like Frazer, Harrison belonged to the Ritualists group, who believed that myths and Classical drama originated in ritual. She was also a pacifist and a feminist who favoured women's suffrage but did not intend to vote herself.

Harrison believed in an ancient matrifocal society, one in which women were the leaders, a different kind of society from the male-dominated cultures of the ancient world. Harrison did not initiate this idea – it was becoming more common among academics and archaeologists in the late nineteenth century, and Frazer was one of these. Sir Arthur Evans, for instance, came to believe that a single great goddess had been worshipped in Crete as a result of his 1901 excavations at Knossos.

In *Themis: A Study of the Social Origins of Greek Religion* (1912), Harrison expanded on Frazer's idea of a 'year god' who dies and is reborn, and who is the son of a mythical Great Mother.[4] For some of Harrison's male colleagues, this was a step too far: both sides accused each other of being subjective and emotional. The idea of an ancient matriarchy has developed significant traction throughout the twentieth century, mainly in feminist circles, but there is little direct evidence for it – charitably, we might see it as an example of 'poetic truth', however shaky this might be in epistemological terms. Harrison's notions of an ancient fertility religion did, however, also feed into folklorists' views on old British customs.

Margaret Murray, born in 1863, was the first female lecturer of archaeology in Britain and believed that the witch trials that took place across England, Wales and especially Scotland were actually attempts to stamp out a pre-Christian pagan fertility religion in Europe. This cult, she said, worshipped the Horned God and a moon goddess, and she wrote an article for *Folklore*, the official journal of the Folklore Society, in 1917. Her work *The Witch-Cult in Western Europe* was also influential.[5]

Ronald Hutton points out that her work was based on a relatively small sample of research. He is not alone in his reservations. They are shared by Jacqueline Simpson, President of the Folklore Society, who wrote in 1994:

> No British folklorist can remember Dr Margaret Murray without embarrassment and a sense of paradox. She is one of the few folklorists whose name became widely known to the public, but among scholars her reputation is deservedly low; her theory that witches were members of a huge secret society preserving a prehistoric fertility cult through the centuries is now seen to be based on deeply flawed methods and illogical arguments. The fact that, in her old age and after three increasingly eccentric books, she was made President of the Folklore Society, must certainly have harmed the reputation of the Society and possibly the status of folkloristics in this country; it helps to explain the mistrust some historians still feel towards our discipline.[6]

These 'ancient origins' theories gained traction in the 1890s, with the growing popularity of the idealization of rural England and the work of people like folklorist Cecil Sharp. Some of this tied into emerging left-wing thought, which romanticized the British working classes and their ways of life.

Robert Graves, born in 1895, was the son of an Irish poet, Alfred Graves, who was interested in the Gaelic revival. He introduced his son to Irish mythology, and Robert remained intrigued; he published *The White Goddess* in 1948.[7] It is an exploration of Celtic and Classical mythology – idiosyncratic, based on poetic feeling rather than historical fact; beautifully intricate but not an academically rigorous work. Nonetheless, it, too, carried forward the idea that some of the customs we practice today are rooted in the ancient past. Graves was keen on the idea of ancient ritual seasonal battles, usually between summer and winter, for example, and although these did take place in some areas, such as the Isle of Man in the eighteenth century around May Day, there's again no evidence that these are anything other than comparatively modern.

These authors all proved influential, and the idea of an ancient fertility cult as the basis for our folk customs still crops up today, not so much among academics but among those who practice those customs and the press, who tend to repeat tropes over and over again with little attempt to dig deeper. But it has been largely discredited among folklore scholars, a move that began in the 1970s and '80s, when folklorists began to take a much more rigorous look at the actual history and were perhaps guided less by personal bees in the bonnet. This endeavour was capped in 1996 by Ronald Hutton's seminal work *Stations of the Sun*, which looks at the festivals of the British year in a chronological order, beginning with Christmas, and delves into the history of each one. I regard it as a crucial work for anyone interested in seasonal customs in the UK.

There's simply too little evidence for any ancient pagan roots and, on top of that, the historical origins of many practices are actually known: most date from after the Norman Conquest at the very earliest, and if they do have roots that go back before that, those roots lie in speculation rather than evidence. We'll take a look at some of those customs now.

TWO

Jacks in the Green

Anyone who has a passing familiarity with English churches will be familiar with the figure of the Green Man: the foliate heads that stare cheerfully, mockingly, down from the rafters. Vines and tendrils grow from the Green Man's mouth and sometimes from his eyes; he is surrounded by leaves and vegetation. He comes in three different versions. As a foliate head, he is covered in green leaves. As a disgorging head, vegetation emerges from his mouth, and as a bloodsucker head, all of the orifices of his head spout leafy greenery. Foliate heads are found not only in European churches, but in eleventh-century Templar churches in Jerusalem and in an eighth-century Jain temple in Rajasthan. There is a very familiar-looking green man on the ruins of a temple in Hatra, in modern Iraq, dating from the second century. There are a handful of Green Women, too, but these are less common and any transgressive role they might have had has been usurped by the image of the Sheela-na-gig, which we will mention later on.

But is the Green Man really a pagan figure, appearing surprisingly as he does in churches, and is he connected to the figures of the Jack in the Green who accompany Morris dancing sides throughout May Day celebrations across the land? We have said that the remit of this book is transgression – but surely the Green Man, peeping cheekily down from the clerical rafters, is a very mild form of transgressive representation? One might think so, but the cousins of these apparently benign foliate heads manifest far more alarming behaviour: violence, the capture and eating of children, an anti-Norman guerrilla movement. In this chapter, we're going to be looking at the origins of the Green Man, of the Jacks in the Green themselves and at a much more recent royal row.

Foliate Heads

The pagan origins of the Green Man seem plausible at first glance. He 'feels' pagan, with his grinning mouth and the festoons of greenery that surround him. Did stonemasons secretly following ancient pagan ways slip him into churches, hiding him in misericords and at the tops of pillars in the clerical gloom that must have held sway before the advent of electric light? Is his very presence a secret transgressive act, a smuggling of nature into the austere home of the Christian God? Does he represent the fertile powers of the natural world? Certainly, the Green Man does give a sense that the wild has crept into the church, to lurk there, just out of sight.

The Green Man is obviously old: many Green Men could be found in churches by the seventeenth century, just before the Reformation, and he also appears in some unexpected places. But does he represent some ancient pagan woodland god, symbolizing the cycle of death and rebirth, as writers such as Frazer or Graves would have it, or is he just a stonemason's whimsy? Or does he represent something else entirely?

The first use of the term 'Green Man' in connection with foliate heads was probably in an article by Julia Somerset, Lady

Raglan, who was likely to have been inspired by carvings at St Jerome's Church in Llangwm, Monmouthshire.[1] She was not a prolific commentator on folklore matters, for it was the only article on folklore that she ever wrote – but its content was certainly enduring. Raglan linked the heads found in churches to the green men found in May Day celebrations throughout both Britain and Europe, and ultimately to Robin Hood, that perennially popular outlaw of Sherwood Forest and champion of the poor and oppressed.

Raglan's paper is, as she says herself, 'scrappy', and it is brief; these are ideas jotted down by an interested amateur rather than an in-depth thesis written by a trained scholar. Some of those scholars have taken issue with claims that the name of the Green Man dates back only so far as the 1930s.[2] Lady Raglan did indeed write about the figure in this period, but she did not invent the term 'Green Man' – her role was simply to be the first to apply it to foliate heads in churches. The term crops up in an earlier passage in 1903 by E. K. Chambers.[3] Moreover, some commentators think that we are conducting our search too narrowly by limiting it to the figures found in churches.[4] We should also be looking out on the streets of British towns and cities – for the Green Man is to be found here, too.

Whifflers and Wild Men

The term 'Green Man' was in use by the sixteenth century and appears to have referred initially to a 'whiffler', someone who is hired to clear a space in which a play or other performance is to be held.[5] To speed this up, the whiffler sometimes carried a club studded with fireworks (which would clear a space pretty quickly, one would think). For example, in George Whetstone's play *The Second Parte of the Famous Historie of Promos and Cassandra* (1578) this passage appears:

> Actus. 1. Scena. 6. Phallax, Two men, apparrelled, lyke greene men at the Mayors feast, with clubbes of fyre worke.
>
> Phal. This geare fadgeth now, that these fellowes peare,
>   Friendes where weight you?
>
> First. In Jesus Street to keepe a passadge cleare,
>   That the King and his trayne, may passe with ease.[6]

In 1347, a mumming performance at Edward III's court included performers wearing 'wild man' masks/heads, as well as animal heads such as dragons and swans.

Raph Cobler, the main character in the play *The Cobler's Prophecy* (1594) by Robert Wilson, says that he plans to keep well out of the way of the 'greene men' in case his clothes catch fire, which may well be a reference to the dangers presented by the fireworks in the whiffler's club.[7] It's uncommon in the UK these days to run about the street actually waving fireworks, even in places like Lewes on Bonfire Night, but I remember attending a street festival in the Gracia district of Barcelona in the 1990s that featured enormous dragons carried on sticks. Each dragon had lighted fireworks stuffed up their nostrils and the local boys were daring each other to run under the dragons' noses, draped in old coats that soon bore a constellation of little smouldering holes. So one could speculate that similar antics might have been undertaken around the whifflers (and as we'll see presently, model fire-breathing dragons are not unknown in British pageantry, either).

However, because everyone was well versed in what a Green Man actually looked like, there aren't any descriptions of them.[8] Thomas Nashe, in his play *Summer's Last Will and Testament* (1600), has his seasonally named title character Will Summer say to the audience, 'The rest of the green men have reasonable voices, good to sing catches or the great Jowben by the fire's side in a winter's evening.'[9]

Both satyrs and nymphs also appear in this play; it is to be assumed that the nymphs would, in the customary manner of the Elizabethan stage, be played by boys, hence both satyrs and nymphs in the play are described as 'green men' (we'll take a look at cross-dressing in British folk customs a little later on). Later in the play they reappear, in the train of Vertumnus, and we are told that they wear suits covered in green grass.

In a St George's Day celebration in 1610, designed for a visit by Prince Henry to Chester, the green men appear again:

> ii men in greene leaves set with work upon their other habet with black heare & black beards very owgly to behould, and garlands upon their heads with great clubs in their hands with fireworks to scatter abroad to maintaine way for the rest of the show.[10]

Robert Amorye, the enterprising ironmonger who set up this event, later goes into more detail. Thanks to him and accounts such as the one above, we do get a more complete impression of these figures, as the following description indicates:

Two disguised, called Greene-men, their habit Embroy-
dred and Stitch'd on with Ivie-leaves with blacke-side,
having hanging to their shoulders, a huge black shaggie
Hayre, Savage-like, with Ivie Garlands upon their heads,
bearing Herculian Clubbes in their hands . . . (Chester's
Triumph in honor of her prince As it was performed
vpon S. Georges Day 1610. in the foresaid citie.)[11]

In 1553, there's a description by scholar Robert Withington
of a London Mayor's Feast that also refers to green men but
calls them 'wodyn'.[12] This was a Middle English term for wild
men and we may speculate that it could be related to the old
god Woden, who gave us our name for Wednesday – but it's
more likely to come from the Old English 'wude-wāsa', later
more commonly transcribed as 'wood wose'. We will be looking into the phenomenon of the woodwose in a moment. A
seventeenth-century account notes: 'ij grett wodyn, [armed] with
ij grett clubes all in grene, and with skwybes borning [carrying
squibs, or firecrackers], with gret berds and syd here, and ij targets
a-pon ther bake.'[13]

At Anne Boleyn's coronation pageant, wild men also
featured. This was a massive, four-day event, kicking off with a
river pageant that included a model dragon on a wherry, surrounded by wild men who later took part in the procession on
land. They wore green leaves and their role, as above, was to
clear the way for the main parade; they carried the customary
clubs and firecrackers.

Woodwoses

Whether in a Royal pageant or the Lord Mayor's feast, these green men must have been alarming figures, with their leafy costumes, big beards and bangers, playing upon fears of the 'wild men of the woods', the 'woodwoses', which crop up in medieval literature and art and have a role similar to the satyrs of the classical countryside: part man and part animal, with affiliations to actual beasts. Historian Matt Salusbury describes them as 'Tarzan-style'.[14] Their feral nature and links with animals render them dangerous, and they are not to be trusted. Representations of these wild men also appear in churches: they are not the same being as the foliate heads, but they seem to be connected. They sometimes appear in churches battling wyverns, the small dragon-like creatures who occasionally crop up on coats of arms, or lions. They turn up on fonts, although many have been defaced during various Protestant reformations. In some cases, they were plastered over until the danger to them had passed. Salusbury, in his informative account of woodwoses in Suffolk churches, notes:

> The standard woodwose-on-a-font configuration is four woodwoses facing outward, rarely more than a foot high, generally flanked by sitting lions, along with the angels and winged animals representing the Four Evangelists – Saints Matthew, Mark, Luke and John. Most of Suffolk's woodwose-bearing fonts conform surprisingly closely to this arrangement. The head of the bull signifying St John in Halesworth Church looks strangely satanic, while some of Halesworth's

font woodwoses stand with their legs crossed, their clubs resting on the ground.[15]

Sometimes, though not as far as I know in churches, they were depicted with a child tied to their club. This is a classic 'bogeyman' image used either to frighten disobedient children or, conceivably, to scare them away from any idea of wandering off into the dangerous forest. Woodwoses were said not only to eat straying children, but to abduct women and rape them, too, because they had insatiable sexual appetites. (The majority of woodwoses are masculine but there is at least one depiction of a female woodwose, and these were said to be able to take more conventional, presumably less hairy, form in order to seduce human men. They are thus a form of succubus.) Although they were held in legend to be deaf to the word of the Lord, they could be converted to Christianity, at least in theory.

Nowadays, in spite of the occasional random murder burial, we tend to see woods as sylvan places, filled with bluebells, and havens for local dog walkers. But in medieval times, in a landscape that was still heavily wooded, interspersed with dense impenetrable tangles of scrub and undergrowth, there lurked many dangers, both real and imaginary. Wolves and boar were still a feature of the British forest then, and one has to wonder how many people who were either responding to the pressures of life, mentally ill, or simply born into remote, isolated and in-bred forest communities, resided in these places, giving rise to subsequent myths of wild or inhuman people. The Celtic legends contain many references to kings or other high-status figures who go mad and spend time in the forests. It happens to the magician Merlin, who, driven insane after a battle, forgets who he is and heads into the forest to live among a herd of wild pigs. In Irish legend, King Suibhne tries to expel a saint from his lands; the saint curses him, causing him to go mad and wander throughout the world. This theme crops up so often in Celtic tales that it seems oddly compulsory, as though a period spent living so close to the dangerous natural world conferred some kind of magical or spiritual depth to these noble individuals.

The Norwegian *Konungs skuggsjá* (King's Mirror) mentions such a real-life feral person in 1250:

> It once happened in that country (and this seems indeed strange) that a living creature was caught in the forest as to which no one could say definitely whether it was a man or some other animal; for no one could get a word from it or be sure that it understood human speech. It had the human shape, however, in every detail, both as to hands and face and feet; but the entire body was covered with hair as the beasts are, and down the back it had a long coarse mane like that of a horse, which fell to both sides and trailed along the ground when the creature stooped in walking.[16]

How widespread the phenomenon of actual wild men in the woods may have been is debatable, however. Matt Salusbury says:

> It's tempting to think [that] Suffolk's woodwoses remember an actual briefly captive wildman, or even a species of relict hominid living among us in the flat plains of East Anglia, but folklorist Gregory Forth points

out that unlike the Asian and American traditions of Bigfoot ... there are very few surviving accounts of actual sightings of hairy wildmen in Europe.[17]

But there are some local stories of weird hairy beings, around Rendlesham, for instance, an area that is also prone to UFO and alien sightings – I am not the first writer to suggest that maybe they're connected to the same phenomenon, whatever that is. And an actual wild man was captured at Orford, in Suffolk, around 1161 CE. The event is noted by the thirteenth-century Cistercian abbot Ralph of Coggeshall:

> In the time of King Henry II, when Bartholomew de Glanville was in charge of the castle at Orford, it happened that some fishermen fishing in the sea there caught in their nets a wild man. He was naked and was like a man in all his members, covered with hair and with a long shaggy beard.[18]

This unfortunate person was tortured, but could not speak, and was also thrown into the sea (to see how he behaved). He survived and later escaped.

Another similar wild man appeared at Sproughton, near Ipswich, and alarmed some medieval builders; he is commemorated in a local pub called the Wild Man. In the same county, there is also the famous story of the Green Children of Woolpit: two children with greenish-grey skin who had been found wandering in the village, speaking an unfamiliar language. The boy died, but once the girl had learned English, she told people that they came from a place called St Martin's Land, where the sun never shone and where everything was green. This odd story also appears in Ralph of Coggeshall's work, and it's impossible to get to whatever truth lies behind it – whether the green children are connected with the legends of the woodwose in some way, or whether this was an allegorical tale (such as the fourteenth-century story of Gawain and the Green Knight), or whether it was a real event that became heavily embellished with a supernatural gloss (the prevalence of urban legends today shows us how easily this can happen).[19] Even quite early accounts suggested that they might have been aliens, either fallen from heaven (like the Bishop of Hereford's 1638 story *The Man in the Moone*) or teleported from another planet (this suggestion appeared in *Analog* magazine in the 1960s).[20] But genuinely feral children do pop up even in contemporary cultures today, usually as a consequence of bereavement or other abandonment by their parents, so perhaps the Woolpit children were an example of this. Outside the UK, there's even a woodwose saint: the fourth-century Egyptian St Onuphrius, who lived as a hermit and is depicted wearing a loincloth of leaves.

Why on earth, the reader may be asking at this point, are representations of child-eating hirsute maniacs so commonplace in the respectable confines of the church? It's understandable that some irreverent stonemason sneaked in a foliate head high in the shadowy rafters, but the woodwoses are in plain sight and often placed on fonts, which are by definition going to be the focal point of at least one church ceremony (the woses do appear elsewhere in churches, too, such as in porches). Salusbury points out that beasts and mythological beings have an allegorical function in medieval times, and woodwoses represent strength, so perhaps some of their wild power was supposed to filter upwards into the baby who was being christened? But he also remarks that on a more practical level they are simply a useful shape for a font, usually being depicted as tall and thin.

The Green Man as guerrilla

In response to Salusbury's own theories, Stephen Mickelewright of Hampshire sent a letter to the *Fortean Times* suggesting that the woodwoses depicted in East Anglian churches might be folk memories of the 'Silvatici', who continued to fight on after the arrival of the Normans and become adept at woodland camouflage.[21] This guerrilla movement, known by the Latin name for the 'men of the woods', is a real phenomenon – many people in England, after the defeat of Harold, did not take the Conquest lying down. The movement is said to have lasted for a decade after the arrival of the Normans, formed of underground and probably unconnected resistance groups that took to the woods (such as Robin Hood and his Merry Men) or the moors and fens. 'Wild Eadric' in Shropshire is an example of one of these rebel leaders and later, like Robin Hood, he became linked with the legends of the Wild Hunt, the eldritch mythical party of hounds and men who track down the souls of wrongdoers. (He's also said to have come across a household of succubi in one forest and sired a son on one of these obliging female demons. Maybe she was a woodwose?) Here we see this alliance between the supernatural and the political: resistance to the established order or to the oppressor becomes wedded to archetypal and allegorical, or simply unearthly, forces.

One only has to pick up a copy of the *Fortean Times* or *National Enquirer* to see the enduring appeal of the wild man today, in the form of Sasquatch, Bigfoot or Yeti. As well as a possible reference to actual feral people, the 'manimal' image has a wider metaphorical role – an obvious one. The wild man is the opposite to the civilized man: he is hairy (even when 'he' is female!), sexualized, violent, bestial. So the 'greene men' in English celebrations have layers of meaning; to their audiences, they would have been likely to appear far more sinister than they do to us today (and even today, some of the Osses and Jacks can still give rise to a frisson of fear, a phenomenon that has not escaped those writers and artists who subscribe to the modern genre of folk horror). Woodwoses occasionally turn up in fiction, such as the acclaimed fantasy novels of the *Mythago Wood* series by the late Robert Holdstock, in which the woodwoses are gentle, benign nature spirits in spring and summer, but in winter take the form of humanoids made of bare branches and sharp teeth who attack unwary travellers. This, to me, sums up the eerie, otherworldly nature of the woodwose, but it is likely that, in reality, their real-life progenitors were lost souls eking out an existence in the cold and dangerous forests of the Middle Ages. Wild men are, after all, found in every culture and every historical period; some societies, such as India with its wandering sadhus, regarded as holy men and given alms, deal with these people perhaps better than others – although one must wonder about some of the early Celtic saints.

A Kind of Hercules

Throughout the seventeenth century, commentators and playwrights continue to refer to the Green Men: John Kirke, James Shirley, Matthew Taubman and others comment on these wild green figures with their fiery squibs. Winick makes the direct connection, pointing out that by the later 1600s the image of the Green Man on pub signs was becoming known as the Wild Man: 'a kind of Hercules with a green club and green leaves about his pudenda and head, as we use to paint the signe of the greene man'.[22] He wears leaves here, as indicated, but other examples of these images show a bearded, hairy figure, naked save for his crown and modesty-preserving foliage.

The pub sign of the Green Man probably also arose during this century, with the familiar foliate head, but there were also some variants, such as an actual forester, an Indigenous American or Robin Hood. The 'wild man' symbol came to be representative of the distilling trade (think of the average Saturday night in any British urban centre and you'll begin to realize why). There are still plenty of pubs called the Green Man across the country and a fair number of beers that use the familiar foliate head as a logo (there is likely to have been some crossover between the images in churches and pub signs: the latter may have drawn on the carvings in churches for their inspiration). A rough count that I undertook for the purposes of this book revealed that there are still close to one hundred pubs with this name, mainly in the Midlands and the south of England. John Bagford (1651–1716) wrote:

> They are called woudmen, or wildmen, thou' at thes day we in ye signe [trade] call them Green Men, couered with grene boues: and are used for singes by stiflers of strong watters ... and a fit emblem for those that use that intosticating licker which berefts them of their sennes.[23]

Thus there were plenty of references for Lady Raglan to have drawn on for her groundbreaking, if perhaps over-enthusiastic article. The Green Man crops up everywhere: in churches, on pub signs and on the streets themselves, wielding his fiery club. We may argue that he has another manifestation, too, as the Jack in the Green who appears around May Day celebrations (and at other times of the year, too) across the country. We will take a look at these shortly, after a brief digression on another unlikely figure to be found in churches.

Sheela-na-gig

Visitors to some British and Irish churches, such as Kilpeck in Gloucestershire, are often startled to look up and see a naked, bald, old stone woman displaying the open lips of her enormous vulva. She is grinning at them from the stonework. These eyebrow-raising figures are Sheela-na-gigs, and they are found not only in Britain and Ireland, but across Europe. The majority, however, are in Ireland – a strikingly anomalous image, one would think, for a Catholic country with strict sexual morals.

What *are* the Sheelas? The green men seem benign – some could be regarded as slightly sinister yet in a jolly, impish way, but in spite of the possible woodwose connection, they don't seem malevolent. The Sheelas are just plain rude and definitely fit our remit of transgression. There are various theories about their origins. Some speculation holds that – like other grotesque figures such as gargoyles – they are set around church roofs in order to frighten away evil spirits, although some of them are almost hidden. Others hold that they are a dire warning to women about the evils of masturbation or other sexual 'transgressions' – it'll make your hair fall out! And some say that they refer to a pre-Christian goddess-based religion and are a symbol of fertility. Like green men, they almost certainly don't, although some of the freestanding ones seem to have been adopted by Irish women hoping to improve their childbearing chances, but they have been taken up by the contemporary Pagan movement today as symbols of female empowerment, as we will see below. And there is a custom in which Irish farmers present ewes to the local Sheela to aid in lambing, lending credence to the fertility thesis, though whether this is a 'chicken and egg' situation is yet to be proven. An image of a Sheela appeared on a ceremonial apron worn by one of the Eel Sisters in the recent 2023 sitcom *The Change*, described by *The Guardian*, its tongue firmly in cheek, as 'Sheela-na-gig chic'.[24] Scholar Barbara Freitag believes that they were originally separate from the Church, as later clerics call for them to be removed, but this isn't straightforward cause and effect: it might simply reflect differing attitudes within the Church itself.[25]

Some scholars say that the carvings seem to be linked to the Anglo-Norman conquest. The origin of the name also remains somewhat mysterious: it may come from Sighle na gCíoch ('the old hag of the breasts') or Síle ina Giob, meaning 'Sheila/Cecelia on her hunkers'. It may also come from a slang term for women's genitals, or from a dance (a jig). Naval records show that a ship of the same name in the 1840s refers to it as an Irish female sprite.[26] There are some illustrations of women exposing their genitals to scare off demons, and in Greek legend the goddess of mirth, Baubo, cheers up the mourning Demeter after the abduction of her daughter Persephone by lifting her skirt and exposing herself in a humorous way. But any classical allusion to the Sheelas has long since evaporated, if indeed it ever existed.

Yet her transgressive aspect continues. In 2021, Project Sheela took place across Ireland, conceived (no pun intended) by an anonymous ceramicist. Images of the figure were placed in areas that the project felt were particularly relevant to misogyny and abuse, such as outside one of the Magdalene laundries, the infamous mother and baby homes that are a blot on Ireland's historical landscape:

We wanted to honour the women who suffered there. The reason women were sent to these laundries was because of the Catholic church seeing women's sexuality as dangerous and sinful – the women were punished and abused by the nuns, who believed they were evil.[27]

Are there male equivalents of the Sheelas? Yes: one of the churches in Devizes has a masturbating male gargoyle, and it seems probable that phallic images accompanied some of the Sheelas in churches but were later destroyed.

The Jacks and May Day

Similar though he might seem to the Green Men, the Jack in the Green has different origins and a different character. His beginnings may lie not in the wild woodwose, but in the garlands and decorated pails carried by milkmaids in their May Day celebrations. Over time, this rather charming tradition was adopted by other professions, such as chimney sweeps and bunters (female rag pickers). Samuel Pepys records one of these in his diary – he came across a milkmaids' procession while on his way to Westminster on May Day in 1667.[28] At this event the milkmaids danced behind a fiddler. In 1712 *The Spectator* referred to 'the ruddy Milk-Maid exerting herself in a most sprightly style under a Pyramid of Silver Tankards' – the maids would borrow silver cups and tankards to hang on their pails, presumably because they caught the sunlight, and clanked and jangled. In addition to the milkmaids, chimney sweep parades in which sweeps sometimes cross-dressed were popular, although the sweeps generally did not carry garlands, and eventually the two seem to have merged together into the Jack in the Green celebrations.

The rationale for this was not just having fun by dressing up or rivalry between different professions, but money – crowds would throw coins to reward particularly spectacular costumes. Thus, over time, the modest pails turned into head-dresses: floral pyramids that became larger and larger until they ended up worn as a frame concealing everything except the bearer's lower legs and feet, rather like an ambulant Christmas tree, but decorated with green leaves and spring flowers instead of baubles and tinsel. One such figure appears in this account from Joseph Strutt:

> This piece of pageantry consists of a hollow frame of wood, or wicker-work, made in the form of a sugar loaf, but open at the bottom, and sufficiently large and high to receive a man. The frame is covered with green leaves and bunches of flowers interwoven with each other, so that the man within may be completely concealed, who dances with his companions, and the populace

are mightily pleased with the oddity of the moving pyramid.[29]

The Jack appears in an anonymous illustration from the late eighteenth century, being led along by a guardian (it's hard to see when you're under one of those things). The 'milkmaid' origin story of the Jack is not unchallenged, however: some historians believe that the links between the milkmaid's head-dresses and the later, full-body Jack in the Green is coincidental. What is clear, however, is that by this time, the Jack was an established figure in May Day celebrations, as in this comment from *The Morning Chronicle and London Advertiser* in 1775: 'Jack of the Green had made his garland by five in the morning, and got under his fhady building by seven.'[30]

In Hastings, the Jack in the Green festival has been a Maytide celebration for many years, although it is not as old as some. I attended it myself in the 1990s, but it began in 1983. It is one of a number of similar festivals; contemporary Jack in the Greens appear in Oxford, Knutsford, Evercreech and several other towns. Hastings' Jack in the Green celebration lasts for four days across the May Bank Holiday weekend. The main event takes place on the Bank Holiday Monday, in which Jack is 'released'. He has a retinue, consisting of bogies (people in greenface and costumes of rags who have been described as part man, part bush and part alcohol), Black Sal and the Fat Man, plus Mad Jack's Morris dancers, giants, drummers and other Morris sides. The procession proceeds through the town and ends on the West Hill where Jack is 'slain' to 'release the spirit of summer'.

It was also home in the 1990s to a group known as 'the Gay Bogies on Acid' – a small group of gay men who included Simon

Costin, now director of the Museum of Witchcraft and Magic at Boscastle. Costin's fellow bogie, Marti Dean, recalls being 'completely blown away by the friendliness, magic, and the vibe', and the pair were joined by two more friends, gay men finding a space in this leafy celebration at a time when it was still difficult for members of the LGBT community to gain acceptance.[31]

For this book, I interviewed a number of people who take part in the various celebrations that appear here. Our first is with Jacqueline Durban, who identifies as a Hedgepriestess, a category of priestess within modern Paganism.

Interview with Jacqueline Durban, Hedgepriestess

It feels like a lifetime and more since I walked every year in the Bank Holiday Monday procession at the Hastings Jack-in-the-Green festival, but I still remember the anticipation of waiting for the Jack to be released from the fishermen's huts in the Old Town, to a rousing and rippling cry of 'Jack's alive!', before processing through the town and up to the castle to be symbolically slain with much merrymaking and good-spirited mayhem.

I was part of the procession with the Raven Drummers for ten years and it was a sacred joy. I loved the feeling of gathering community, and one of my favourite and most sacred moments of the year was when I bowed to the Jack as he passed by, knowing that he walked out as a willing sacrifice to the pulse of Life and all that's good. One year he bowed back to me and I still haven't quite recovered. In that moment it was absolutely real; the Jack was, and is, the Spirit of the Land walking ...

We live in a culture where the pull is to celebrate pomp and war, rather than the lives and traditions, and the resistance, of the common people. The Hastings Jack and others like him are symbols of that resistance, reborn each year. So many of our May Day traditions are born out of a determination to reconnect to a land and a way of being that had been in many ways lost/stolen from us when we sold ourselves into the lie of prosperity in the towns and cities during the Industrial Revolution, just as carvings of the Green Man may have developed as a protest against Norman oppression eight hundred years before that. Jack in the Green reminds us that we were not born to be slaves.

And so this is a reminder that, every year, on the West Hill of Hastings at around half past three on May Bank Holiday Monday, the Jack in the Green is symbolically slain and the Spirit of Summer is released to dance through every leaf and branch, every petal and root; every wing, paw and fin; every heart, mind and voice; every mycelial thread and shimmering web; every stagnant corner where power is undeservedly and cruelly held; every place where injustice seeks to take root.

Beltane

We began our exploration of these green men, woodwoses, Jack in the Greens and foliate heads with Lady Raglan, and we now return to her. Jacqueline Durban, as a modern Pagan, celebrates the Jack in the Green as a pagan image: an avatar of the spring itself. As we mentioned earlier, Lady Raglan subscribed to the 'pagan origins' view of the Green Man promulgated by Frazer, among others. But the enigmatic green figures who appear throughout British history seem much more recent than this, manifesting principally in the past few hundred years. There is very little evidence that they have any kind of pagan origin. The main thrust of the case for a May custom link with ancient paganism comes from the view, after Frazer, that 'the spirit of vegetation is blent with a personification of the season at which his powers are most strikingly manifested.'[32]

The issue here is that May Day is, even given climate change, pretty much the peak of spring in the UK. I am writing this on May Eve, and despite a faint mist and the fact that it's actually quite a chilly day, the sheer exuberance of everything I can see from this window – apple blossom, hawthorn blossom, tulips and grass that's growing almost as you watch it – is overwhelming. So no wonder that the logical assumption for many people is that the Green Man *must* have some connection with all of this. This is also where the modern Pagan celebration of Beltane kicks in, which is seen as a fertility festival, because writers such as Frazer have had an impact on contemporary spiritual practices when it comes to nature religions such as modern Druidry and Wicca. But was it always linked with fertility?

The earliest mention of Beltane was in the *Sanas Chormaic*, a medieval glossary – written around 900 CE – which mentions 'lucky fires'. It seems to have been a fire festival, comprising two bonfires through which cattle were herded to protect them before they were taken up to their summer pastures. This may have been linked to a god named Bel, Bil or Baal.

But in ancient times, this festival may not have had the same meaning that it does today. The Celts seem to have held that this was a time of year when the veil between the worlds was thin, a time when spirits, ghosts and the fairy folk were abroad – a chancy time when it might be safer to stay at home. In traditional folklore throughout the medieval and Elizabethan periods, May Eve had many of the connotations that we now associate with Hallowe'en. The Welsh festival Calan Mai is linked to this kind of supernatural activity, and according to the tale of Culhwch and Olwen, the heroes Gwythyr and Gwyn ap Nudd are fated to do battle on May Eve – summer defeating winter. In the early nineteenth century, festivals involving cattle and fires were held throughout Ireland. Women jumped the fire to ensure that they would meet a husband and (here at last is the fertility bit) wives did so to ensure that they would have children.

So there is some link between May Day and fertility, although it's not as firm or as obvious as one might think, and I think it's understandable that at this visibly fecund time of the year, some writers have made connections between the green men and old religions, even if that link falls apart under close examination.

Edinburgh Fire Festival

These days, Beltane and May Day is, for contemporary Pagans, more closely linked to love and romance, and to sex. The Glastonbury Pagan community was rather startled, some years ago, to be accused of planning a Beltane orgy in the letters column of the local press (the most common response to this was 'Why wasn't I invited?'). Some private Pagan rituals do involve ritual sex; public Pagan Beltane rituals do not, and many of those hark back to their folkloric roots, anointing a May Queen and a May King, and celebrating fertility as a central concept. These customs have, in the modern age, been adopted and transformed into other kinds of festival. One of these, perhaps the best known in the British Isles, is in Scotland: the Edinburgh Fire Festival.

The Fire Festival, the world's largest Beltane celebration, dates back to 1988, sparked by the community arts collective Test Dept and the School of Scottish Studies at the University of Edinburgh. It now involves around three hundred performers and is usually a sell-out. The organizers say that:

> While the festival draws on a variety of historical, mythological and literary influences, the organizers do not claim it to be anything other than a modern celebration of Beltane, evolving with its participants. The purpose of our festival is not to recreate ancient practices but to continue in the spirit of our ancient forebears and create our own connection to the cycles of nature.[33]

The festival starts at the National Monument on Calton Hill in Edinburgh and moves anti-clockwise around the hill. It's led by the May Queen and the Green Man, who initiate proceedings by lighting a bonfire that symbolizes the birth of summer. Performers then interrupt the May Queen and the Green Man on their progress until everyone congregates in a communal space known as the Bower. The performance celebrates the marriage between the sun and the earth.

The Beltane Fire Society not only focuses on Beltane, their first and main festival, but also on the other 'quarter days' of the year: Samhain (Hallowe'en), Lughnasadh (1 August) and Imbolc (1 February). Although there is a ritual element to these festivities, they are not Pagan rites as such, but are arts and performance-based, including fire dancing and drumming; Trinidadian Carnival plays a role in inspiring the event, for example. Participant Chloe Dear, who has performed as both a White Woman and a Blue Man, told the Edinburgh Guide:

> I first performed in 1993 as a White Woman, which completely blew me away. I was a creature transformed. Talk about a cathartic episode: it was one of my most life-changing experiences, and eventually led to me leaving my job as a drugs worker and becoming a full-time producer for te pooka, the performance company which has grown out of Beltane ... White Women are warriors, defenders of the May Queen and the orderly passage of Winter into Summer. Although the May Queen is the catalyst for the transition, she is dependent on her entourage to see that she carries out her role ... We had had lots of prep and a very ritualistic warm-up ... I felt quite calm until we were on the way up the hill in the truck and then the tension started to rise. I did feel safe behind my White Woman exterior and we had been well prepared in how to deal with crowds. Thousands of them. Lots off their faces too! There is a lot of tension (good, not bad) built into the event: the slow build-up to the killing of the Green Man and then the dancing with the Red Men ...
>
> I had mucked about before as a performer, but it was nothing compared to Beltane that first time. I came away quite different ... it wasn't just being up all night

dancing, it wasn't the intensity of a two hour performance . . . there was something quite powerful about
remaining focused and intent on carrying out a ritual in
front of so many people. I was not myself which is what
gave me that power to see it through . . . and people did
not recognise me, or if they did, recognised I was in a
different state that night – I was a White Woman, not
Chloe. And all without the aid of any drugs whatsoever
– just the whole joyous spirit of Beltane.[34]

Dear is clear, in her interview, that she does not regard herself
as a Pagan or as a New Ager, remarking that Beltane is mean-
ingful to her on a 'primal' level and not as something that she's
just read about.

The Green Man and a Royal Row

As I was writing this book, the Green Man popped up again
in a slightly unexpected place: the formal invitation to King
Charles III's coronation in May 2023. Amid a plethora of spring
flowers and heraldic images, the Green Man appears at the
bottom of the invitation. He is crowned with a pair of leaves
that look like delicate horns and there is an acorn balanced on
top of his head. So far, so good – we've seen that the Green
Man appears in many forms. The royal family's own Twitter
account stated: 'Designed by Andrew Jamieson, the invitation
features the Green Man, an ancient figure from British folklore,
symbolic of spring and rebirth, to celebrate the new reign.'[35]
However, controversy was kicked off in the national press by
a complaint from that bastion of theological conservatism

Winston Marshall, former member of the band Mumford and Sons, who tweeted:

> Why is the Jolly Green Giant more prominent on the Coronation invite than any Christian symbols? He's the head of the church. Has he forgotten the first commandment? 'Thou shalt have no other gods before me' This is paganism. Shame.[36]

His complaint was swiftly countered by a welter of quite well-informed commentary, some of it (by Alice Roberts, professor of Public Engagement in Science and a prominent historian on British media) citing Lady Raglan herself. Overseas Minister Zac Goldsmith tweeted:

> [the] Green Man is one of the most ancient symbols of all, and appears on countless churches across the land and beyond. It is a symbol, among other things, of our relationship with the natural world (or in Christian terms, God's creation). This is beautiful.[37]

It's also not entirely a surprising choice from a monarch who has had a decades-long interest in environmentalism and the natural world. The symbol may also be a nod to the location of the coronation, since there is a Green Man in Westminster Abbey, at the top of the quire screen facade. (The invitation also features a robin and a wren; as we shall see in the section devoted to the custom known as the Hunting of the Wren, this little bird is also seen in folklore as a symbol of rebirth.)

The tiny acorn on top of the Green Man's head might be a tribute to the Princess of Wales, whose coat of arms was designed to include acorns, since she is from Berkshire and the county has a number of oak woods. Some commentators, however, have interpreted it as a symbol of Oak Apple Day, also known as Restoration Day, Shick Shack Day (an old name for oak galls/apples) or Oak and Nettle Day, which was the 29 May holiday to commemorate the restoration of King Charles II. The story goes that the king escaped death at the hands of the Roundheads by hiding in an oak tree at Boscobel. This celebration had a transgressive element all of its own: in some areas, if you were not seen to be wearing an oak gall or a sprig of oak leaves, you were thrashed with nettles or bombarded with birds' eggs, and in Sussex you could be pinched, hence the local name of Pinch Bum Day.

This mild violence came to an end in 1859 when the celebration was officially abolished, but some parishes still hold it today: Upton-on-Severn in Worcestershire, Membury in Devon and St Neot in Cornwall among them. These days it is a sedate affair, involving the church and sometimes a small parade of worthies such as the local Mayor, but there is a Civil War re-enactment at Moseley Old Hall in the Midlands – one of the houses where Charles was said to have taken shelter during his flight from Cromwell's men. In Fownhope, Herefordshire, the Heart of Oak Society also keep this old tradition going; this is another example of revival, since the Society was re-instigated in 1989, and is also an instance of an event that has seen an increase in popularity over the years.

The town of Glastonbury, in which I live, is at the forefront of modern British Pagan practices, and arguably has the highest number of actual Pagans per capita of anywhere in the country. In Charles III's coronation year, 2023, it briskly dispensed with any reservations expressed by minor British indie stars and seamlessly bolted together the town's annual Pagan events (a maypole, two red and white processing papier-mâché dragons, the crowning of a May King and Queen) to the events surrounding the coronation at the end of the first week in May, such as the national community lunch. Using Andrew Jamieson's delightful design, including the Green Man, the local council advertised Beltane/May Day and the coronation in one handy leaflet, thus integrating the old and the new. The Green Man may not be coming full circle, exactly, but he is certainly developing. Even if the foliate head that peeks down at us from the roof bosses of our old churches or the bell-shaped playful Jack who capers about the clifftops of Hastings were not pagan symbols long ago – they are now.

THREE

The Mari Lwyd and Animal Figures

If you had been in the Welsh Border town of Chepstow on a Saturday in January some years ago, you would have been able to meet some unusual visitors: the world's biggest group of Mari Lwyds (I'm not sure if this got into the Guinness Book of Records, but perhaps it should have done). This event started in a local pub, the Greenman Backpackers – a coincidental but, to my mind, rather nice link with the previous chapter – from which, in due course, emerged a host of people concealed in sheets, wearing horses' skulls, decked in ribbons and with clattering jaws. A pure piece of folk horror, surely, which would make any normal person take to their heels – but in many Welsh villages in the past, and even today, this is a familiar sight that brings a smile to the face rather than a grimace of fear.

The peculiar old Welsh custom of the Mari Lwyd has been revived in recent years and for a while became a definite point in the Chepstow calendar and that of other Welsh towns, as well as being popular among British Pagans, some of whom have come to honour the Mari as a form of *genius loci*. Unfortunately, the Chepstow celebrations went into abeyance as a result of the COVID-19 pandemic lockdown and restrictions placed on public gatherings by the Welsh Assembly, but the practice is now returning and undergoing a revival in other parts of the country as well. The Mari Lwyd celebrations have long been associated with the Wassailing customs popular throughout the southwest and Gloucestershire, a celebration of the apple harvest, and we will look at this shortly as well. Both these customs are old – but when did they begin? And what is the meaning of this sinister skull-topped figure?

The 'Mari' is a form of guising or mumming, a custom that involves groups of men (traditionally) travelling from house to house and collecting money, assembled around the central figure of the Mari Lwyd, a man draped in a sheet and carrying a horse's skull, like a spectral pantomime horse. The term 'mumming', which we will encounter a lot throughout our narrative, refers to being masked, possibly based on the Greek word 'mommo', which means 'a mask'. They would sing and enter into a 'call and response' with the householder, who was traditionally supposed to deny them entry, finding a variety of excuses to keep them out (a process known as a 'pwnco').

It might begin:

Wel dyma ni'n dwad
Gy-feillion di-niwad
I ofyn am gennad
I ofyn am gennad
I ofyn am gennad i ganu.

Well, here we come
Innocent friends
To ask leave
To ask leave
To ask leave to sing.

The householder was expected to relent eventually – or run out of excuses! – and let the Mari and her followers in, and give them food and drink. Once in the house, the Mari runs about, snapping her jaws and frightening the kids, while the rest of the team play music and sing. Not all Mari performances involved the call and response: in Llangynwyd, the troupe were simply invited in after they had sung their first song. When they left, they sang a blessing:

Dy-mun wn I'ch lawenydd,
I gynnal blwyddyu Newydd,
Tra paro'r gwr I dincian cloch
well, well, y bo'ch chwi beunydd.

We wish you joy
To sustain a new year
While the man continues to ring a bell
May you prosper more every day.

The custom was first recorded in 1800, in J. Evans's *A Tour Through Part of North Wales*, but is generally considered to be older, and the etymology of the name is open to some debate: folklorist Edwin Cawte suggested that it refers to the Welsh for 'Grey Mare', but other origins have been proposed, too.[1] Earlier folklorists posited it as a pre-Christian rite, but there is a lack of evidence for this, as we have already noted to be the case with many rural folk customs. For example, Ronald Hutton was informed in 1985 by people in Padstow that their Oss derives from a prehistoric fertility rite in which a man was sacrificed;[2] this seems to have been an invention by the Folklore Society some decades earlier and suffers somewhat from a complete lack of proof (for example, there is no evidence for the custom in late medieval writing). This 'ancient pagan ritual' theory probably derives, Hutton suggests, from a theory held by Lord Raglan of the Folklore Society, who was influenced by the hypotheses of James Frazer in *The Golden Bough* – as we have seen above, the source of much confusion within British folklore. If the name 'Raglan' seems familiar, we've already met Lord Raglan's wife, Julia; she was the writer of the Green Man article mentioned in the previous chapter. Raglan himself was a keen amateur folklorist and was president of the Folklore Society from 1945 to 1947.

Violet Alford and Edwin Cawte, also of the Folklore Society but (at least in the case of Cawte) significantly more rigorous scholars than Lord and Lady Raglan, undertook a considerable amount of research into these horse effigies. They held that in the first half of the nineteenth century the horse figure was known as 'Y March' ('The Horse') or 'Y Gynfas-farch' ('The Canvas Horse'). Cawte believed that the name means 'Grey Mare'. 'Llwyd' means 'grey' and is associated with the common Welsh name 'Lloyd', as in Lloyds Bank, but the word for 'mare', in Welsh, is 'caseg' and from this, unless the Welsh borrowed the English word 'mare', it seems a little more likely that 'Mari' means 'Mary', in which case the claim made by folklorist Iorwerth C. Peate is more probable: that the name means 'holy Mary'.[3] However, it's a bit of a stretch to see why the Mother of God is being represented by a horse's skull – surely that's a bit blasphemous? The word 'Mari' was not commonly used for the Virgin in Wales, but it does appear in the Black Book of Carmarthen in the mid-fourteenth century and in some traditional Welsh Wassailing songs.[4] It's often known today as

Y Fari Lwyd (the definite article in Welsh sometimes mutates 'm' to 'f'). So the origins of the name of the horse-skulled figure in this custom remain murky and unresolved.

The custom itself has somewhat more distinct origins, however. There are suggestions that the 'hooded animal' custom – the Maris, the Hodening of Kent and the Cotswolds 'Broad' – derive from the popularity of hobby horses in the sixteenth and seventeenth centuries, and are not confined to Wales. The Mari Lwyd herself is mainly a southern Welsh custom, and there's no apparent correlation between Welsh language speaking areas and the practice (south Pembrokeshire has long been primarily English speaking, for instance). However, it does seem to have been more popular in mining districts, possibly related to a need to establish a regional identity after the decline of local industry (it was revived in parts of south Wales during the 1980s), and possibly due to the inspiring presence of the Folk Museum at St Fagan's.[5]

The central figure is not just equine, although the horse is the most common costume used. However, as we've commented, some of the mummers dressed as bulls, and at least one bull appeared at Chepstow when I was there. Not all the Maris were made from an actual horse's skull: in the Pembrokeshire village of Solva in the mid-nineteenth century, the Mari's head was made out of a sheet stuffed with hay, with button eyes, and some of the heads were carved from wood – like hobby horses. From accounts of the custom in the village of Llangynwyd, again in the mid-nineteenth century, it seems that a lot of local people were involved in decorating the Mari: it was a communal effort.

We've noted that the Mari does not go forth alone; like the Jacks in the Green with their bogies, she has a retinue with her, usually consisting of around half a dozen men who are dressed similarly to Morris men, their garments decorated with colourful ribbons but without the bells. One of these is a leader, with a staff or a whip, and the group might be accompanied by Punch and Judy, or other figures such as the 'Merrymen' who played music. Peate has suggested that these events were influenced by English mystery plays.[6] But the Old Tup tradition, in Derbyshire and Yorkshire, is a little similar, with a sheep's head rather than a horse's skull, while festivities in Gloucestershire and Dorset feature a bull. (Hutton was charmed to meet the bull's effigy at Chepstow, but was subsequently somewhat disconcerted when he questioned the man holding it, who replied airily that he had got the idea from a book written by some chap named Hutton – this is perhaps the fate of the professional folklore historian, who inspires as well as explains.)

Cawte mentions the Hooden Horse in Kent, first recorded around 1807, which is a wooden horse's head on a pole that also comes with an accompanying team and a 'Mollie', who dresses as a woman and carries a broom.[7] Similarly, there is the Old Horse in the mining districts of Nottinghamshire, Yorkshire and Derbyshire, a practice that died out around the turn of the century (a fragment of its song migrated to south Wales and became part of the Mari's songs on the Gower). These other 'hooded animal' traditions all also take place at Christmas-tide, like the Maris themselves.

There is also a Manx equivalent – the Laare Vane, which is a wooden horse's head painted white. Again, this is a New Year custom where the 'White Horse' would chase the female members of a household, one of whom would then carry the horse's head while a dance was conducted and a fiddler played. The fiddler was put through a make-believe execution and his head was placed in the woman's lap; he would then have to answer questions about the year to come, rather like an oracle. This is very similar to an Irish custom of the same name, the Láir Bhán, which was found throughout Ireland but particularly in County Kerry. She, too, accompanied a Wren Hunt, which we'll come to shortly. The Láir Bhán in Ballycotton, County Cork, took place at Hallowe'en, not midwinter, and money was collected in her name for the giant boar known as the Muck Olla (it's not clear what he planned to spend it on!).

But the custom is not just found in the British Isles and Ireland. Krakow has a hobby horse of its own, called Lajkonik, which is said to be seven hundred years old, and hobby horses are found at Spanish festivals, too. They appear across the world and there are enough of them to put an in-depth study beyond our remit here, due to issues of length, but if we are looking for connections, I'd suggest that these are more likely to be found in Europe than, for example, Asia.

The Mari Lwyd custom declined throughout the twenti-eth century, possibly as a result of Christian disapproval; the Baptist Reverend William Roberts of Blaenau in Gwent called it 'a mixture of old Pagan and Popish ceremonies ... I wish of this folly, and all similar follies, that they find no place anywhere apart from the museum of the historian and antiquary.'[8] Hutton reports that by the start of the twentieth century the custom had died out, but it was revived in the mid-twentieth century and has become increasingly popular ever since – in this, it follows the increased popularity of Wassailing itself.[9] At Chepstow, the official literature described the custom as the 'newest old tradition in Wales, or perhaps the oldest new tradition'.

Padstow and its Oss

The May Day celebrations in Padstow, Cornwall were marked by tragedy in 2019 when a young mother died, possibly as a result of an accident involving one of the traditional figures of the Padstow Obby Oss, a large wheel-shaped structure carried by a man at its centre. This must surely be one of the most bizarre causes of death in the UK in recent years, as well as being, of course, an extremely sad episode.

Having collapsed in a lane in the port, 34-year-old neonatal nurse Laura Smallwood was found unresponsive and airlifted to Plymouth Hospital but died from neck injuries on the morning of Saturday, 4 May, after attending the Padstow May festivities on the first of the month. There were suggestions that she may have been assaulted by another woman earlier in the evening, but the authorities also had to look at the possibility that her injuries were caused by an interaction with the Oss itself.

The Oss was examined by police and returned, and the Health and Safety Executive was also informed. An employee of a restaurant close to where Mrs Smallwood was found said that the festivities can often attract rowdy and aggressive behaviour. A local woman, Rose Barker, was quoted as saying,

> There was a lot of pushing and shoving. A lot of people had too much to drink and one man passed out in the middle of the street near the harbour. I got shoved as I was walking to work.[10]

Smallwood inadvertently suffered a glancing blow from the Oss, which in this case was being carried by a man named Kevin

Constance. He stepped backwards, slipped and the heavy edge of the Oss struck Smallwood in the head or neck. She became dizzy and later collapsed.

In this age of social media, tributes to Mrs Smallwood and to the town flooded in, with more than a hundred messages of support left on the *Cornwall Live* Facebook page. Padstow was said to be 'shocked and heartbroken' by the death and some residents feared for the event's future. A resident who wished to remain anonymous told *Cornwall Live,*

> People get minor injuries every year. I saw a woman with a gashed arm this year. But for something like this to happen is truly shocking. I was speaking to someone who said they've seen this coming for years.[11]

Another resident was quoted as saying, 'I've always worried someone might get seriously hurt by an oss. They are very heavy and people get so close.'[12] One of the Padstow shop owners also commented:

> It will be a real shame if this has a serious effect in the future, especially knowing what Health and Safety did to carnivals. This is very sad for the lady involved and very sad for the Obby Oss and Padstow.[13]

A suggestion was made at the time, however, that future Osses could be made from cardboard, which is obviously much lighter, but it doesn't seem that this was actually carried out. Some health and safety measures were brought in: the distance between the Oss and spectators has been increased after the coroner criticized a lack of best practice at Smallwood's inquest. This concluded that she died of a brain stem stroke caused by being struck in the head by the Oss, although she had sustained a minor arterial tear ten days previously and the blow to the head opened it up again, causing her death. The coroner's report stated:

> At inquest, I heard that there is still no one willing to act as an 'Event Organiser' for the May Day event as a whole despite repeated requests from the police for this to happen. As a consequence, there is no single point of contact for the police or others and no one who is engaged with the LSAG to look at public safety.[14]

This tragic episode is not the only violent incident at Padstow; tourists who have mocked the practice are said to have been thrown into the harbour. But Smallwood's death garnered headlines, for the Padstow May celebrations are famous throughout Britain. According to a local historian, 83-year-old John Buckingham, the May Day celebration is 'Christmas and birthdays and everything rolled into one for most people'. He adds, 'there are young people in the town who can't wait to carry the Oss, it's a rite of passage. Cool or not, I do not know, but it's cool if you're a young Padstownian.'[15]

The festivities, which attract up to 4,000 people, begin on May Eve at midnight, when townsfolk gather outside the Golden Lion pub in Padstow and sing the 'Night Song'. Two groups are involved, one featuring the 'Old' Oss and one with the 'Blue Ribbon Oss' (it was the latter that was involved in Mrs Smallwood's death). The Oss consists of a wooden horse's head and a large round structure over which a black oilskin cape is hung; the Blue Ribbon Oss is actually made from a table top. It is thus a sort of cousin to the Mari Lwyd, an example of a hooded animal custom, although in form it is possibly closer to a Jack in the Green. Although it's always called an 'Oss', it really doesn't look much like an actual horse apart from its head; it probably represents a man riding a horse, possibly caparisoned like a medieval steed in a tournament. Young women are encouraged to duck under the Oss (some folklorists hold that there is an obvious sexual subtext to this). The horses are accompanied by 'Teasers', who try to catch young women as they pass through the town on a twelve-hour circuit, initiated by the 'Morning' or 'Day Song'. The two horses meet at a may-pole whereupon the horses return to their 'stables'. They are said to die, and be resurrected on the following May Eve.

Whether the Obby Oss ceremony is genuinely ancient is debatable. There are extensive mentions of May Day festivities in the sixteenth century, but the first mention of the Padstow celebrations comes in the early nineteenth century, and it's possibly no older than the eighteenth century. There have been suggestions that such events originally come from Beltane celebrations; certainly, many newer rites such as the Glastonbury Dragons Parade are recent and are explicitly Beltane-related, but as we saw when we looked at the Jacks in the Green, there's unlikely to be a direct line of descent. Ronald Hutton says that when he visited Padstow in 1985, locals described the event as coming from an ancient fertility rite, but, as we've mentioned, they probably got this belief from early twentieth-century historians influenced by Frazer.[16] Alex Merry, of Stroud's Boss Morris side, says:

I think beasts predate Morris dancing, from the little that I know about it. I think it's a very old tradition. When I was first getting into Morris dancing, I would make a beeline for any beast that was at any event. I totally fell in love with all these weird hobby horses and strange goggly-eyed clacky things on the sidelines.[17]

The Stroud Morris side themselves feature creatures, such as Ewegenie the sheep, harking back to Stroud's wool trade, and (rather randomly) a giant owl.

Certainly, the Blue Ribbon Oss itself is of recent origins, devised by the Temperance Movement in the late nineteenth century to try to discourage the excessive drinking that accompanied the event (there's no evidence that this has succeeded). After the First World War, it was known as the 'Peace Oss'.

The Padstow event is not the only one that involves an Oss. Minehead also has a similar celebration involving two boat-shaped costumes, and we've already looked extensively at the revival of the Mari Lwyd.

To have a death at this kind of event is unusual, but injuries are not infrequently reported at folk events like mass street football matches, such as Haxey Hood in Lincolnshire, or the Cooper's Hill cheese-rolling competition, as we will note later on.

Interview with Daniel McKenzie, Order of Bards, Ovates and Druids

Daniel is a member of one of the modern Druid orders, the Order of Bards, Ovates and Druids, and took part in a ritual re-enactment involving a masked horned figure.

I was once part of a Wild Hunt in Wales and became the actual Horned One, not being aware what else was expected of me.

I got 'married' to the Moon's daughter and we were led to a bower to . . .

Well, I had a very nice chat with the lady in question and we became good friends. She introduced me to OBOD.

But we kept our hands to ourselves.

It was part of a folk customs/witchcraft retreat in a very nice country estate. It was held there every year and spawned several interesting stories. The 'hounds' had to wear actual dog masks. Once they came across a car in a ditch and wanted to help, forgetting they were dressed as canines. It was already dusk. They scared the living daylights out of the poor driver.

Interview with Marion Pitman

Which folk customs do you engage with or practice?
I watch and used to do Morris dancing. I go to Padstow for May Day each year.

What do you enjoy about them?

Mostly the people. Also, there is a degree of anti-establishmentism which I enjoy, though it is being forcibly reduced.

What do you think other people think of your involvement? Do they approve, or do you get criticized for it?

A great many of the people I know do the same sort of thing; others think I'm barmy.

What role do you think these customs play in the modern world? Do you think they are still important (or just a bit of fun), and if so, why?

I think they are important, as well as fun, since by and large they are done by the people at ground level, not organized from above. They are also a reminder of how things change, and that they weren't always like this and won't always be like this. There is a tendency to think that whatever is now is what will be forever, and even that it always was.

Is your chosen folk custom important to your identity?

Not as such. I don't really grasp this idea – my identity is me, whatever I do. I feel more like Granny Weatherwax in the hall of mirrors: 'Which is the real you?' 'This one.'

How has your chosen custom changed during your engagement with it? Has it become more diverse, for instance?

Morris dancing has certainly become more diverse, both in the people doing it and the types of dancing. May Day has changed more subtly, perhaps; I hope it may have become kinder. Padstow has changed hugely, but May Day is still for the people who have always been there, although I have seen Rick Stein having a drink out the London Inn. Elements of the day and following day change quite a lot.

Do you think your interest in your folk custom is diminishing or growing?

Certainly not diminishing, possibly growing. I am always interested in anything out of the ordinary.

Is there a transgressive element to your chosen custom?

Definitely in May Day, though as I say, it has been forced to be less transgressive recently. I don't know if they still throw people in the harbour if they get in the way. I am not privy to everything that goes on. Anyone trying to drive through the town while it's going on gets short shrift.

Morris dancing also holds up the traffic. (When I say Morris I am including Molly dancing, which I used to do, and all the other kinds.)

The Dorset Ooser

The Dorset Ooser, described by Hutton as a 'magnificent enigma', is a hollow wooden head about two feet in width.[18] It takes the form of a man with bull's horns, and is said to have originated in the Dorset village of Melbury Osmond. The word 'ooser' crops up in the novels of Thomas Hardy, and has been defined as 'a wooden horned mask used for folkloric and magical purposes'. William Barnes, the nineteenth-century Dorset dialect poet, says that the ooser, oose or wurse is 'a mask . . . with grim jaws, put on with a cow's skin to frighten folk. "Wurse" . . . is a name of the arch-fiend."[19] Daniel Patrick Quinn, whose research we will be looking at below, notes that it is not clear whether the term 'ooser' refers to the mask itself or to the person wearing it, but it's probably easier to treat it as the mask itself.[20] Oosers feature in the novels *The Return of the Native* (1878) and *The Mayor of Casterbridge* (1886), in which Hardy describes 'skimmity riding' or 'Rough Music', which we will address in due course. In *The Return of the Native*, a character says, 'What have made you so down? Have you seen a ooser?' Hardy also once told an acquaintance that the ooser was a 'sort of bogeyman' used to frighten children into obedience.[21]

The head could technically be worn, but would need someone to guide the person wearing it as there is no way to see out, although it was constructed in such a way that the jaw could be made to clack up and down. It was wide, as we noted above, and if you wore it, the top of its head would be over 2 metres (7 feet) off the ground; it would also have been very heavy. The image of the Ooser has been taken up by at least one Morris side, the Blackthorn Morris, which also features a Mari Lwyd. In these instances, it is a processional figure, carried but not worn, although some of the replicas might be wearable if made out of papier mâché and not the original heavy wood and horn.

The original head itself was owned by the Cave family of Holt Farm in Melbury Osmond and was allegedly used to frighten children trespassing on the farm near the malt house. Contemporary members of the Cave family say that the mask was very old and had been in the family since 'time out of mind', but that they didn't know what its original purpose had been. Having resided for years in the malt house itself, the mask was probably moved to Holt Farm at some point in the 1870s, as there was an application from a local man to use the malt house as a chapel. Mr B. W. Milward of Sawbridgeworth, Hertfordshire, and Tom Cave's cousin remembers getting a fright from the Ooser in 1875 when he met his cousin wearing it in the garden in the dark. But it might have gone back to the new chapel: Hardy, in his short story 'The First Countess of Wessex' (1889), refers to the Ooser as 'being in the church vestry'.[22]

Since the story is set in Melbury Osmond, this gives us a clue, but fiction writers often conflate locations and events, and perhaps Hardy thought that the alarming mask might have more dramatic impact if it was in a clerical context rather than just a farm. H.S.L. Dewar relates that a stablehand was so terrified by the Ooser that he leaped through a window and severely injured himself.[23]

After this, the head was taken up to Somerset by one of the family, Dr Edward Cave, who was working in Crewkerne. His brother Thomas attempted to sell it in 1891, advertising it to antiquarians and asking for 50 guineas, without success.

In 1897, the head went missing. Edward Thomas had apparently moved to Bath and left the mask in the care of a coachman, but when he subsequently tried to retrieve it, the mask was nowhere to be found. Rumours suggest that either the coachman sold it, to someone unknown, or that the mask was left in the charge of a Dr Webber, who had been in partnership with Edward Cave. A woman named Elizabeth Ramsden made enquiries in 1935 and her research suggests that Cave's coachman went to work for Dr Webber. The coachman said that he recalled the Ooser hanging in Dr Webber's loft, but by this time the poor Ooser had lost its horns and its hair was coming out in tufts. However, the coachman wore it at a carnival in Crewkerne, and this seems to be the final mention of the Dorset Ooser. Dr Webber's house was eventually pulled down and replaced with a Post Office, but there was no sign of the Ooser. It is possible that the old mask simply fell apart and the remains were disposed of. However, Webber's daughter, Mrs N. H. Marshall, told an acquaintance in 1962 that her father had told her that the coachman had sold it (maybe he got an offer at the carnival?). Another source is quoted by folklorist Christina Hole as saying:

> Some years ago when they moved from Crewkerne it
> was left behind with other property and stored in a loft.
> Later it could not be found, and a groom admitted that
> a man from 'up Chinnock way' had asked to buy it, and
> he, thinking it rubbish, had let him have it. It was not
> known why the stranger bought it or what he intended
> to do with so peculiar an object, since, from the groom's
> description, he did not appear to be a collector of curiosities. All inquiries at East Chinnock proved entirely
> fruitless; the Dorset Ooser has not been heard of since
> and is probably lost for ever.[24]

A replica is now held in a local museum and taken out by
Morris sides for St George's Day and May Day. The original
head initiated a widespread discussion among folklorists. Was
it a representation of the Devil, as some claim? Or an ancient
fertility god?

The folklorists Frederick Thomas Elworthy and H.S.L.
Dewar believed that the head represented the Devil, and maintained that its deployment in local shaming practices, which
we'll come to later, was to reinforce conventional Christian
morality, frightening wrong-doers with a reminder of the torments to come if that morality should be abandoned.[25] We
should take this as a hypothesis, as it is not clear what evidence
Elworthy and Dewar had for their claim.

A commendable effort to track down the history of the
Ooser has been made by Daniel Patrick Quinn, who made

several visits to Holt Farm in the early 2000s and spoke with a woman named Margaret Courage, who lived in Thomas Cave's old house. She recalled meeting older villagers in the 1960s who remembered folk talking about the Ooser. However, they were rather reluctant to do so themselves; there seems to have been a miasma of fear around the old mask, and it was regarded with suspicion (apart from one old lady who seems to have found it hilarious but there's always someone who is fearless in regard to these matters!). Quinn describes the Ooser thus: 'The appearance of the Ooser is certainly one of deep, other-worldly despair.'[26]

Charles Herbert Mayo, Canon of Longburton Rectory and the Dorset editor of *Somerset and Dorset Notes and Queries*, described it in 1891:

> a wooden mask, of large size, with features grotesquely human, long flowing locks of hair on either side of the head, a beard, and a pair of bullock's horns, projecting right and left of the forehead. The mask or ooser is cut from a solid block, excepting the lower jaw, which is movable, and connected with the upper by a pair of leathern hinges. A string, attached to this movable jaw, passes through a hole in the upper jaw, and is then allowed to fall into the cavity. The Ooser is so formed that a man's head may be placed in it, and thus carry or support it while he is in motion. No provision, however, is made for his seeing through the eyes of the mask, which are not pierced. By pulling the string the lower jaw is drawn up and closed against the upper, and when the string is slackened it descends.[27]

There are two photographs in existence, both taken by John W. Chaffin and Sons of Yeovil at some point between 1883 and 1891, and we can assume that these might have been part of the efforts of Thomas Cave to sell the mask.

Between the eyes, the Ooser has a round lump, sometimes suggested to represent a third eye (there is absolutely no evidence that this was the intended symbolism and we have to treat this as entirely fanciful). Anyone wearing the mask would not be able to see out through the eyes in any case, as they are set too far apart; the head is simply too big. However, some have suggested that the wearer might be able to see out through the mouth.[28] It's also possible from earlier accounts that one horn was painted white and the other red. Poet William Barnes, cited above, claimed that the wearer would also be garbed in a calfskin cloak.

Being made of wood and hair, the mask is unlikely to have been ancient – possibly dating back no further than the middle of the eighteenth century. We know that horned masks were made in places such as Hungary and it is possible that some adventurous member of the Cave family might have brought it back as a souvenir. I did a little digging into some of these old masks – there are images on the Internet, and certainly the Ooser seems to be a cousin of these, if not identical. He also looks rather similar to images of a Javanese Barong Naga mask; this isn't completely beyond the realms of possibility given the degree of trade between East Asia and Britain during the nineteenth century and earlier. All it takes is an enquiring-minded traveller to pick up some curio in a bazaar, and for that origin to be lost to memory. It's a shame we don't have a sample of the wood of which the Ooser was made, for that might have provided some valuable clues. Although there might have been previous Oosers, we have no evidence for their existence.

H.S.L. Dewar became enthused about practices such as the Abbots Bromley Horn Dance, citing also the antler skull caps found at Starr Carr, and made the far-reaching claim that the Devil, and thus the Dorset Ooser, was originally a fertility figure.[29] As usual, there's no proof of this. There's also no real evidence that the Ooser represents the Devil; it could do, but it might just be a fanciful bogeyman.

Quinn cites a comment made by Henry Joseph Moule of Dorchester, who wrote to *Somerset and Dorset Notes and Queries* in 1892 regarding the Ooser and mummers:

> The note about the Ooser calls back old times. In my childhood he was doing service – at Christmas mummings surely it was. Our Cerne Abbas nurse was quite up in all relating to the 'Wurser', as I should spell it phonetically. I did not know of the horns, indeed in our embryo Latinity we thought the word an attempt at Ursa, if I remember rightly. What crowds of odd bits I could note if, alas, I did but 'remember rightly' all the nurse's folk-lore and folk-speeches.[30]

Whether this was the actual Dorset Ooser, minus his horns, is unclear, but there were other masked heads used in mumming in the locality, such as the Shillingford Bull. The Ooser's face is humanoid, rather than animal, although we have seen above mention of the calfskin cape.

Wessex Morris side are the current owners of the remodelled Dorset Ooser:

The side are the owners of the infamous Dorset Ooser (or Oozer), the new one that is, a giant of a creature with a large wooden head and even larger horns, carved from a passing log by John Byfleet using a small pen-knife. It is cloaked in the hide of a peripatetic calf, supported on a stick, and ceremonially embedded in the groin of a Wessex Morris Man. Poor old Alan Cheesman always draws the short straw when it comes to carrying the Ooser, something to do with the fact he is the only bloke big enough and strong enough to lift it. Other people have tried on numerous occasions and ended up with bleeding sores on their shoulders, even Alan has a rough time of it and has to stop and rest at regular intervals. This is the main reason the Ooser is only seen on May Day and St Georges Day. It is said, by some, to be the Dorset manifestation of the Horned God; also known as Herne the Hunter, Cerne, Cernnunos, etc. The new version was made by John Byfleet in 1973 and can be seen at The Dorset County Museum in Dorchester. If you want to see the Ooser in action you will have to get up very early on May Day and meet us at the top of the Cerne Giant before sunrise.[31]

Hunting the Wren

Another custom that sits alongside the Mari Lwyd in south Welsh villages, and in other places, too, is the practice of hunting the wren. Here, groups of boys and young men would go forth either on St Stephen's Day, also known as Boxing Day, on 26 December, or in the early days of January, and catch a wren, then bear it around houses on a bier (sometimes it was killed, but sometimes not). The custom occasionally crops up in literature, appearing to eerie effect in a dream in Susan Cooper's well-known children's novel *The Dark Is Rising*.[32] In the book, it is clear that the wren is a personification of the Lady, a goddess or spirit of the land. Steeleye Span also did a song relating to the custom.

In the Isle of Man, the justification for this cruel practice was that a wicked woman of the fairy folk came to the island and drowned a number of men, then to evade capture, changed shape into a wren and flew away. The custom is said to have originated to commemorate the event and punish the witch each year. There are other origin stories, too – that a wren alerted an enemy force by pecking crumbs that had fallen onto a drum, for instance. On the Isle of Man, the wren was hunted on Christmas Eve night and then buried in a mock ceremony in the churchyard; the feathers were used as a charm against shipwreck and were carried by fishermen throughout the year.

Although the custom was popular on the Isle of Man, the wren population must have breathed a sigh of relief when, by the 1880s, the little bird itself was no longer hunted (although some groups used a large rat instead) and only the wren pole itself was carried around the district. In other parts of the UK and Ireland, a potato was substituted. As with so many of these customs at this time of year, the main aim was to earn a few pennies. And with many customs, blacking up and wearing women's clothing was also a feature of some wren dances.

The custom has been revived. It takes place once a year in Glastonbury, for example, but the focus has changed, to honour the wren and the winter spirits, and a felt wren or other replica is used instead. Wren hunting just fits our 'transgression' remit; it's only a controversial custom now because of the element of animal cruelty.

FOUR

Wassail, Wassail, All Over the Town

We have looked at the various traditions surrounding the Mari Lwyd as part of the wider context of Wassail, but what does Wassailing itself involve? The word 'wassail' comes from the Saxon Wæs þu hæl, meaning 'be thou hale (healthy)'. Geoffrey of Monmouth's *History of the Kings of Britain* claims that:

> While Vortigern was being entertained at a royal banquet, the young lady came out of her chamber bearing a golden cup of wine, with which she approached the king, and making a low curtsey, said 'Lauerd King wacht heil!' The king, at the sight of the lady's face, was on a sudden both surprised and inflamed by her beauty; and calling for his interpreter asked him what he said and what answer he should make her.
>
> 'She called you, Lord King,' said the interpreter, "and offered to drink your health. Your answer to her should be 'drinc heil'! Vortigern accordingly answered 'drinc hail' and bade her drink; after which he took the cup from her hand, kissed her, and drank himself. From that time to this, it has been the custom in Britain, that he who drinks to anyone says 'wacht heil' and he that pledges him, answers 'drinc hail'.[1]

In a later version of this story, the king and Rowena drink alternately from the cup.

The drink itself is claimed by some to be a descendent of the spiced Roman hypocras – a beverage for the wealthy alone, given that spices such as cinnamon had to be imported into Britain. But sometimes it took the form of a drink called Lambs' Wool, in which roasted crab apples are placed in ale. These puff up and burst, forming a froth reminiscent of the woolly strands of a lamb's coat. We find mention of this in Shakespeare's plays:

Sometimes lurk I in the gossip's bowl
In very likeness of a roasted crab
And when she drinks, against her lips I bob,
And down her withered dewlap pours the ale.[2]

This comes from *A Midsummer Night's Dream*, and in *Love's Labour's Lost* we find:

When all aloud the wind doth blow
And coughing drowns the parson's saw
And birds sit brooding in the snow
And Marian's nose looks red and raw,
When roasted crabs hiss in the bowl,
Then nightly sings the staring owl, Tu-whit,
Tu-who – a merry note,
While greasy Joan doth keel the pot.[3]

We also find mention in Robert Herrick's seventeenth-century poem *Twelfth Night; or, King and Queen*:

Now, now the mirth comes
With the cake full of plums,
Where bean's the king of the sport here;
Beside we must know,
The pea also
Must revel, as queen, in the court here.

Begin then to choose,
This night as ye use,
Who shall for the present delight here,
Be a king by the lot,
And who shall not
Be Twelfth-day queen for the night here.

Which known, let us make
Joy-sops with the cake;
And let not a man then be seen here,
Who unurg'd will not drink
To the base from the brink
A health to the king and queen here.

Next crown a bowl full
With gentle lamb's wool:
Add sugar, nutmeg, and ginger,
With store of ale too;
And thus ye must do
To make the wassail a swinger.

Give then to the king
And queen wassailing:

And though with ale ye be whet here,
   Yet part from hence
   As free from offence
As when ye innocent met here.[4]

The first mention of the 'Wassail cup' itself comes in the thirteenth century. The drink is described as having small pieces of bread floated in it, hence the claim that this is the origin of the term to 'toast' someone. One of the folk stories of Somerset tells of the Apple Tree Man: the spirit of the oldest tree in the orchard, who is given the orchard owner's last glass of mulled cider and, in thanks, shows him the way to buried treasure. Some communities still have their original nineteenth-century cups but most of the old Wassail cups in existence today date from the last forty years of the seventeenth century; during Cromwell's rule, Christmas and thus Wassailing were banned, but after the Restoration, the old trappings of such customs became popular once more. Dyrham Park in Gloucestershire has a magnificent Wassail cup made out of lignum vitae. This, like others of its kind, dates from the eighteenth century when Britain's colonial reach began to see interesting woods brought in from abroad. Lignum vitae is supposed to have medicinal properties (it is held to be able to cure gout and syphilis, for a start) and is a hard wood that can easily contain hot liquids; drinking from a cup made out of a 'health giving' wood was evidently appealing in a custom designed to bring good health for the year to come. Some of the cups, such as the one made by the Worshipful Company of Grocers in the seventeenth century, are decorated with silver.

There are three kinds of Wassailing that have emerged over the centuries: House Wassailing, Orchard Wassailing and

Cattle Wassailing, in which the Wassail bowl was taken into the byre where the oxen lay and a toast drunk to their health. Fire Wassailing was also practised in some areas, in which torches were lit around the orchards, but this has died out. Orchard Wassailing is not a universal British custom, being found, as one might expect, predominantly in those areas where apple and pear orchards are a major agricultural feature: primarily, therefore, the southwest of the UK – Gloucestershire, Herefordshire and Somerset, and also the island of Jersey. Originally, as the name indicates and as we've noted above, it is supposed to have been a Saxon custom, to thank the spirits of the trees for their bounty, but in the twentieth and twenty-first centuries it has become simply a family evening out; a number of farms arrange Wassailing events in mid-January, usually around Old Twelfth Night on the seventeenth. In earlier times, Christmas itself would end on 6 January, at Epiphany, and Wassailing would commence from then onwards.

This is one of a number of customs that have been increasing in popularity in recent years – partly for farmers to make money, since they usually charge an entrance fee, and partly, I think, because it's a fun activity for parents to do with the kids in the long dark month after Christmas. Some Wassail celebrations can draw quite a large crowd, up to several hundred people in the case of the larger commercial orchards and cider farms.

During the course of the Wassailing, mulled cider and wine are given out, sometimes in a 'loving cup' (which has two handles, so that two people can drink from it at the same time). A Wassail king and queen are elected, usually by means of the ancient method of a bean found in a piece of cake. A shotgun is fired into the trees and pans are banged to frighten away evil

spirits, and an offering of toast and cider is made to propiti-
ate the good spirits of the orchards. Then Wassail carols might
be sung:

> Here's to thee, old apple tree,
> That blooms well, bears well.
> Hats full, caps full,
> Three bushel bags full,
> An' all under one tree.
> Hurrah! Hurrah!

The Gloucestershire Wassail Song' ('Wassail! Wassail, all over
the town, our toast it is white and our ale it is brown') and
'The Wassailer's Carol' ('Here we come a-Wassailing among
the leaves so green') are among the best known today. House
Wassailing, too, used to follow a call and response format, like
the Mari Lwyd, reminding the householder,

> we are not daily beggars that beg from door to door
> But we are friendly neighbours whom you have seen
> before.

Many of us who have been carol singing will have experienced this as a charitable exercise; monies gathered will be
donated to good causes, but when I was a child it was considered acceptable to keep the money that people gave you. (My
partner and his cousins, with some degree of cynicism, took an
angelic-looking little sister with them on their carol singing
outings, which took place on the London Underground, all the
way round the Circle Line. They sang and the little girl, brought

there to look winsome and thus induce commuters to part with their cash, was bribed with sweets). 'We Wish You a Merry Christmas' is a Wassailing-type of song, entreating households for provender such as food and drink.

Carhampton, Dunster and Glastonbury all hold regular Wassail events in Somerset, and so do Whimple and Sandford in Devon. Clevedon, near Bristol, hosts one and this is combined with dancing from the local Morris side, who also feature a grumpy pantomime horse – not quite a Mari Lwyd, but definitely related. I attended the one held at Glastonbury's Rural Life Museum some years ago. This involved the firing of a shotgun and, since the museum is set on a busy junction, nearly resulted in a passing Belgian lorry driver running his truck off the road – fortunately, he recovered in the nick of time. In the context of a book that considers the transgressive element of folk customs, weapons fire definitely fits the bill in the modern climate!

We Won't Go Until We've Got Some

House Wassailing used to be a common practice, but over the past hundred years this has mainly been replaced by carol singing. But there was a darker side to House Wassailing, involving groups of rowdy young men who might, if refused entry or food, not only curse the householder but vandalize the property as well. This falls into the 'emergent property' category of transgression: it's not an intrinsic part of the custom, but something that developed from it. Some enterprising souls also used the practice as a further money-making scheme, taking the drink that they'd been given and selling it on to households further down the road. This isn't confined to Wassail and the other mid-winter customs; it is also found at other times of the year, such as Pace Egging at Easter, the various Shrovetide customs and, as we will see in a later chapter, in modern times at Hallowe'en. (It will become clear as we proceed that the basis of a lot of these customs is financial: providing entertainment in a difficult economic time of the year, to make a few pence to tide oneself over. Once society started becoming more organized – for example, instituting basic forms of national insurance – a lot of these customs started to die away until revived by twentieth-century folk enthusiasts for other reasons.)

A late-seventeenth-century journalist complained: 'Wenches . . . by their Wassels at New-years-tide . . . present you with a Cup, and you must drink of the slabby stuff; but the meaning is, you must give them Moneys.'[5] In a more lawabiding society, this aspect of the practice is thankfully no more. An account of Wassailing written by the head curator of the National Trust, Sally-Anne Huxtable, comments:

> The noisy banishing of spirits seems to bear a close relationship to the rural folk custom of Charivari, or skimmington ride, in which a wrongdoer would be shamed by a large group of people parading around their house, making loud and discordant music.[6]

That's an interesting point, given that we are going to look at the charivari later, but here we encounter again the tendency of many folk customs to have an in-built aspect of menace. The seemingly innocuous apple-celebration of Wassail is no exception.

This line of the carol 'We Wish You a Merry Christmas' always seemed to me to be imbued with a faint sense of threat. We've noted that Wassailing, like other customs, used to have something of a poor reputation due to the behaviour of groups of young men, who would, indeed, not go 'until they'd got some'. Current moral panics – sometimes justified, sometimes not – about the modern incarnation at Hallowe'en of trick or treating bear a considerable resemblance to the issues that surrounded Wassailing. Complaints were made throughout the history of the practice about rowdy young men who forced their way into people's homes and demanded money or drink, both in the UK and in the USA; from the early nineteenth century, more respectable Americans were calling for the custom to be banned.

They were not alone. On the other side of the Atlantic, in Wassailing's original home, sixteenth-century English bishop Hugh Latimer (despite coming from a sect that celebrated Christmas), remarked sourly, 'Men dishonour Christ more in the twelve days of Christmas, than in all the twelve months besides.'[7]

There's a class element to original Wassailing: as we've seen, poorer members of the community would go to their wealthier neighbours to ask for alms. Essentially, although they remind the householder (as in the Wassail song above) that they are not beggars, the custom has often been a licensed, more socially acceptable form of begging, with money kept by the wassailers rather than given to charity, as it often is today. In the USA, the Puritans sought to stamp out the custom altogether; Governor William Bradford in the Plymouth Colony punished anyone who celebrated Christmas. In 1659, the General Court of the Massachusetts Bay Colony upheld the ban:

It is therefore ordered by this court and the authority thereof that whoever shall be found observing, by abstinence of labor, feasting, or in any other way, any such day such as Christmas . . . shall pay for every such offense five shillings as a fine.[8]

Part of the reasoning given was to keep in check 'disorders arising in several places within the jurisdiction by reason of some still observing such festivities, as were superstitiously kept in other countries, to the dishonor of God and the offense of others.'[9]

Wassailing was at the forefront of these 'disorders'. Wassailers sometimes entered a house uninvited, demanding drink. In 1679 in Salem, in the unfortunate case of an elderly couple, John Rowden and his wife, who were renowned for their perry, four Wassailers were given beer but demanded more. They were sent packing, but returned a short time later and tried to pass off a piece of lead as payment. The Rowdens' adopted son, Daniel Poole, took issue with them and violence broke out:

They threw stones, bones, and other things at Poole in the doorway and against the house. They beat down much of the daubing in several places and continued to throw stones for an hour and a half with little intermission. They also broke down about a pole and a half of fence, being stone wall, and a cellar, without the house, distant about four or five rods, was broken open through the door, and five or six pecks of apples were stolen.[10]

On 22 December 1794, almost a hundred years later, a Massachusetts shopkeeper named John Birge noted in his shop accounts that 'Nightwalkers – or rather blockheads' had turned up, ostensibly to Wassail, but actually to break into the shop and ransack it. He questioned, not unreasonably under the circumstances, how the custom differed from actual burglary.

In Cornwall, guising at Christmas in Penzance was banned in the late nineteenth century for similar reasons. The revellers were described as a 'lawless mob' who yelled and hooted, and because they were masked, old scores could be settled anonymously, which led to further violence.[11] Both Wassailing and guising, which are similar customs (sometimes at the same and sometimes at different times of the year) carried out originally for money and goods, have suffered throughout their history from associated violence. In Bradford, in 1868, a guiser assaulted a couple on their own doorstep. Hutton comments that 'What had presumably begun as a tradition by which communal solidarity was reaffirmed had become one of social confrontation and aggression.'[12]

In Britain, the law against Christmas was not repealed until 1681, but although religious ideology played a role in the original legislation, it was also designed to eradicate what was perceived to be a significant social problem. In 1761, almost a century later, the press was exhorting people to keep Christmas as a 'most solemn festival [without] disorder or immorality'.[13] One of the New England ministers backed this up, saying that in 'the keeping [of Christmas as] a matter of devotion, let them keep to their houses, but there should be no gaming or revelling in the streets'.[14]

Christmas as many Americans now know it – a Norman Rockwell vision of apple-cheeked children greeting their Christmas stockings with joy, sleigh rides to church through the snow and the decorating of the Christmas tree – did not really begin until the nineteenth century, and it was much the same in England. Thomas Nast, editor of *Harper's Weekly* from 1862 to 1887, did much to cement this wholesome, not-at-all-unruly vision of Christmas in the minds of the American public. Dickens's novels feature the Wassail bowl, and so does the work of Washington Irving:

Now Christmas is come
Let's beat up the drum,
And call all our neighbors together,
And when they appear,
Let us make them such cheer
As will keep out the wind and the weather.[15]

In Shetland around Hallowe'en or Yule, mummers – local folk in disguise for the purposes of performance – known as skeklers or gulicks, their bodies concealed in straw costumes, would wear hankies to hide their faces and would fire a shot upon approaching a farm. Elsewhere in Scotland people would black their faces (boys and girls in some places) and wear false beards before guising. They would sometimes play practical jokes. In England there are similar customs, again with blackened or reddened faces.

In the 1930s and '40s, children in New York City would blacken their faces with soot and go from door to door, asking for pennies (though not, one hopes, drink). In the UK, the practice remained in a few rural areas but, as we have noted, has since been revived, without the blackface and hopefully without the menaces. We're going to look later on at the issues surrounding blacking up – whether it is a result of wanting to adopt a disguise and remain anonymous, or whether there are other causes for the practice – when we come to consider Morris dancing, since blacking up has more recently been an issue in Morris dancing rather than in Wassailing, in which it is no longer practised.

But there is more to this question of rowdy behaviour. In certain periods it has gone beyond demanding money with menaces and vandalism. In 1631, Wassailing was associated with social unrest, on an occasion in which the Wassailers assembled 'with two rummes, two coulers, and one fife in a warlike and outrageoud manner assemble themselves, together armed with gunnes, pykes, halberds, and other weapons'.[16]

How did a midwinter custom intended to celebrate the apple harvest become a form of activism, of social protest, of lawlessness – and why? Let's take a deeper look at this now.

The World Turned Upside Down

At some point, commentators on the social role of Wassailing, the Mari Llywd and similar midwinter customs often mention 'misrule'. What exactly do they mean by this?

The central conceit of misrule is what English Heritage rather charmingly refers to as 'holiday misbehaviour'. English Heritage properties historian Michael Clarke suggests that this dates back to the Roman custom of Saturnalia, focusing on a rite held on 17 December in honour of the god Saturn.[17] This, in turn, derived from a similar Greek festival, the Kronia, but that took place in midsummer. Saturnalia initially lasted for one day but by the late Republic (133–31 BCE) it had lengthened, extending across seven days and featuring a socially licensed form of transgression: masters would serve food and drink to their servants, for example. Schools and law courts were closed, and much business was suspended for the duration of the festival. Gambling was practised. People filled their homes with greenery – something that seems to be a feature of this time of year. When the Roman Empire became Christianized, some customs remained, held over from older times, and by the medieval period the Feast of Fools had taken the place of the Saturnalia, lasting from 26 to 28 December. Here, junior members of the clergy served their seniors, but there was more to the custom than this decorous reversal – the Bishop of Lincoln, Robert Grosseteste, had to forbid clergy from pretending to worship demons during the Feast of Fools period in the thirteenth century.

People wore colourful clothes and gave one another gifts of cerei (wax tapers) and, on the final day, the sigillaria, gave gifts of little terracotta figurines. Catullus describes the Saturnalia as 'the best of times' but it did not appeal to Pliny, who allegedly constructed a soundproof room so that he could continue working without being disturbed.[18] Modern urban dwellers may sympathize.

Households elected a 'Saturnalicius princeps', a lord of misrule, perhaps from among the lower ranking servants. This person might be chosen by hiding a coin or other small object in a cake (like the later Wassail cake). He would essentially organise the festivities and be responsible for a degree of mayhem (insulting guests, for instance). This is a time when the social hierarchy is turned upside down and chaos becomes the order of the day, but even chaos has rules – there were presumably limits to the mayhem that was allowed, which everyone would understand. Lucian, in his *Saturnalia*, has Cronos say,

> Mine is a limited monarchy, you see. To begin with, it only lasts a week; that over, I am a private person, just a man in the street. Secondly, during my week the serious is barred; no business allowed. Drinking and being drunk, noise and games and dice, appointing of kings and feasting of slaves, singing naked, clapping of tremulous hands, an occasional ducking of corked faces in icy water, – such are the functions over which I preside.[19]

It is generally held that many of the customs of Saturnalia became absorbed into early forms of Christmas in the Roman Empire – the candles, the gift giving, the presentation of special verses and the greenery. However, Christmas is a much more orderly affair without the social role reversals (the braver reader can test this by roundly insulting their Christmas Day guests and seeing how that goes down nowadays). Yet perhaps elements of that transgressiveness recur in the rowdiness of Wassail at the end of the Christmas period, although we must not make any claim that it descends directly from the Saturnalia itself. Hutton comments that later folk customs in the British Isles merely 'evoked the anarchic spirit of the ancient Saturnalia and Kalendae'.[20]

The city of Rome is considered to have celebrated Saturnalia a hundred years or so after it became Christianized (it officially became Christian in 313 CE), but the religious side of the festival gradually faded away until it revived again, this time with a Christian aspect, around the second century. Christ's actual birthdate – if he existed – is obviously unknown, but it is possible that Christmas derives from the Roman festival of dies natalis solis invicti ('day of the birth of the unconquered sun') around the winter solstice. This festival was celebrated on 25 December; Roman authorities were not quite sure when the winter solstice actually took place. Ronald Hutton suggests that this was a relatively minor celebration and the main festivities took place every four years in October.[21] The Emperor Aurelian devised the cult of Sol Invictus in 274 CE, replacing earlier worship of Sol Indiges, the older sun god of a Syrian cult (this is not uncontentious, by the way – authorities disagree on the origins of these deities). Constantine, in 321 CE, also decreed Sol's day – Sunday – as a day of rest, which we still maintain today.

The Unconquered Sun was celebrated primarily by chariot races, symbolizing the god's passage across the sky. Initially, the cult was obviously mainly Roman since Rome was where the Emperor was based, but it spread out across the Empire. We have images of Sol's chariot in mosaics from Colchester among other places; worship of Sol Invictus was therefore known in Britain. However, the cult of the Unconquered Sun did not last long, as it was replaced by Christianity in 313 CE.

It is probably a stretch to claim that later customs stem directly from the Saturnalia. Examples of Wassailing getting out of hand probably have more to do with young men drinking too much and letting off steam, sometimes in a nasty way. Whatever the actual origins, however, practices such as disguise (guising), cross-dressing, the temporary overturning of social hierarchies, transgressive behaviour such as insulting people, demanding money or kisses, and the presence of a designated fool or other leader are core to these winter festivities.

This 'world turned upside down' feature of misrule was not confined to Christmas. It was a Hocktide (the second Monday and Tuesday after Easter) custom in some parts of Britain, in which the war between the sexes was carried literally into the streets; groups of men would kidnap women on Hocktide Monday and hold them to ransom, and on the following day, the roles were reversed. What could possibly go wrong? It seems to have been particularly popular among the women of the parish, with 'goodwives' being some of the main organizers. The custom of 'hokking' experienced serious pushback from the Church from as early as the fifteenth century, although the practice was also used to raise money for church funds. In some parts this custom turned into 'heaving' – sometimes carrying a person around on a chair (possibly to symbolize the elevation of Christ), but sometimes resembling more the 'bumps' that used to be carried out on a child's birthday at school and that I, for one, always dreaded. Similar dread was experienced by a number of men of the middle classes and of a more timid disposition, terrorized by working class 'amorous Amazons' in various parts of the country. Some men were targeted year after year. While there is an obvious class and gender element to this, it also rather too often seems to have been generated by female revenge and degenerated into simple bullying, with squires and vicars keeping to their houses or having to fight off a small horde of determined local women. It died out in the nineteenth century.

John Canoe

There are also similarities between Wassailing and Junkanoo (which you may have seen in the Bond movie *Thunderball* – that's actually Junkanoo, not Mardi Gras as it is often described). This celebration is sometimes termed 'John Canoe', possibly after an Ahanta king who defeated the Germans in Ghana in the eighteenth century but who was then captured and taken to Jamaica as a prisoner of war and subsequently enslaved. Stephen Nissenbaum notes:

> Essentially, it involved a band of black men – generally young – who dressed themselves in ornate and often bizarre costumes. Each band was led by a man who was variously dressed in animal horns, elaborate rags, female disguise, whiteface (and wearing a gentleman's wig!), or simply his 'Sunday-go-to-meeting-suit'. Accompanied by music, the band marched along the roads from plantation to plantation, town to town, accosting whites along the way and sometimes even entering their houses. In the process the men performed elaborate and (to white observers) grotesque dances that were probably of African origin. And in return for this performance they always demanded money (the leader generally carried 'a small bowl or tin cup' for this purpose), though whiskey was an acceptable substitute.[22]

We obviously need to take care around attributing connections in cases which might simply result from parallel development, but the resemblance between the two customs,

Wassail and Junkanoo, and the subtext of misrule and unrest, are interesting when we consider them in the context of the USA. Some planters in the Southern states, like the aristocratic landowners of England, opened their houses to their slaves, to receive food and drink. Frederick Douglass and Booker T. Washington, both former slaves, wrote of this festivity as a time in which white owners encouraged their slaves to get drunk.[23] Whether this was to provide a form of licensed catharsis, or whether it was a cynical measure to reinforce bigoted notions of the emotional instability and poor moral character of Black slaves, is moot.

Interview with Nick Ford, Wassailer and mummer

I Wassail my fruit trees (not just the apples), and engage with others who also Wassail theirs, elsewhere in this county and the next (Shropshire and Herefordshire). I have played with three mummers' groups, and would like to start a fourth where I am now.

What do you enjoy about them?
A. (Wassailing) The timeless acknowledgement of a symbiosis, and of course its festal aspect, especially the singing and the drinking.
B. (Mumming) The interactive street theatre of public performances, and the lasered creativity the constraints that the canon of the play afford. I enjoy entertaining people and causing reflection as well as laughter and wonderment. There is also a sense of privilege in being part of a timeless tradition. Oh, and then there's the singing and the drinking.

What do other people think of your involvement? Do they approve, or do you get criticized for it?

A. I used to work on a community farm down in Hampshire, and one or two of the more Pagan-minded of the members introduced apple tree Wassailing to our newly planted orchard of rare traditional varieties. One of the directors, an evangelical Christian, would have nothing to do with it because of its assumed Pagan antecedents, even though no deity or elemental was explicitly invoked in the ritual (and I've never been to or done a Wassailing that ever did). Mostly people came and enjoyed the social occasion, which continues.

B. Some passersby seem to regard street mumming as an inconvenience, and/or scurry past as if they don't know how they should handle it. A few will make smartarse comments but usually wish they hadn't when we engage with them. Mostly we have received benign, passive approval though on one occasion security guards insisted we vacate a shopping mall. The ultimate social sanction, though, is when one makes a collection from the audience in aid of a charity. We've also had a few grumbles from locals when we've played pubs and all they want is a quiet pint and a game of dominoes when these bizarrely clad lunatics engage in ritual combat and miracle working on the saloon bar floor. But the word of the landlord or landlady who welcomes us is law: if you don't like this kind of live entertainment, you don't have to stick around for it.

What role do you think these customs play in the modern world? Do you think they are still important (or just a bit of fun), and if so, why?

A. Wassailing works if you do it right: the trees bear well and are disease-free the following year. Besides which, it behoves us to show some gratitude to what I will call The Secret Commonwealth, now and again. So Wassailing is important. It also helps bind a community as any religious ritual does. Showing gratitude and bestowing cider, toast and blessings on trees is, in my view, not only a religious act but thoroughly interfaith and ecumenical. If they had had apple tree Wassailing in the time, place and culture of any of the prophets of our several religions, I reckon they would have joined in – I can't see Jesus, Muhammad, Gautama Buddha, Guru Nanak, Krishna or Zarathushtra considering it in any way unseemly.

B. The Mummers' Play allows the public exposition of concepts of good and evil, moral and political, and permits serious social comment behind a mask of satirical comedy. It's sneaky that way. For example, the last group I was in – the Hampshire-based Carnival of Crows – produced a particular play in which the previously unrecognisably helmeted Saint George is a lesbian (and demands a civil partnership with the rescued maiden), the Doctor is a Californian New-Age quack called Bluesky Birkenstock, and the Dragon is Welsh and has a lot to say about the rights of cultural minorities and endangered species (and Six Nations Rugby).

Is your chosen folk custom important to your identity?

What I do is a large part of what I am, so yes – both of them are. Wassailing because to give back for what you have received is a fundamental precept of mine, and the mumming is because basically I'm a show-off who thinks he has important things to say.

How has your chosen custom changed during your engagement with it? Has it become more diverse, for instance?

A. When we moved from Hampshire, I had to sell off my old cider press because there isn't the space to make my own where we now live, and the neighbours and their livestock don't like gunfire or crackers hung in the trees (a method we used at the community farm), so my own Wassailing is now a quiet, private domestic ritual.

B. The first mummers' group (Shirley Mummers) started out with a few friends connected to the University of Southampton. We performed a play that was highly traditional in that it was a careful amalgam using all the elements common to all the plays recorded as having been performed in Hampshire. As we performed it, improvizations of a more topical nature began to creep in but it remained basically a trad play. When the mummers' group dispersed it was adopted by a Southampton Morris side who continue to perform it year on year, decades later. It is very gratifying to have invented a tradition in this way. The second (Dorset Knobs) was a Dorset-based Hobby Horse play made up from two or three originals, and again it was fairly traditional and performed more or less the same every time according to the wishes of the originator. I have to say I didn't get too much out of that one. The third, by Carnival of Crows, was a gloriously anarchic compendium of the creative genius of each player, who pretty much wrote and improvised on his or her part, and was highly satirical in a self-deprecating way. These performances seemed to be noticeably more popular because I feel the spirit in which we did them was highly infectious to our audiences.

Do you think interest in your folk custom is diminishing or growing?

Growing, without a doubt. Apple tree wassailing especially.

Is there a transgressive element to your chosen custom?

A. No.

B. It is passing fine to dress as a magnificent, beautiful, handsome and manly red dragon and admire one's reflection in cafe windows like a narcissistic saurian Tom Jones, leer in through open shop doorways and chase young girls screaming down the street in the market towns of Middle England. Saint George and I were sparring partners and we choreographed our fights very carefully, though, which was necessary as Saint George is disarmed by the dragon but in her moment of peril, grabs a convenient pre-fractured screw top bottle and cracks him over the head, effecting the dragon's temporary demise until Birkenstock resurrects him with a chakra-balancing phone app. Theatre has always had a vital transgressive element, at least ever since the comedies performed at the Athenian Dionysia festival from the fifth century BCE. If it doesn't shock a bit and surprise and challenge, what's the point? I think you've lost the spirit of the tradition otherwise.

Interview with Liz Cruse, Druid
What folk customs do you engage with or practice?

Wassailing, May Day/Beltane celebrations, Morris, Summer
and Winter Solstice public celebrations at Stanton Drew,
and other eightfold wheel of the year festivals: Imbolc,
Alban Eiler, Alban Hefin, Alban Elfed, Alban Arthan as
per OBOD and Dobunni infinite variations. Not sure if you
count these as folk customs since they are relatively new
rituals, but they obviously contain folk elements – Brigid's
crosses, for example.

What do you enjoy about them?

Joyful, slightly anarchic. I went to the May morning celebration in the Ashdown Forest that included Morris sides
and at one point the youngest and fairest – an American
girl – was grabbed from the crowd and lifted up by the
dancers. No crowning as Queen or anything. There was
a great sense of exuberance, and her face was a picture of
shock and pleasure. I suppose some might object to this,
but I couldn't see any sexual harassment going on. I don't
know how long this celebration has been going on.

I watch Morris dancers – my knees won't permit joining
in, alas – and get a similar sense of pleasure.

Most of these customs are celebrated outside, which
gives me a sense of connection to the natural world and
the turning of the earth through the solar cycle. Thus I am
linked with the old, indigenous people of these islands who
probably also celebrated key times in the year. But obviously we don't really know how they might have framed
this in, for example, the neolithic period.

What do other people think of your involvement? Do they approve, or do you get criticized for it?

My non-Druid friends regard it all with some bemusement, I think. My feeling is that most regard it all as a bit silly and are puzzled as to how I came to be involved with such things. Attitudes vary from ridicule to tolerance. Obviously Pagan-orientated friends don't find it problematic.

What role do you think these customs play in the modern world? Do you think they are still important (or just a bit of fun), and if so, why?

I think it's important to have some aspects of society that are still rooted in communities and that, no matter how weakly, put two fingers up to a homogenous society dominated by capitalism. These celebrations are not 'provided' for people in exchange for money. They are part of the life of a community, albeit there will always be organizers.

Is your chosen folk custom important to your identity?

Since I see all these customs as related to my version of Druidry, as they are linked to the natural cycles of the world, then absolutely. But I am not a Morris dancer or anything more than a bystander, except for OBOD rituals.

How has your chosen custom changed during your engagement with it? Has it become more diverse, for instance?

The Glastonbury Wassail ceremony seems to be much the same in the years I've been attending, and when I went to one in the Midlands some years ago it didn't seem much different – toast in trees, etc. Same at Chew Magna Community Farm.

There has been controversy about blackface Morris dancing. I'm OK with this given the historical explanation given to me but I can see it might be a sensitive point for Black people. I myself have ghastly memories of the Black and White Minstrel Show, which of course wasn't that controversial in the 1960s.

These customs are mostly in the countryside so there's not a lot of ethnic diversity. A Black friend of mine (Caribbean) visited an event with me that included Druid-based ritual. She likened the community in which it took place to her experiences with rural communities in the Caribbean who have folk customs too (though different obviously, harking back to African culture). I don't think she felt any urge to become further involved in [the] UK though.

Do you think interest in your folk custom is diminishing or growing?

It seems to me that more people are coming to the ceremonies at Stanton Drew and when I have been in a role of handing out blessings (such as pieces of mistletoe), I sense almost a hunger for something that expresses a non-material reality. But this is purely subjective and intuitive. Druidry per se seems to have a steady growth.

Is there a transgressive element to your chosen custom?

The very act of getting up at dawn to do a ceremony is transgressive in a way but most of the ceremonies I attend feel quite safe, if somewhat boisterous.

Beltane has been controversial given the shifting attitudes towards gender roles. Our White Horse Camp ceremonies have been through many revisions over recent years and we have had women become the May King/ Lord of the Land. Not so far the other way round, although this happened at Dobunni when a trans woman stepped forward to take the role of the Lady of the May and someone objected strongly on traditional gender grounds. The atmosphere became very uneasy – no one stepped forward to do the Lord of the Green Wood role until I did. For myself, I don't mind since I think anyone can channel the relevant energy, but many disagree and some people have stopped coming to White Horse Beltane Camp over this very issue (sadly).

The Mari Lwyd figure I find very creepy and I'm not sure I'd want to be at that event. I suppose processing around with an animal skeleton is a bit transgressive when it's not plastic and made in China as it is for many Hallowe'en events.

FIVE

Morris and Molly

Morris dancing is perhaps the folk custom that is most familiar to the English. It pops up all over the place: on Bank Holidays outside pubs, at Christmas and at village fetes. It's such a common sight that perhaps we don't think to question how it arose in the first place. But we know from historical records that the origins of Morris lie both in the court dances of the fifteenth and sixteenth centuries, and also as a form of village green entertainment. Hutton suggests that the form began in noble households from around 1458–1540, then moved into the towns between 1540 and 1600, and from then on became mainly a village pastime.[1]

Seven shillings were paid to a Morris side in 1448 by the Goldsmiths Company, and it was used by Henry VIII in his many court masques. He may have come across the custom in France, and he was not only familiar with the custom but had a gold salt cellar that depicted a Morris dance. Royal support was continued by Edward VI. In 1552 his official Lord of Misrule, George Ferrers, organized Morris dancing as part of the festivities, thus linking Morris with the Christmas 'misrule' period that we looked at above. William Kempe, a Shakespearean performer, undertook an epic Morris dance from London to Norwich, apparently as a publicity stunt after falling out with the great Bard himself. (His feat was replicated in 2015 by Rick

Jones of Catford, not actually a Morris dancer himself – he told the BBC that he intended to 'sort of skip' most of the distance.)[2] It is possible that Morris took on some of the elements of medieval folk dance – we don't have a very clear idea as to what this would have looked like, although some commentators have suggested that it might have been influenced by Italian dances of the period, imported by the aristocracy.

There is also a likelihood that Morris was influenced by the earlier Robin Hood plays, featuring the familiar Sherwood Forest outlaw and his Merry Men. Margaret Murray and Lord Raglan regarded Robin as a kind of nature spirit, but there's little or no evidence that he was seen in this light throughout the Middle Ages. In 1498, a Robin Hood play ended in a riot and a number of deaths, and increasingly they were banned.[3] They faded in the seventeenth century, leaving Maid Marian behind for the Morris, a man dressed up and played for comic effect.

Like most folk customs, Morris has experienced periods of diminishment followed by revival. It was interrupted by the Civil War and the accompanying dictats against religious festivals and then went into abeyance after the Industrial Revolution, a period in which so many people moved from rural areas into the cities. By the late nineteenth century it had largely disappeared, but was revived by a handful of enthusiasts such as folklorist Cecil Sharp, who started to collect folk songs after seeing a Morris dance at Headington Hall in Oxfordshire, and Cheltenham-based music teacher and pageant organizer D'Arcy Ferris (aka de Ferrars). The latter became intrigued with Morris dancing in the 1880s when undertaking research for an Elizabethan revel and revived the Bideford side, which had ceased to perform some decades previously, and then entered into correspondence with Sharp.

Morris became, and remains, a purely grassroots form of expression, which, apart from its early royal connections, has never attracted a great deal of state support; some would claim that this is a good thing, as it means that Morris dancing has remained truly of the people, regardless of its courtly origins. However, as with many customs, it has a number of origin stories.

In 1801, claims were made that the word 'Morris' derives from 'Morys', or 'Moorish'.[4] Whether this means that dancers were actually blacked up, or whether the choreography of the dances themselves resembled that of Moorish or Spanish dances remains a moot point, as does the connection between the dances on the continent and those in Britain. Cecil Sharp believed that Morris dancing derived from a pan-European dance and further traction was given to the idea that it was actually pagan in origin by Gallop in 1934, who noted that the term 'moor' in the Basque country and parts of Portugal meant 'pagan' and had nothing to do with the Moors of Morocco.[5] Gallop suggested that the dances might be a relic of older choreographed rituals of the battle between summer and winter, but there's very little apparent evidence for this hypothesis, and this, again, may stem from the late nineteenth-century 'ancient origins' hypothesis.

Morris and Modernity

Historically, many Morris sides are quite old, but there are modern versions as well, and we're going to look at both. We tend to think of Morris dancers as men, but there are all-female Morris sides, too, and women have been dancing the Morris since the sixteenth century. There are also references to women dancing the Morris in the nineteenth century in Oxfordshire. When Cecil Sharp began collating Morris dances, he was aided by a woman named Mary Neal, who ran a dress-making co-operative for young working-class women called the Espérance Club and who was in search of suitable dances for club members to perform.

However, when the Morris Ring, the oldest official Morris dancing organization, was set up in 1934 the custom was pre-sented as a purely masculine activity. This is largely due to the influence of folklore revivalist and Nazi sympathizer Rolf Gardiner, who convinced Mary Neal that the dance had pre-viously only been performed by men, although he was not a founder of the Ring itself. Gardiner came out of an alterna-tive form of the Boy Scouts, known as the Kibbo Kift, and had reactionary views regarding women. His influence did not last. Knots of May, an all-female side, started in 1974 in Brighton and the ban didn't mean that women didn't do it; they just didn't do so 'officially'. The rules changed in 2018 and some sides, such as Exeter, have dropped the 'men' part from their name, now being simply Exeter Morris. Exeter's John Armstrong told the press that it was a matter of 'change or die', since not enough men were interested in keeping the tradition going.[6]

Now, a third of the Morris sides in the UK are mixed and half of the country's Morris dancers are female. Hutton suggests that the folk revival of the 1960s made the form more welcoming to women. He comments, in summary:

It may be concluded, therefore, that down to the twentieth century the story of the Morris dance in England has been one of constant evolution and adaptation, according to period, region and social class. It is hard to argue from all this that it has ever possessed an 'authentic' form, still less that it represents an ancient and unchanging rite. The tale of the dance is, rather, one of a triumph of versatility.[7]

In the north of England, Carnival Morris is practised. This was described by *The Guardian* as a combination of Morris dancing and cheerleading.[8] It's sometimes known, perhaps a little derogatively, as 'fluffy Morris'.

These days, Stroud is host to the neon-lipped, gold-lamé-wearing Prog Morris all-female side Boss Morris. This came to the attention of the nation in 2023 when the side performed at the Brit Awards alongside band Wet Leg. Founder Alex Merry started out her dancing career in 2008 in London, at Cecil Sharp House, which had just formed a side called the Belles of London City. She had originally gone there to investigate accordion classes, coming as she did from a folk singing background. When she moved back home to Stroud in Gloucestershire, Merry started her own side in 2015 with some contacts, all of whom had been working for the artist Damien Hirst and several of whom came from the same kind of folk-singing childhood (for example, parents who took them to Sidmouth Folk Festival and the Padstow Obby Oss celebration or Helston Furry Dance). Merry describes Morris as the 'reverse' of that kind of high-end, big money art. Side member Lily Cheetham told Tradfolk.co:

I always feel that it's way more real than any of the pretence, the things associated with money, that we found when we were working in the high-end art world. That's a very different thing. It doesn't feel real. It's about pretence and what people think about other people, whereas, I don't know, folky stuff is laypeople, their stories; it's things handed down, isn't it? It feels much more real.[9]

The courtly origins of Morris formed part of the inspiration for this spectacular, glamorous manifestation of the dance form. Founding member Rhia Davenport told *The Guardian*:

The dancers would have been dressed in the finest glitzy garments, which we take pride in making a nod to, particularly in our gold costume. We also take pride in using symbolism which ties to our local landscape, in the way that many other Morris sides today will display a badge or emblem which represents their locality. Although our costumes don't always appear traditional they do have strong links to place and history. It's just that they mean something to us in a different way.[10]

The only constant element of Morris costuming through the ages is the presence of bells: everything else has been prone to change. But Boss Morris also references Stroud's textile industry (it is one of the old Cotswold wool towns) through some of their costuming. They use face paint and make-up, but this tends to be spontaneous rather than following a set formula. The side says that they like the idea of being connected to a community and the spontaneity allows them to develop flourishes within the dance, 'patterns' that thus make it local to Stroud. Morris was above all a community activity, with dances that were specific to particular villages and towns, and using 'songs with a postcode'. It is, says Alex Merry, a little like using a very old pattern to knit a smart new Aran sweater.

Brighton's Knots of May are a little more historically minded in terms of their costume, wearing clothes that are inspired by the dress of the 1890s, plus an apron. At the time, the group were dancing Lancashire Morris and their clogs and aprons were a nod to those of the Lancashire mill girls. They also performed dances from Cheshire, using sticks – they say that these were originally the bobbins from mill work, with cotton plumes on the ends. Over the years, the group have sourced dances from areas beyond the UK, such as France and Flanders, and some of the choreography is wholly new. The group has the distinction of having a local beer named after them: Harvey's Brewery of Lewes has produced an ale named Knots of May, perhaps appropriately, given the cultural connection between real ale and Morris dancing. Knots of May have been more interested in the dances than what to wear: 'Until the arrival of Boss Morris many younger teams were more interested in playing with the collected dance form itself, creating visually complex choreography rather than re-imagining the dance through costumes.'[11]

Boss Morris were not originally on a mission to showcase female-dominated avant-garde Morris dancing. They were aiming to have fun. Merry and Cheetham say,

> AM: I think it surprised all of us that we're in the position to ... comment on stuff. But, no, we didn't sit down and say, 'Right, we're going to change how people perceive

Morris dancing'. It's very much like Lily says: it's a kind of organic recipe combining all of us together that we've cooked up.

LC: It has kind of become a bit of a mission, but a true mission, really. Something that feels like something we should be doing, rather than it being a prescribed constitution or anything like that.[12]

Their mission – should they choose to accept it – is to take Morris to diverse as well as to traditional audiences, and to places where Morris dancing is not expected to be. Morris, Merry notes, has a 'nerdy' reputation that they enjoy challenging. As well as their radical costumes, they have some electronic versions of old Morris songs, incorporating drum 'n' bass.

I don't know where we get the idea that Morris dancing is an uncool thing to be doing. I suppose for my age group, it has to do with going to country fetes when I was a kid and seeing middle-aged and older men, out of shape, dancing badly. But when I took my daughter to Sidmouth about four years ago – she was about nine at the time – we got off the bus in the town centre and we could hear a Morris side walking around the corner. We couldn't see them yet, but we could hear the bells and she was so excited. It was like Father Christmas was coming. So I wonder if there's a way that we can bypass that bit where we get a bit jaded about Morris dancers and retain that sense that we're seeing something a little bit magic.[13]

There is a definite demographic trend in this country and elsewhere, in which a wide range of groups, not just folk custom groups, are finding it difficult to attract younger members. I spoke to historian Ronald Hutton about this in a private conversation and he said that he had made something of an informal study of it, and the phenomenon was across the board, from historical re-enactment organizations such as the Sealed Knot, to contemporary Druidry, to 'old people's' activities such as Morris. Part of this may be due to the pressures of work among the younger generation (although their grandparents and parents must have worked as hard) and part is perhaps due to the wide availability of other forms of entertainment, the Internet and Netflix among them. Some of it is due to a decline in service provision in something of a chicken and egg situation: the number of youth clubs in London, according to *The Guardian*, fell by a hundred between 2011 and 2019, a consequence of austerity being applied to local councils' budgets.[14] Whatever the case, this is a distinct trend and one that is lamented across a range of previously thriving activities.

The *Daily Mail* ran a characteristic 'our way of life is dying out' piece in 2009 reporting that young people were reluctant to join Morris sides because they were 'too embarrassed'.[15] This was inspired by a remark from Morris ring member Charlie Corcoran, to the effect that Morris dancing could die out in the next twenty years. There was significant pushback to this comment. Matt Morris, of Hammersmith Morris men the Smiffs, told My London:

> We have been going for nearly 50 years, and we've definitely not found that Morris dancing is dying out. Our

youngest member is 19, and our members range in age up to about 60 years old. We're finding that the next generation of Morris dancers is coming through, with sons and grandsons of members starting to join.[16]

He did note, though, that the practice was tough on the knees. Boss Morris members noted that their grandmothers had 'dressed up' when the Morris sides came to town, drawn by fit young men – the fact that Morris dancing is actually quite athletic perhaps needs to be noted here!

Boss Morris rely on the Morris 'Bible', Lionel Bacon's *A Handbook of Morris Dances*. They say that negative reactions to their dancing from other, more traditional Morris sides has been relatively slight. There are purists out there – Barry Care from the Moulton Morris Men terms female sides 'pound-shop Morris', asserting that women have a different centre of gravity from men and that all-male Morris is an art form in itself, like ballet.[17] Richard Macer, who interviewed Care for *The Guardian*, did, however, make a point that I think is a relevant one: men who want to be in an all-male group may not be deliberately excluding women, even if they are not in favour of the inclusion of women. They may just want to be in a masculine environment, just as some women would prefer at times to be in all-female company. This point tends to get lost in the current climate, but although it may be adjacent to institutionalized sexism, I don't think that it is invariably a direct manifestation of it.

The worry among traditional Morris sides is that new ways of performing might just be a gimmick, but this concern has dissipated over time. Boss Morris has now been going for six years and they say that people can see that they are serious about the dancing; local Stroud Morris man Steve Rowley had considerable input into Boss Morris. There is said to be a correlation between how much a side dresses up and how badly they dance, but that's probably more of an in-joke than a Morris purist's slur. They also say that although it's harder to attract young men to the practice, young women – as we have seen – have been forming their own sides, so Morris seems to be undergoing something of a gender flip revival. But there has apparently been talk of a young men's side starting in Stroud – perhaps determined not to be outdone by the girls!

Interview with Julia Hawkes-Moore, Morris dancer

One Sidmouth Farewell Torchlit Procession, I was aged just 16. I accidentally turned up, dressed in a floor-length white Broderie Anglaise gown with a crown of flowers, which I had been saving for best. The two Morris sides I had been tagging along with all week had asked me to dress in something special for the last night!

As soon as I arrived, the Morris Men grabbed me and surrounded me with flaming torches, then set off downhill to escort me to the sea and along the esplanade.

At one point, there was a high wall alongside it with a family leaning over the barrier to watch. The little boy called out 'Dad! Who is that girl?' His father sighed, and announced, 'Son, she is this year's Sacrificial Virgin'.

There was much laughter from my flaming escorts. But as all of them surrounded me closely all night until I was returned safely to my parents, no actual ritual defloration occurred. That year.

Interview with Lynne Tan-Watson, Morris dancer

I am part of a group who sing and dance as the sun comes up on May Day morning. It was started by Packington Morrismen, who now don't exist as a side but some of them still go up the hill and dance along with a fairly disparate group of people. The custom started something like fifty years ago. It's widespread now and is known as 'Dancing the sun up'. We also got to the Bull and Lion in Packington, Leicestershire in the afternoon where Pennyroyal Garland Dancers and Anstey Morrismen dance in the car park. The children of the local school decorate May sticks, which are judged, and also select a May Queen who is crowned as part of the afternoon. Unfortunately, there is nothing in the region of transgression that I can think of!

I also help organize a Wassail event in our village orchard, which has been going on now for thirteen years. No transgression there either!

I enjoy the feeling that we are continuing something that, in some form or another, has been going on for centuries. I also enjoy the community spirit they engender and the fact that they are fun.

Can't say I've ever been criticized for it, though people often think we are mad to get up at 4.30am to 'Go up the Hill'! As far as the Wassail goes, a large part of the village participates.

I think people are actually craving these celebrations of the turning of the year. The fact that there are people in some places still continuing celebrations that have been going on for hundreds of years, and that people so readily jump onto anything like this, as witness the massive spread of Wassailing events in the past few years, indicates to me that it is something very basic that they want to be part of.

Is your chosen folk custom important to your identity?

Er . . . probably. I am a folkie first and foremost and this is all part of that persona.

How has your chosen custom changed during your engagement with it? Has it become more diverse, for instance?

The only change to the 'dancing the sun up' is that it was organized by the Morrismen and is now organized by me. The afternoon celebration changed because the school stopped doing the May sticks, but we have resurrected that in the past couple of years.

The only change to the Wassail is that we used to have LED balloons to light the lane and the orchard but now, in the interest of preserving the environment, we have willow lanterns and tin can lanterns made by the local guides and youth club. As far as diversity goes, I don't think either has become more diverse but folkies are a very welcoming lot and no one would be discriminated against in any way.

Do you think interest in your folk custom is diminishing or growing?

Interest in the May Day events stays much the same I think. Our own Wassail also stays the same but Wassails generally have grown phenomenally in the past few years.

Is there a transgressive element to your chosen custom?

Not that I can think of. A few years ago someone insisted that we have marshalls in hi-viz in front of and behind the procession as we walk down the lane to the orchard but that person is no longer involved and it doesn't happen anymore.

Molly dancers

In parts of Britain, some of the people who danced for Wassail were known as Mollie/Molly dancers, or Bessie dancers – both of these terms refer to men who dress as women. 'Molly' has been used since the eighteenth century to refer to an effeminate man, while 'Molly House' referred to a brothel in which men cross-dressed. Pig Dyke boss Tony Forster quotes eighteenth-century journalist Ned Ward, who described the Molly Houses in 1709:

> There are a particular Gang of Sodomitical Wretches in this Town, who call themselves the Mollies and are so far degenerated from all masculine deportment, or manly Exercises, that they rather fancy themselves Women, imitating all the little Vanities that custom has reconciled to the female sex, affecting to speak, walk, tattle, curtsey, cry, scold, and to mimick all manner of Effiminacy, that ever has fallen within their several Observations; not omitting the Indecencies of lewd Women, that they may tempt one another.[18]

Molly dancing itself appeared across the Midlands and East Anglia, and was usually organized by ploughboys. One of its last appearances was in Downham Market in Norfolk in the 1930s, in a performance that featured a cross-dressing tango. Russell Whortley and Cyril Papworth, both folklore and dance enthusiasts, recorded some of these dances, to tunes which included 'George Green's College Hornpipe'. However, the custom of Molly continued in the north, minus the dancing, with boys dressed as girls going from door to door and asking for money. This lasted until the 1960s, but the final nail in its coffin appears to have been housing reconstruction, which got rid of the rows of terraces and resulted in the disruption of local communities.

Originally the custom was associated with Plough Monday and seems to have started as a way for unemployed ploughboys, 'Plough Jags', to make some money in the fallow period between Christmas and Plough Monday, the first Monday after Epiphany (6 January), and is thus linked to the Twelfth Night period. It is the old beginning of the agricultural year. As with other of the customs we have looked at, refusal to give alms was sometimes punished – for example, having a furrow driven across a landowner's lawn. Sybil Marshall, writing in the *Fenland Chronicle*, notes:

> There always seems to have been at least a potential element of coercion in the custom, as it was conducted by a group of young men, seeking money or some equivalent donation towards a feast, and equipped with a piece of machinery which could inflict damage to property.[19]

'Plough Bullocks' were sometimes prosecuted for ploughing up people's drives and mention is made of the menacing behaviour that often marred their arrival. But some of the participants, at least, saw the custom rather differently:

> Living where we did and how we did, we used to make the most of anything a bit out o' the ordinary, and we looked for'ard from one special day to the next. Looking back on it now, I'm surprised to see how many high days and holidays there were during the year that we kept, and we certainly made the most of any that children could take part in at all … The Molly Dancers 'ould come round the fen from Ramsey and Walton all dressed up. One would have a fiddle and another a dulcimer or perhaps a concertina and play while the rest danced. This were really special for Christmas Eve, but o' course the dancers cou'n't be everywhere at once on one day, so they used to go about on any other special day to make up for it. They'd go from pub to pub, and when they'd finished there, they'd go to any houses or cottages where they stood a chance o' getting anything. If we ha'n't got any money to give 'em, at least they never went away without getting a hot drink.[20]

Nowadays, Molly dancing has made a revivalist come-back as a form of Morris. There are Molly performances at the Whittlesea Straw Bear festival, and dances performed by the Deptford Fowlers Troop also feature a Jack in the Green. Today, the troupes include women, who may cross-dress as men. Other troupes include the Norwich Shitwitches (renamed the Kit Witches after a decade, when they realized that the 'Sh' from the original text was actually a 'K') and Pig

Dyke Molly. But there are many more: Seven Champions Molly Dancers, Ouse Washes Molly Dancers, Gog Magog Molly, Old Glory, Soken Molly Gang, Green River Tap & Die, Brummie Gems, Black Dog Molly, Good Easter Molly Gang, Mepal Molly, Midlands Molly, Misfit Molly, Oxblood Molly and Old Hunts Molly. Not all of these are in the UK – the revived custom has crossed the Atlantic, and there are Molly sides in New Jersey and California. William Arderon, writing in the mid-1700s, says:

> In Christmas time, and especially on Plough Monday, several Men dresse themselves in Womens Close and goes from House to House a Dancing along with fiddles where they beg for Money. These are called Kitwitches.[21]

Donning women's clothing was common, as above, but other forms of costume were used, including dressing as Indigenous Americans or with a fake humpback. These forms of costume were supposed to be grotesque, to mock and mimic rather than to pass as the opposite gender, although the Old Glory Molly troupe suggests that men may have dressed as women to escape arrest.

Some Fenland sides also used full animal heads, a custom reminiscent of the Mari Lwyd and other hooded animal customs. And women cross-dressed, too, such as the guising in the Scilly Isles in which young women either dressed as men or both sexes part-dressed in both male and female attire, or St Andrew's Day in some areas, which was celebrated by cross-dressing of both sexes. There were specific prohibitions against this in some areas, particularly in Scotland where the kirk prohibited men from putting on women's clothes but also women putting on men's clothes.

Taking a closer look at a Molly side, the Kit Witches' website says that the word 'Kitwitch' refers to a buffoon. The word is also found in Great Yarmouth, where there was a Kittywitches pub and Kittywitches Row, which ran from Middlegate to King Street. In 'The Folk Lore of East Anglia', Enid Porter reports that in this area women dressed as men and smeared blood on their faces, then did the rounds of houses asking for money (which was then spent on alcohol).[22]

It is possible that the term 'Kitty Witch' comes from the Dutch *kitwijk*, which means a house of ill repute. The Dutch used to attend the Yarmouth Free Fair and may have introduced the word to the locals. However, it may simply come from the name of Christopher Wyche, who lived in the area in the early eighteenth century. Or it might have another origin entirely: Hazlitt's *Dictionary of Faiths and Folklore* (1895) says 'In Norfolk, and perhaps elsewhere, a female attired in some grotesque and frightful manner is called a Kitch-witch.'[23] Whether this is a direct reference to actual witchcraft is doubtful; it is more likely to be a reference to an old hag, of the sort stereotypically associated with witches.

When reviving their dances, the Norwich Kit Witches – a spin-off from a Cotswold Morris side – looked into the history of the tradition and decided that they would only perform around midwinter/Twelfth Night. (There were practical as well as traditional reasons for this, as members were also attached to other Morris sides and didn't want to become overstretched.) There is some uncertainty as to where the dances come from: folklorist Cecil Sharp was apparently prone to regarding various forms of Morris as 'degenerate' versions of the Cotswold form, but the Molly dances might have come from their own traditions and not from the Cotswold form.

Mr and Mrs Wright of Great Sampford, Essex, informed Russell Wortley that 'some of the men were dressed as women with bonnets etc' and at Castle Camps he was told of 'men with blacked faces, some wearing skirts'.[24] But the dances are relatively simple and may just have come from country dances, rather than a specific kind of Morris itself. We simply do not know, as relatively little is known for certain about the origins of this form of Morris dance or its music:

> If there was little indication of how the dances were performed, there was nothing to indicate what the music was like, or what it was played on. For this recreated tradition we decided to use original tunes, slow polkas, written by our musicians, although as the years developed the 'Bonzo Dog Do-Dah Band's 'Jollity Farm' seemed to slip in.[25]

The Kit Witches were then faced with the question of what to actually wear. They selected women's clothing of choice over a white shirt and black trousers – the lack of uniformity seemed, Jon Hooton says, to be suited to the somewhat shambolic nature of the dances. Since some members of the troupe were female, they also had women dressed as men dressed as women, all with a sort of pantomime dame make-up to exaggerate the effect. This had the benefit of sidestepping the question of whether to black-up dancers' faces, which is traditional in some areas but is currently fraught due to questions of racism and cultural appropriation, which we've noted above and will address in due course. In this, they are akin to a number of Morris and Molly sides, who have legitimate concerns about being conflated with, for instance, the Black and White Minstrel Show. The Pig Dyke have similarly chosen an exaggerated face paint. Tony Forster explains:

> Molly dancers in the past blacked their faces for disguise, weirdness, and loss of personal identity: we achieve that ... Pig Dyke is proud to be weird, proud to amuse, proud to confuse, proud to entertain (we hope) through our whole performance, including the lies that introduce the dances. We believe we are true to Molly's anarchic roots and have created something for audiences of the twenty-first century to enjoy – even or especially the ones who hate folk.[26]

The Kit Witches have also dispensed with bells, but do include a besom in some dances, referencing the traditional flying aid of the witch. Sides have developed their own dances, based, for example in the case of the Ouse Washes Molly, on local Fenland folklore: marsh spirits, giants, murder and retribution.

The Pig Dyke side point out that the local papers did not approve of Molly dancing:

> The annual vagabondry of the plough witches took place on Monday, to the annoyance of a great number of the inhabitants. These witches principally represent themselves to be agricultural labourers from the neigh-bouring villages, and disguised in women's clothes or

with blackened faces, make pertinacious demands to all meet for money, entering your house with the greatest effrontery if they can do so unmolested. We really think that this custom would be more honoured in the breach than the observance; all responsible workmen now hold themselves aloof from this idle practice and it is confined chiefly to the lazy and the dissolute, against whom the police might swiftly put in force their authority for the quiet of the town.[27]

Whatever its origins, Molly dancing is, like other forms of Morris, going from strength to strength, and its diversity is currently key to its success. In an age that has become increasingly conscious of diversity in gender, however, and in which the various issues surrounding transgenderism have become a cultural hot potato, what are we to make of Molly dancing?

Cross-dressing

Sexual morality has changed substantially across the centuries in Britain. There is a tendency to see our forebears as prudish and respectable, if with an underlying hypocrisy, but if you look at the historical record of such matters, it is clear that sexual morals have altered a great deal, from the prudishness of the Puritans to the sexual licence of the Georgians (a period in which erotic literature might be read aloud in pubs and prototype contraceptives were for sale in Covent Garden), reverting to the uptight Victorians and thence to the helter skelter of the 1920s and 1960s. We might see the turn of the twenty-first century as a particularly lax time with some (to many) baffling new gender identifications, but in parts of the Global North – Texas, for example – society's sexual morals are closer to *The Handmaid's Tale*. The notion of being transgender would have astounded some of our ancestors, but along with transgender people, transvestites have always been with us.

Male fashion has in any case altered radically over the years. Wearing make-up used to be commonplace for men, for example. Whig statesman Charles James Fox routinely appeared in public in high heels with blue hair. He may not actually have cross-dressed (heels were fashionable for men), but he certainly caused a stir, and other 'macaronis' (fashionable young men) were regarded as effete; a series of sodomy scandals ensued among the set, for homosexual behaviour was against the law if widely practised and sodomy was a hanging offence. John Cooper, a gentleman's valet in the eighteenth century, was a well-known cross-dresser who went by the name of Princess Seraphina. His friend, pub landlady Mary Poplet, remarked that:

> I have known her Highness a pretty while, she us'd to come to my House from Mr. Tull, to enquire after some Gentlemen of no very good Character; I have seen her several times in Women's Cloaths, she commonly us'd to wear a white Gown, and a scarlet Cloak, with her Hair frizzled and curl'd all round her Forehead; and then she would so flutter her Fan, and make such fine Curt'sies, that you would not have known her from a Woman.[28]

Private drag balls known as 'Festival Nights' were held at Molly houses in the eighteenth century, around Christmas and New Year.

Nor was cross-dressing limited to men: a number of women also adopted men's clothing, not restricted to some famous cases who joined the army, but also those who ran public houses or worked as ballad singers. This sometimes appears to have been a social measure – to enable women to gain access to a particular profession, such as becoming a soldier, or to enter into lesbian 'marriages' and pass as a man, for example – but it also seems to have been a genuine form of personal expression.

Rictor Norton comments on the opportunities for cross-dressing that masquerades gave to gay men:

As commercial masquerades became fashionable for the wider public, it is only to be expected that some gay men would have exploited their opportunities. Such masquerades were first organized by the impresario John James Heidegger at the Haymarket Theatre from 1717 onwards. His 'Midnight Masquerades' were tremendously successful, and drew 800 people a week. They provided many people with the opportunity to explore fetishism and transvestism. Men disguised themselves as witches, bawds, nursing maids and shepherdesses, while women dressed as hussars, sailors, cardinals and Mozartian boys. In the early days of the fashion, Richard Steele, co-founder of the early periodical *The Tatler*, went to one where a parson called him a 'pretty fellow' and tried to pick him up, and Horace Walpole, antiquarian and builder of Strawberry Hill, passed for an old woman at a masquerade in 1742. The opportunities for illicit assignations provoked a host of anti-masquerade satires, and some tracts attacked the mollies or sodomites who allegedly attended them, supposedly imitating infamous homosexual cross-dressers such as Sporus, Caligula, and Heliogabalus.[29]

Some targets of public shaming due to dress codes now seem simply bizarre. Jonas Hanway, an Englishman recently returned from France in the 1750s, was reviled in the street by the general public. His crime? Being the first public user of an umbrella. Why was he reviled? Clearly, he was a weak, effeminate man; a 'mincing Frenchman' unable to cope with the robust weather of his native country. Carrying an umbrella was initially regarded as an effete foreign custom, unsuited to the robust English character. Much of the abuse stemmed from coach drivers, who had a vested interest in protesting – their cabs had little canopies to keep customers dry and the offensive umbrella represented a threat to their business. Hanway was subjected to verbal abuse, pelted with rubbish and one coach driver even tried to run him over. Hanway responded with a secondary use of his umbrella: he gave the driver a good thrashing with it.

Hanway, who had already drawn attention to himself by denouncing the introduction of tea, stuck to his guns, however, and as we know (since most of us own one), the umbrella caught on. Shortly after Hanway's death, an umbrella factory opened in London, advertising a device with a handy spring lock, and the umbrella was on course to become a household essential.

But I digress. It is very hard to get into the mindset of someone in any historical period who is now dead and who cannot answer for themselves, and who may have left no record. It seems obvious to me that transgenderism has been present in most societies, if not all, throughout history, and so has transvestism, which is different, as well as the various sections of the QUILTBAG rainbow. The quotations above regarding Molly houses serve as just one example. However, although I am sympathetic to the queer person's need to reclaim aspects of queer history, not everyone can be shoe-horned into it. So, although I think that the presence of non-cisgendered and non-heterosexual individuals cannot be questioned, this does not mean that we can claim everyone who Morris danced in women's clothing for the trans cause, but neither does it mean that we can categorically state that everyone who danced Molly dances was entirely cis-gendered or heterosexual either. We just don't know and those claims need to remain in the realm of speculation, not historical appropriation. People dress up for all manner of reasons and it is plausible that one person should have taken to Molly dancing as a socially licensed expression of their inner gender identity, while another did so as part of a socially licensed exploration of a sexual fetish, while another did so simply to have a laugh and out of an anarchic sense of fun. These are all portals that allow transgression of various sorts to enter. I think 'disguise' might be stretching it as an explanation in this particular context, however; unlike, say, within poaching or civil unrest, villages are small places and even dressed up in your wife's second-best bonnet, you'd still be perfectly recognizable. It is possible, though, that by adopting a different costume, people were also adopting a different persona.

The expressive rights of transgender people have, despite the best rabble-rousing efforts of some newspapers, largely remained something that is tolerated by the British public (as shown in a survey undertaken by More In Common in 2022),[30] despite some very real and very unpleasant threats from what

I suspect to be a relatively small group of bigots. A lot of older people are genuinely baffled by the alphabet soup of modern gender norms, but they're also bemused by the fuss that is made in the USA about 'men' dressed as 'women'. To a generation who grew up with Dick Emery, Monty Python, Dame Edna and Lily Savage, not to mention the annual Christmas panto, a moral panic about drag hasn't quite gained the traction that it might do in another nation, and long may that be the case; tolerance is, after all, supposed to be a British virtue. This is not to downplay the vulnerability of this particular group, however: transgender people face genuine dangers, not least from a vitriolic press.

Blacking up

Here, we are going to take a look at one of the most contentious contemporary elements of folk customs such as Morris dancing: the issue of blacking up. Before we head into a discussion of concerns such as racism and cultural appropriation, however, we need to take a look at the role of the chimney sweep in British folklore, as this does have a bearing on some of the practices that we are contemplating.

Sweeps

Sweeps are considered to be lucky, hence the old custom of having a sweep turn up at one's wedding (probably alarming to anyone who is wearing an expensive white dress, but there we go). Legend has it that a sweep saved the life of King George II by grabbing the bridle of his bolting horse; the king issued a royal decree to proclaim sweeps as lucky people. This may be apocryphal, but what is definitely the case is that sweeps still perform a crucial role in a society that has open fires and soot-encrusted chimneys.

Rochester Sweeps Festival is one of the biggest Morris celebrations in Europe and the clue is in the name; these festivities are said to date from the days when chimney sweeps would have one day off a year, namely May Day, and would parade through the streets. This used to be known as Chimney Sweepers' Day. Some folklore commentators suggest that the more modern celebrations emerge from this and from an earlier amalgamation of a milkmaid's celebration, in which the maids would carry elaborate garlands – eventually, as we have seen in an earlier chapter, these may have become transformed into the enormous May Day costumed figures such as the Jacks in the Green.

This is a celebration involving particular trades, and it originally fell foul of health and safety legislation. The Chimney Sweeper's Act in 1875 put paid to the practice of sending small boys up chimneys. Readers may remember Charles Kingsley's *The Water Babies*, which today contains some contentious elements in terms of racial slurs, but that functioned at the time as a tract against child labour and that had an influence upon the 1875 Act.[31] The new legislation also required chimney sweeps to register with the police. This tightening of controls over the profession had an impact on the May Day celebrations, which had already proved unpopular with some of the more respectable members of Victorian society (as a working-class festivity, often accompanied by rowdy behaviour). Even in the mid-nineteenth century, some of the 'Jacks' were more respectable revivals in a middle-class, sanitized version of May Day.

The tabloid press in the UK have, in recent years, been fond of running 'moral panic' articles relating to Morris sides being obliged to abandon the old custom of blacking their faces during performances, as a result of wokery/political correctness gone mad/abandonment of common sense and a variety of other reactionary responses. As we have noted, however, many Morris sides have given up the custom and adopted a number of alternatives (blue face, green face or the exaggerated panto dame make-up that we mention above in the case of Molly sides). It should also be noted that in 2020, only 1 per cent of Morris dancers were of non-white extraction; this is unarguably a white-dominated form of dance.[32]

The arguments against the loss of the tradition are succinctly made in a *Guardian* article from 2019:

> Those in favour say the face-painting has nothing to do with racism, the Black and White Minstrels [Show] or the lampooning of anyone of black and minority ethnic backgrounds. It is 'history' or a 'bit of fun', they claim. They argue that the practice dates back centuries to well before the time Morris dancers might have encountered blacked-up performers from overseas. They are dressing up as chimney sweeps or miners, a ploy that originated with agricultural workers trying to disguise themselves from their employers when they went out to sing and dance for a few extra pennies, when begging was illegal. It has nothing to do with race, they say. The chancellor, Sajid Javid, defended the practice in 2017, when he was communities secretary, saying he was 'proud' of a group in Alvechurch in his Bromsgrove constituency. 'They are as racist as I am', he tweeted.[33]

Are these arguments for the origins of blackface actually sound, however? Blacking up mainly occurs in the form of the dance known as Border Morris. The earliest reference to Morris dancing, as we've noted above, occurs in 1448, but Nicholas Wall asserts that blacking up did not become commonplace until the mid-nineteenth century and the first reference to it comes from 1855. Wall observes that 'an onlooker's comment makes it clear that it results from the influence of blackface minstrelsy'.[34] However, Wall may be confining his comments to Britain, since Thoinot Arbeau, the *nom de plume* of French cleric Jehan Tabourot, who commented extensively on forms of dance, wrote in the late sixteenth century:

> In fashionable society when I was young, a small boy, his face daubed with black and his forehead swathed in a white or yellow handkerchief, would make an appearance after supper. He wore leggings covered with little bells and performed a morris.[35]

Henry VIII's Shrovetide banquet for ambassadors in 1509 featured torchbearers who 'were appareyled in crymosen satyne and grene lyke Moreskoes, their faces blacke'.[36] Black people were present in Britain at this time, as the reference to Moors suggests, and as historian David Olusoga's comprehensive work *Black Britain* ably demonstrates. Whether the presence of blackface at this time represents a form of mockery is moot: a nuanced understanding of how non-white people were perceived at the time needs to be taken into consideration.

There is, however, also quite well-documented evidence for blackface being used as a ruse to avoid detection when engaged in antisocial activities. The first 'black act' against poaching when disguised was passed in 1486 in a response to acts of organized mass poaching, such as the slaughter of 82 deer belonging to the Duke of Buckingham in Kent in 1450. These, in turn, were reactions to enclosure legislation: the poachers not only blacked their faces but also adopted women's clothing and would give their names only as 'servants of the Queen of the Fairies'.

By 1723, using a disguise, either 'by mask or by blackened face', became a capital offence under the Waltham 'Black Act'. Again, this was in response to mass poaching by groups known as 'the Blacks' in Hampshire and Windsor Great Park, itself a partial consequence of the economic downturn created by the collapse of the South Sea Bubble. The Blacks were also rumoured to have been smuggling brandy and planning a Jacobite uprising, so there was an extra political dimension to their activities.

So it seems that there is plenty of evidence for blacking up as a precaution against identification, and some documentary evidence that the practice was also employed in Morris dancing from quite an early stage in its development. But we must be careful here. It is also possible that early Morris dancers used blackface as a legacy of disguise or for some other reason (Moorish influence, for example, or the copying of popular sweeps' parades), then the practice fell out of favour when later laws came in against blacking up because of its presence in antisocial behaviour, and then, later still, Border Morris sides resumed the practice as a result of influence from minstrel shows. I've addressed the 'disguise' question above – the explanation doesn't make a great deal of sense in a small community where everyone knows you, and why would you need to be disguised in any case if you're just dancing on the village green? Maybe if you're drunk and it's dark there might be a justification, and there certainly would be for poaching, but that's an entirely different set of activities.

The Cheltenham Mummers told the former head of campaigns for the Commission for Racial Equality, Nicholas Milton, who attended one of their performances, that they had originally started blacking up in order to disguise themselves from employers, since mummers were 'not renowned for their sobriety',[37] but I refer my honourable reader to the 'still easily recognisable' argument. I suspect it's more a case of tradition: we've 'always done it' so we're going to carry on doing it (even if 'we' haven't always done it).

We have seen that the majority of traditional and folk practices (the Mari Lwyd is a case in point) do not have an unbroken linear heritage from their inception to the present day, but are more commonly hallmarked by stops, starts, abandonment or decline, followed by revival, and even something as seemingly unchanging and perpetual as the Morris actually goes through a number of incremental changes and sometimes some quite major shifts. Unless this is documented, we tend not to be aware of it.

However, although tradition can be used as a justification for contemporary practices, this is not to say that it *should* be. Critics of the practice point out that for many people today, blacking up symbolizes not disguise, but mockery; both the reason for the practice (tradition) and its interpretation (racism) have changed. Some commentators also suggest that blackface is a product of institutional racism, in which society as a whole is inherently colonialist or racist, regardless of individual intent.

This is perhaps more plausible than the view that Morris is directly racist and an expression of the anti-Black attitudes of its members; I actually don't think that this is the case. Racism might be an emergent property out of the use of blackface, but it's debatable whether it was the reason for it. (If it does come from an emulation of minstrelsy, I suspect that this was more because minstrelsy was popular with audiences than because it was explicitly racist, although the argument can be reversed; it was clearly racist, relying as it did on unpleasant stereotypes of Black Americans, so perhaps that's *why* it was popular.)

Canadian academic Pauline Greenhill, commenting on Morris dancing in Canada, writes that:

> it seems unlikely that North American audiences, who encounter Morris at dance-outs at local shopping centres, pubs, and so on, far from geographical associations with coal miners, would see in blackface dances anything other than a white peoples' representation of black culture. Unfamiliar with the localized and historicized explanations of Morris tradition used by dancers, audiences might historically contextualise blackface in terms of entertainment forms such as vaudeville and view it in light of the overtly or covertly racist ideas associated with these practices. Or they might locate it in a slightly more up-to-date scenario of riots and gangs.[38]

Sophie Morris writes:

> History is interesting. Origin stories fascinate people. All of these arguments are well-worn. But the more I listen

to how critics and supporters slice, dice and muddle the evidence, the more tempted I am to say to hell with all of it. What relevance has origin in what is perceived as outwardly – often proudly – racist behaviour?[39]

A number of Morris sides either concur or perhaps feel that the practice has now become so controversial that it's not worth persevering with. It's not the central element of Morris – that would be the dances themselves and the music – and it may not be the hill on which a Morris side wishes to die. One side that has dispensed with blacking up and gone over to blueface is the Hook Eagle side from Fleet, in Hampshire. Member John Ellis told *The Guardian*, 'We adopted this idea because the dancing is really easy, good fun and we quite like the idea of dancing in disguise.'[40]

Hook Eagle did this in response to a call in June 2020 from the cross-country Joint Morris Organisations (comprising the Morris Federation, the Morris Ring and Open Morris) to dispense with blackface in light of the Black Lives Matter movement. In leading up to this statement, they gave comprehensive reasons for the change:

> Our traditions do not operate in a vacuum. While no Morris dancer wants to cause offence, we must recognise that full-face black or other skin tone make-up is a practice that has the potential to cause deep hurt. Morris is a living tradition and it is right that it has always adapted and evolved to reflect society. In 2016, we issued guidance to our members with respect to using face paint as a disguise, and we welcome the fact that

many long-standing teams who used to wear full-face black makeup have chosen to use masks, alternative colours, or other forms of disguise. We now believe we must take further steps to ensure the continued relevance and inclusivity of the tradition. Morris is a unique cultural tradition of which we should be rightly proud. We want people from all races and backgrounds to share in this pride and not be made to feel unwelcome or uncomfortable by any element of a performance.

As a committee we have come to the conclusion that it is no longer a matter of personal preference but of taking a stand. Accordingly, a motion will be put forward to the AGM in September to ask member teams to review their policies and practices and move that The Morris Federation should not renew membership for teams where individuals still continue to use full-face skin tone makeup.

This decision has been considered for a long time and we do not take this action lightly. While not a direct reaction to recent nationalist articles, we should recognise that the use of full-face black make-up can encourage and embolden these sentiments.

We understand that such a move may distress and upset people we know as friends. We would like to reach out to member teams to engage with us on this matter so that we can move forward together.

We will be urging all of our members to consider this issue seriously and to vote on the motion that will be discussed at the upcoming virtual AGM to be held on Saturday 26 September 2020.

We expect that this story will be picked up by the press and we would urge all members to be aware of the wider issues when engaging with the media or in their use of social media. We understand that no member seeks to contradict our aims for inclusivity, but it is not each dancer's intent that matters, rather how they – and the Morris – are perceived by the outside world.[41]

So, although the origins of blackface in the context of Morris dancing remain unclear and probably derive from a variety of disparate influences, contemporary views on the practice must still be taken into consideration, and the various Morris organizations have proven proactive in suggesting alternatives. As with so many customs, Morris dancing not only moved with the times throughout its long history but continues to do so.

Darkie Day

The midwinter festival held in Padstow, Cornwall used to be known as Darkie Day. It's now called Mummers' Day and it's actually two days, held on Boxing Day and at New Year. The old name is said to come from 'Darking Day'; the blacked-up faces represent the dark half of the year, as opposed to the 'white', light half of the year.

I have entered into debate with people who believe that our fear of the 'dark' is in itself racist. This may be the case or it may not; I tend to believe that it comes from living in a northern climate in which long nights and dark forests are places of danger, but I am open to alternative explanations if they're based on evidence. We've looked at blacking up in connection with Morris dancing, but concerns about Darkie Day were being aired in the 1970s, given that the celebration used a number of minstrel songs; these have now been discontinued and replaced with more traditional Cornish songs.

With reference to the Oss celebrations at the other side of the year, there have been claims that the songs around the Blue Oss are in support of Black rights, basically because the spirituals sung in the celebration originate in Methodist support of Black American rights. There's also a local legend about a slave ship moored in Padstow in the seventeenth century, where the slaves, either allowed out for exercise or in escape, taught a dance to the locals, who have blacked up in solidarity ever since. Another version relates that the locals saw slaves singing and dancing on the ship and copied them. I am not alone in finding this improbable for a variety of reasons – slaves being allowed to fraternize with the locals being one of them, and I don't think anyone on the run from enforced servitude would pause to teach choreography. I find the protests that Darkie Day is nothing to do with race somewhat strenuous, given that minstrel songs were such a feature of the celebration, with lines like 'He's gone where the good n*****s go,' and given that people were prone to wearing Afro wigs and 'mammy' turbans, which I don't somehow feel were widespread features of English mumming in the seventeenth or eighteenth centuries.

In 2006, MP Diane Abbott tabled a motion in Parliament asking for the Padstow celebration to be banned, but it was unsuccessful. The local MP, Dan Rogerson, defended blacking up on the 'disguise' justification. The festivity is still held, but has been renamed 'Mummer's Day'.

SIX

Mystery Plays

We might wonder whether mystery plays have a role in a book that's all about folklore and transgression. Surely re-enactments of biblical tales are there to reinforce religious order and maintain the status quo? But perhaps we should now take a deeper look into these once popular events and their history.

Mystery plays are among the earliest English plays. The name might come from 'miracle' (though, as we shall shortly see, miracle plays are a little bit different) or from the word 'ministerium', or 'craft', as these plays were often performed by guilds. (It has nothing to do with our modern use of the word, which obviously refers to sundry types of detective fiction.) In medieval times, a mystery play would be enacted in a church and might take the form of a tableau representing some biblical event, such as the creation story, accompanied by music. They began as a little addition to the main service but spread in popularity until they were enacted by professional companies outside the church, still focusing on the Bible and its set pieces. One early example is the *Quem Quaeritis*, the *Whom Do You Seek*, based on four lines of the Easter liturgy (it originally comes from John 18:7). It's very simple, taking the form of a question, an answer and a command:

Question [by the Angels]: Whom do ye seek in the
    sepulchre, O followers of Christ?
Answer [by the Marys]: Jesus of Nazareth, the
    Crucified, O heavenly ones.
The Angels: He is not here; he is risen, just as he
    foretold. Go, announce that he is risen from the
    sepulchre.[1]

Yet this simple biblical episode spawned a huge variety
of mystery plays over the next 650 years and it was only the
Reformation that caused this liturgical juggernaut to grind to
a halt. Initially, around the ninth century, the actors, writers
and directors of these performances would have been monks,
but in 1210 Pope Innocent III became wary of the increasing popularity of mystery plays and delivered an edict that
banned clergy from performing on the public stage. This set-
back did not succeed in putting a stop to the plays, though;
their performance passed from the Church to the town guilds,
who took them over. The language of the plays changed under
their new producers, too, from Latin into the vernacular, and
the plays now started to contain elements which were other
than biblical and which were sometimes comic. Freed from
the constraints of the Church, the mystery play was allowed
to develop and grow – sometimes in surprising directions.
Special effects were sometimes added, and some plays were
enacted on carts, which could be taken from place to place, a
bit like a mobile cinema (these performances took place across
Europe and were not solely an English phenomenon). They
might have been an early example of amateur dramatics, but
they were nonetheless big productions: the York cycles, for

instance, were re-enacted around the Feast of Corpus Christi and could take up to twenty hours to perform, spread across several days. In England, they include:

- The York cycles: 48 pageants
- The Towneley cycles: 32 pageants
- The Chester cycles: 24 pageants and probably an Elizabethan reconstruction of earlier plays
- The Ludus Coventriae (also known as the N-town cycle or the Hegge cycle): probably a compilation of three distinct plays

Apart from these main cycles, there are also additional individual plays, from Norwich and Newcastle, for example, and three from Cornwall in Cornish (the Ordinalia). All of them contain well-known Bible stories. For example, the York cycle consists of the following:

- The Creation of the Angels and the Fall of Lucifer
- The Creation through the Fifth Day
- The Creation of Adam and Eve
- The Prohibition of the Tree of Knowledge
- The Fall
- The Expulsion from the Garden
- Sacrificium Cayme et Abell
- The Building of Noah's Ark

Some guilds took on plays featuring episodes that are most closely related to their own professions: bakery guilds would take on the loaves and fishes story, for example, and goldsmiths would take responsibility for plays featuring the Adoration of the Magi with their gifts of frankincense, gold and myrrh.

The Towneley plays originated in Wakefield and some were the work of the 'Wakefield Master', an anonymous author who was probably a cleric of some description. But it's debatable how many of the plays he actually wrote. The plays include what we would now call comedy skits, such as the Second Shepherds' Pageant, which features a sheep thief, Mak, and his wife. Before paying their respects to the infant Christ at the Nativity, the shepherds first have to find and liberate one of their sheep, which the thief has stolen and hidden – his wife disguises it as a baby in case the irate shepherds come and search the house. This turns the whole thing into a bit of a farce; medieval humour was often broad, to put it mildly. There's a lot of bawdy advice to young men about the intricacies and problems of wooing. One of the shepherds has a rant about his wife (hard drinking, controlling, abusive). Another complains about being oppressed by the rich – a message that one imagines would have been well received by the audience, who were in the main likely to have been illiterate and poor. The shepherds do find their stolen sheep, and they punish Mak by tossing him up and down in a blanket, but they don't beat him up or kill him. In a reward for their forbearance, an angel appears and tells them about the birth of Jesus, whom they then go to see. The moral message is straightforward: good deeds are rewarded and bad ones punished.

In discussing these mystery cycles with a group of fellow writers, one of them described the mystery plays to me as 'biblical fanfic', and there's certainly an element of truth in this; the initial stories, once liberated from the constraints placed

upon their performance by the Church, are used as a spring-
board for comedy, political comment and the concerns of the
day, rather as a village pantomime might use local in-jokes and
easily recognizable local characters. This is not necessarily an act
of intentional transgression, but a natural extension of creativity,
using tropes that would be familiar to everyone in the context
of a Christian society and with the aim of providing laughs. The
actors would not be distant celebrities, but people whom the
audience knew, recruited by the guilds. Hetta Elizabeth Howes,
medieval literature expert, notes that these plays would draw
upon local events and individuals:

> The players performed their historical stories in up-to-
> date settings, making references to local landmarks,
> disputes and characters in order to root the action not
> only in the contemporary moment, but in their particular
> location. In this way, the players drew their audience into
> the playworld, making the mysteries of God and the
> history of Christianity feel more present and accessible.[2]

Rather than private theatres, enclosed in the round like the
Globe, these productions were performed in the street – by the
community and for the community. They were, as we have seen
above, often irreverent:

> Students of medieval mystery plays are often surprised,
> even shocked, by their humour. Noah is portrayed as a
> bit of a drunken fool, and his wife as a shrewish nag.
> The York play of the Crucifixion, which concerns Jesus
> being nailed to the Cross, sees the soldiers arguing and

making the audience laugh with their incompetence. This might seem sacrilegious to a modern audience, but it was part and parcel of medieval life and the attitude of medieval Christians to their religion. The comic nature of Noah's character in these plays did not detract from the overall importance and significance of their Christian message: it just amused and entertained the audience on the journey to salvation. The black humour of the York play of the Crucifixion did not risk dampening the awe and glory of Christ rising from the dead, fighting back devils or allocating the saved to Heaven – rather, it amplified his triumph.[3]

In Salisbury in 1614, one Alice Mustian charged her neighbours with the cost of small trinkets (such as pins) to come and watch a play in her back yard. The subject was the adultery of local people.

Alice Mustian's humble provincial performance had obvious affinities with the bawdy satirical jigs found on the London stage, or even with a play like George Chapman's *Old Joiner of Aldgate* whose matrimonial theme was firmly based in real-life events which occurred not a hundred miles from the theatre.[4]

We will be returning to this kind of localized retribution when we come to consider the phenomenon of the charivari.

Not everyone found this acceptable; there are contemporary criticisms of the mystery cycles. Complainants found the fact that Christ was played by an ordinary man to be objectionable, verging on blasphemous and lessening the sacred messages of the Bible. *The Tretise of Miraclis Pleyinge* is an example and the first piece of dramatic criticism in English: 'God takith more venjaunce on us than a lord that sodaynly sleeth his servaunt for he pleyide to homely [familiar] with him.'[5] No one seems to have paid much attention to this apparent blasphemy in Catholic England, but this was to change towards the Reformation, when a more Protestant zeal saw the lens of religious fanaticism turned upon the mystery plays.

Accompanying the phenomenon of the mystery cycles were morality plays, which had the function that their name suggests. These highlighted the nature of sin and repentance, with characters meeting the personifications of virtues and vices. Again, these shorter plays often contained moments of low comedy – particularly, one suspects, when it came to the vices. As an example, the medieval play *The Somonynge of Everyman* features a wealthy gent who is forced by Death to account for his virtues and vices; not surprisingly, the latter far outweigh the former and although the central character tries to enlist personifications of Fellowship and Earthly Goods to help him, they prove of little use (you can't take it with you, in other words). But he does finally squeeze into Heaven, via a last-minute repentance. This is a familiar type of story to Christian audiences and it has been reprised ever since: *Faust*, for instance, is the same kind of tale. The theological sceptic might question the nature of repentance – basically, you can be a complete bastard all your life but still make it into the life eternal at the last minute, and if one were cynical, one might suggest that this is a theological reassurance to the ruling classes, who would also have been aware of the biblical dictum that it is easier for a camel to pass through the eye of a needle than it is for a rich man to enter the kingdom of Heaven. *Everyman* shows that this is possible, but in *Faust*, the central character doesn't repent and must honour his pact with the Devil.

The timeless message of *Everyman* is shown by the fact that it was last produced in 2015, with an updated script by Carol Ann Duffy and with Chiwetel Ejiofor in the lead role. The character celebrates his fortieth birthday with a hedonistic coke-fuelled party until Death comes calling. *The Guardian* said of the update that 'what was originally church propaganda has been turned, in Carol Ann Duffy's stunning adaptation, into a scathing assault on the myopic materialism of the modern age and a reminder of our own mortality.'[6]

Booze and drugs are portrayed as the lesser sin here: Everyman's real failing is his reliance on throwing money at problems in order to solve them and his disregard for the environment – in a secular society, these are seen as more critical sins and the figure of God (here portrayed as a Marigold glove-wearing cleaning lady) is merged with that of the personification of Good Deeds. But in this adaptation, as with the original, the worst underlying sin is perhaps selfishness, a lack of community spirit. 'I thought the Earth was mine to spend, a coin in space,' says Everyman. He learns that no man is an island and the earth is not expendable, and faces death at the last with a new humility and understanding.

The update is interesting, as it shows us how the structure and concerns of the old morality play can be adapted to suit the age. These deep-underlying themes remain a societal preoccupation even in a nation in which religion has lost much of its impact, and new sins (such as lack of respect for the environment) have come to the fore.

The Curious History of the Devil in England

Throughout English history, the Devil appears in folk festivals and folklore in various guises. He carves huge gouges in the landscape, such as Devil's Dyke in Sussex or the Devil's Punchbowl near Hindhead. He seems remarkably active in his efforts to literally transform the English landscape, either by digging vast holes or other earthworks, or by flinging boulders about the place. The curious prehistoric earthwork of Silbury Hill was said in local folklore to have been dropped by the Devil as he was carrying a huge bucket of soil to bury the village of Avebury; the villages prayed for redemption, the Devil dropped his load some distance away and thus they were spared. We can see these as efforts by geographically ignorant locals to explain unusual features of the landscape, such as drumlins left by the retreating ice that once covered so much of this country, or enigmatic monuments left by ancient peoples (Stonehenge is a prime example – the Devil is said to have been its architect). Similar tales are also told about giants, who are attributed with the same kind of landscape-moulding properties. But the presence of the Devil is not confined to large and arbitrary building projects.

Throughout the medieval period and later, the Devil became associated with fairies. In 1579, the Elizabethan preacher Edmond Bicknoll expressed the opinion that a belief in fairies was actually Satanic; the Devil induced people to believe in 'false spirits' and thus lead them away from an understanding of God. Fairies induced people to 'cast of[f] the spirite of grace' so that the Devil will forever be 'the terrour of our conscience'.[7] Thomas Hobbes also connected belief in fairies with the Devil, and both beliefs with 'popery': the king of the fairies was the Devil, and both were associated with Catholicism (Hobbes did not apparently believe in the Devil per se, so this is presumably either metaphorical or cynical, or both). In James i's *Daemonologie* (1597), fairies are one of four categories of devils.

The Devil's alarming horned presence features in mystery plays and as comic relief in pageants, such as the demon Titivillus in the Wakefield or Towneley Mystery Plays, who comments satirically on human foibles. Is he the biblical Satan, however, or does he have different origins?

The standard view of the Devil (or devils) who appear in mystery plays is that they are initially theologically transgressive: they appear when those plays become, as we have seen above, increasingly secular. Devils are obscene, perhaps witty, a bit edgy and ribald. They say the things that respectable people cannot say. This view is, according to writer John Cox, taken on board by Marxist scholars and taken further into an account of devils as remnants of folklore that symbolize the working man and his rebellion against the establishment: 'In this view, the social function of devils is to provide a subversive expression for class frustration and protest.'[8]

Hutton spreads the net wider and comments, in relation to the Antrobus Play (but applicable to other mumming plays as well):

it depends upon the fielding of and increasingly outrageous set of characters who evoke laughter, but also fear, surprise and questioning. All are peripheral to the community, all economically unproductive; they are either menacing outsiders or internal misfits . . . The overall impact is, perhaps, the better definition, and so reinforcement, of the community.[9]

Most mumming plays in which the Devil features take place around Christmas or other holidays such as Hallowe'en, Twelfth Night, All Soul's Day or Plough Monday.

Here comes I Beelzebub
And over my shoulder I carry my club
And in my hand a dripping pan
I think myself a jolly old man.[10]

Peter Millington points out some of the pitfalls in analysing the Devil in mystery plays, based on the instance of an illustration showing a group of juvenile folk play actors that comes from William Sandys's book *Christmastide, its History, Festivities and Carols*.[11] Everyone assumes that the figure on the left is the Devil, but he's actually supposed to be Father Christmas; the author ventures to suggest that you wouldn't want him coming down your chimney.[12]

In folk plays, Father Christmas and Beelzebub have a similar role but are geographically distinct. According to Millington, Father Christmas shows up in plays that are south of a line drawn roughly between the Severn and the Thames, whereas in plays to the north of this line and in Ireland, Beelzebub features instead.[13] In a few places, such as Ovingdean in Sussex, records show that this became hopelessly confused, with Old

Father Beelzebub putting in an appearance in the script. In Berkshire, the character appears as 'Old Beelzebub: As Father Christmas'.[14] This is a great example of a folk play going hopelessly off-piste, possibly for the simple reason that someone wanted to use an existing costume rather than from any deep theological confusion. It's also possible that someone of a more devout bent took on the production and wanted to make the play a little more respectable and Christian.

Are the old mumming plays remnants of a pre-Christian fertility ritual? Almost certainly not, as we've noted above. They do, however, often adopt a standard format, usually taking the form of a hero, such as St George, challenging a villain, such as a dragon, to combat. Someone (not always the villain) is slain, and a quack doctor is then enlisted to revive them.

Contemporary mumming plays often subvert this basic structure, while still retaining elements of it. I attended one written by poet and performer John Constable, aka John Crow, whom we will meet again when we come to look at the Crossbones rites later in this chapter. This was written for the queen's Platinum Jubilee in 2022 and staged at Glastonbury Abbey. In this, St George negotiated with the Dragon and, despite collapsing and having to be brought back by the Doctor, played by the then-mayor, survived. A goddess played a role in helping the Dragon, too, and there was an underlying environmental theme, once again indicating how these old plays can be easily adapted to carry a modern moral message.

In the East Midlands, mumming plays had a different structure, based around the Recruiting Sergeant model, and were usually performed around Plough Monday. Tom Fool introduces the action, which then moves into a three-way operatic scene between a Recruiting Sergeant, a Farmer's Man and the Lady. The Farmer's Man dumps the Lady and joins the army, so his ditched girlfriend marries the Fool instead. After this is a scene between a character known as Old Dame Jane and Beelzebub or Eezum Squeezum. Old Jane is knocked to the floor and it is she who then has to be revived by the Doctor.

The third type of play is a Sword Dance play, found in Yorkshire and other parts of the north of England, which features, rather obviously, a Sword Dance.

Mumming has caused controversy in its time. A coup at Eltham was plotted in the fifteenth century under the cover of a mumming performance and four hundred years later people were still complaining about the trouble it brought in its wake, such as the episode in the late nineteenth century when Wraxhall mumming men were attacked by their Melksham counterparts for performing in the latter's territory. Throughout its history mumming has been periodically banned, for instance in Bristol and London, probably due to the opportunities for crime or antisocial behaviour that were presented by its use of disguise.

Abbots Bromley Horn Dance

One of the most mysterious events in the British folk calendar is the Abbots Bromley Horn dance. It's one of the oldest documented, too, having been first performed in 1226 at the Barthelmy Fair in Abbots Bromley, a little village in Staffordshire. It now takes place on Wakes Monday, 9 September – one of the last vestiges of the old Wakes Weeks, which were originally a religious festival, a period to commemorate the saint to which your local church was dedicated and which then changed to a secular holiday (the summer fortnight in which northern factory workers were given time off).

In medieval times, the Wakes Week in any given district depended on the day to which the local saint was dedicated (the term 'wake' means a vigil, and is the same word for the period immediately before or after a funeral). Many of these fell in the summer, such as St John on 24 June, St Philip and St Paul on 29 June, and St Thomas on 3 July. These commemorations of saints' days were banned in 1571 in the archdiocese of York, due to what must by now be a familiar story to readers of this book; namely, complaints about drunkenness and excess revelry. A few hundred years later in the West Riding, increased transport links compounded the problem – the crowds coming into the wakes by train overpowered the local police.

There were dubious enticements, at least from the point of view of the 'respectable' classes. At Shaw Wake, a local butcher carried out the novel attraction of shattering an iron door with his head and people often encouraged (that should probably read 'incited') crowds to engage in dubious challenges, such as scrabbling for heated coins, head butting competitions or naked men's racing, which was banned pretty quickly in Birmingham. Animal tormenting also became something with which the authorities became increasingly disgusted.

King Charles I smelled a rat about these claims of abusive and rowdy behaviour, however, writing:

Of late, in some counties of our kingdom, we find that, under the pretence of taking away abuses, there hath been a general forbidding . . . of the feasts of the dedication of churches, commonly called wakes. Now our express will and pleasure is, that these feasts, with others, shall be observed.[15]

However, this more relaxed attitude did not survive his reign, and the Wakes Weeks were once more banned entirely by the new regime of Cromwell and the Puritans. Once the Restoration occurred, however, Wakes Weeks were re-established. John Lucas wrote in the early eighteenth century about the feast of St Oswald, on 9 August, in Wharton in Lancashire:

> The feast of dedication . . . is now annually observed on the Sunday nearest to the first of August, and the vain custom of dancing, excessive drinking, etc., on that day being for many years laid aside, the inhabitants and strangers duly spend the day in attending the service of the church and preparing good cheer within the rules of sobriety in private houses . . . They cut hard rushes from the marsh, which they make up into long bundles, and then dress them in fine linen, ribbons, silk, flowers, etc.; afterwards the young women take the burdens upon their heads and begin the procession . . . which is attended with a great multitude of people, with music, drums, ringing bells and all other demonstrations of joy.[16]

The custom of rushbearing, in which the old floor covering of scattered rushes was swept out of the church and replaced with new rushes, was an integral part of Wakes, but Lucas' charming depiction of a sober, cheerful 'summer cleaning' was perhaps somewhat retrospectively optimistic, as one of the Rochdale vicars, a Dr Hind, banned the rushbearing in 1780 for the reasons mentioned above. It saw numerous outbreaks of violence: the decorated carts that bore the rushes were defended according to territory and fights between rival cart bearers, usually young men, often occurred if different carts happened to meet in the street. Despite bans, rushbearing still continued in some places, however, and gradually was joined by other customs such as Morris dancing. One cart remains, borne by a Morris side in Saddleworth, as a revived custom. Georgina Boyes, in the more rigorous approach to folk customs taken by scholars in the 1980s, has debunked any idea that this was an ancient custom.[17]

It seems likely that the Abbots Bromley horn dance became associated with Wakes Week, although previously it was a Christmas dance, performed at Christmas itself, New Year and Twelfth Night. It now takes place between 5–12 September, having been moved to that month by the change of calendar in 1752. We have few records of it, and none before the seventeenth century:

At Abbots, or now rather Pagets Bromley, they had also within memory, a sort of sport, which they celebrated at Christmas (on New-Year and Twelft-day) call'd the Hobby-horse dance, from a person that carryed the image of a horse between his leggs, made of thin boards, and in his hand a bow and arrow, which passing through a hole in the bow, and stopping upon a sholder it had in it, he made a snapping noise as he drew it to and fro, keeping time with the Musick: with this Man danced 6 others, carrying on their shoulders as many Rain deers heads, 3 of them painted white, and 3 red, with the Armes of the cheif families (viz.) of Paget, Bagot, and Wells) to whom the revenews of the Town cheifly belonged, depicted on the palms of them, with which they danced the Hays, and other Country dances. To this Hobbyhorse dance there also belong'd a pot, which was kept by turnes, by 4 or 5 of the cheif of the Town, whom they call'd Reeves, who provided Cakes and Ale to put in this pot; all people who had any kindness for the good intent of the Institution of the sport, giving pence a piece for themselves and families; and so forraigners too, that came to see it: with which Mony (the charge of the Cakes and Ale being defrayed) they not only repaired their Church but kept their poore too: which charges are not now perhaps so cheerfully boarn.[18]

The horns themselves are not the antlers of British deer, but reindeer horns (three white and three brown) attached to more recent wooden heads in the shape of deer, which seem likely to date from the sixteenth century and were probably domestic (forensic analysis shows that they had been gelded). There is also room for coats of arms to be depicted, of the local grand families, notably Paget, Welles and Bagot. The horn dance is very much a family affair, not necessarily involving the aristocracy but certainly performed by local families: the Adeys, Bentleys and Fowells. Laura Fowell, a member of one of these traditionally involved families, stated on the Horn Dance's public Facebook page:

I have grown up with the horn dance, attending my first dance when I was 11 months old (it's in mine and my families blood). One of my fondest memories of Horn Dance day is of my Grandad. We were at Lady Bagots on the lawn, Grandad was playing the accordion, everyone was dancing. Grandad got down on his knees, rolled on to his back, all whilst playing, he looked like a rock star. I watched on thinking that legend is my Grandad.

I'm not the first female to be part of this wonderful tradition and hopefully I won't be the last.

I follow in the foot steps of my Aunties, Mum and Sister. We are all very proud to be part of its history and in our own way, carrying on the 'Fowell family' tradition.[19]

Joe Bailey, a member of another such family, says,

I'm Joe Bailey son of Terry Bailey the Jester, I currently carry the 2nd white horn. This year will be my 24th year doing the Horn Dance. One of my fondest memories involves Doug Fowell, the former Melodeon player, I then played the Triangle and was told to keep close to Doug, to ensure I kept in time. One year we were at a festival in a town centre, and Doug must have just fancied a change of scenery, as midway through a dance, he decided to go into the supermarket, and we all followed, dancing and playing up and down the aisles, as the shoppers looked on in bemusement and security tried to usher us out! I'm very proud to be part of the horn dance, and see it as a great privilege and responsibility to keep this tradition going. With that said, my 3-year-old son is horn dance mad, and [will] hopefully follow in his dads and grandads footsteps.[20]

The apparatus is heavy: some of the horns are more than 3 feet in width and the biggest, Big White, comes in at 11 kilograms (25 lb). One set has been carbon dated to 1065 and is kept in the local church.

Whether there was any dance associated with the horns this far back in history is a very moot point. Some historians have linked them to Wulfric, an adviser to King Ethelred who founded the local Benedictine Abbey in the 1100s, others to the commemoration of the granting of hunting rights to the villagers of Needwood Forest. There have been suggestions that the horns were brought across by the Vikings against whom Ethelred fought. Their longevity is remarkable – it seems likely that they were concealed during the English Civil War and its immediate aftermath – and a number of elk horns were brought back from Turkey by Lord Paget in 1703. The problem with this particular custom is that the date of the horns may not correlate with the date of the dance itself; there is some suggestion that the dance was originally a hobby horse dance and the horns, which could have been brought into the country at any point between the eleventh and seventeenth centuries, were added later on, since the first note that we have of them is from Robert Plot, above.

On Horn Dancing Day, participants receive an early morning blessing from the vicar, around 7.30 a.m., and the dancers then progress around the parish. The dance, which involves locking the horns, is performed at twelve different locations around Abbots Bromley; the dancers' circuit used to cover some 20 miles (it's now shorter, around 10 miles, which is still a sizeable distance, especially given the weight and the cumbersome nature of the horns). It's supposed to bring bad luck if the dancers don't perform at their appointed place, so it's good news if they show up. The horns are returned to the church around 8.15 p.m. and a Compline Service is held.

Dancers are costumed; they apparently used to wear their usual clothes plus a few ribbons, but in the 1850s various wives decided that the dancers needed something a bit more showy and devised a quasi-medieval costume for them, including jerkins. A form of this costume is still worn today.

The dance is accompanied by music, originally a fiddle but now accordions and the mandolin are used. Around 1910, folklorist Cecil Sharp published the tune played on the melodeon, Wheelwright Robinson's tune, in *Sword Dances of Northern Europe*.[21]

Does the horn dance have pagan roots? Theorists sometimes cite the horned 'shaman' in the cave paintings in Lascaux, in France, in support of this claim. These images are around 20,000 years old, but historians have conflicting ideas about them. Ronald Hutton questions the image known as the 'sorceror', the figure with horns, suggesting that the sketch made by Henri Breuil does not accurately represent the image on the cave wall, and that Breuil may have been influenced by his own theories regarding hunting magic.[22]

Attempts to provide definitive proof have not succeeded, although the Siberian region of Yakutia does have a horn dance that has been said to be similar to the one in Abbot's Bromley. But although reindeer play a sacred role among many Siberian tribes, and indeed among all the peoples of the Arctic Circle (such as those in Lapland), there's no proof of any connection with the British dance. The theories regarding the Viking origins of the horns themselves may, however, hold more water given their carbon-dated age.

The dance contains some typically transgressive elements that should by now be familiar to the reader: cross-dressing and the subversive actions of a Fool, and some associated drunkenness has been used as an argument against it in the past. But current participants say that they value it for the sense of community and the bond that it creates between participants. Some say that it has a family feel to it, perhaps unsurprisingly for a tradition that is so anchored in local families, although not all participants are related. It is notable that the dancers start young and have a genuine commitment to, and enthusiasm for, the dance from an early age. Carl Fowell, the current leader, commented on Facebook:

I have been dancing since I was 7 years old, when I was honoured to be able to dance. Although I was expected to be a part of the dance and become the leader I have always wanted to be a part of this dance family. No matter the weather the dance has always been fun for me, the comradery between dancers is what makes it so enjoyable.

A key memory for me was our trip to Germany in 1996 with the likes of Terry Bailey, Jeff Bradbury, Doug Fowell, Tony Fowell, and Clag. The dancers took a coach and ferry for a weekend away, everyone was so welcoming and we had a great laugh with the locals.[23]

The May Horns

Penzance in Cornwall sees the May Horns, an annual event in which locals meet between Penzance and Newlyn at dusk on the first Sunday in May. Dressed in green and white, they blow horns and sycamore whistles in order to drive out 'the devil of winter' and bring the summer in. Playing these instruments, the Mayers walk into Penzance, joined by the Lord and Lady of the May and Old Ned, a man in a crow costume who wears a floral crown, dies and is revived thrice en route.

Despite its atavistic feel and the sinister appearance of Old Ned, the tradition dates back only as far as the nineteenth century and was banned in 1933 after complaints about the level of noise (horn blowing is still banned in Penzance). The event was revived by the Cornish Culture Association. This particular incarnation of the May Horns does not seem to be especially old, but there is a version of the same sort of celebration in Serbia, on the eve of St George's Day (6 May in that nation). Again, horns and whistles, made of willow, are blown to celebrate the return of summer, but these are broken up at the end of the parade.

Hunting the Earl of Rone

This curious custom is a revival and takes place over the last Bank Holiday weekend in May. Legend has it that it refers to the hunting of the Earl of Tyrone, Hugh O'Neill. Prior to the sixteenth century, Irish chieftains were elected according to local 'brehon' laws but the earldom was conferred upon the O'Neill family by the English, in an attempt to establish a direct line of descent (the earl had to swear allegiance to the English monarch). Hugh O'Neill blotted his copy book by rebelling against the English during the Nine Years War and eventually fleeing to Europe, anticipating the invasion of Ireland by the Spanish. He was declared a traitor and his flight from Ireland in 1607 is commemorated in the Devon custom.

This used to take place every year up until the 1830s, when it was banned. It was revived in 1974, based on written accounts of people's memories such as the Reverend Tugwell in 1863, who wrote a full account of the ceremony:

> I am not, however, going to tell you the story of [the earl's] wanderings in the woods, or of his capture, but of the strange annual commemoration thereof which the Combmartin people instituted, and which they kept up with great regularity till the year 1837, when the ceremonial was finally abolished. The 'show' took place yearly on Ascension Day, and the characters or mummers who played in it were the following. The Earl of Rone: wearing a grotesque mask, a smock-frock stuffed or padded with straw, and a string of twelve hard sea-biscuits round his neck. The Hobby-Horse: masked and covered with gaily painted trappings, and armed with an instrument called a 'mapper', which was shaped to represent the mouth of a horse, and was furnished with rude teeth and the means of rapidly opening and closing its formidable jaws. The Fool: also masked and gaudily dressed. A (real) Donkey: decorated with flowers and a necklace of twelve sea-biscuits. A troop of Grenadiers, armed with guns, and wearing tall caps of coloured paper profusely adorned with bunches of ribands.

During the fortnight which preceded Ascension Day the Hobby-Horse and the Fool, in full dress, paraded the parish and levied contributions to defray the cost of the dresses and the other expenses of the show. On the morning of the day itself great numbers of people thronged in from the surrounding parishes, and the whole village turned out in its Sunday garments and put on its liveliest aspect. At three o'clock in the afternoon the Grenadiers marched with all due pomp and circumstance of war to the neighbouring plantation called Lady's Wood, and after much parade of search, discover the fugitive Earl of Rone ineffectually hidden in the low brushwood. They immediately fire a volley, lay hold of their prisoner, set him on the Donkey with his face towards the animal's tail, and thus conduct him in triumph to the village. Here the Hobby-Horse and the Fool, and great numbers of the inhabitants, join in the procession.

At certain stations in the village the Grenadiers fire a volley, when the Earl falls from his Donkey apparently mortally wounded. Hereupon there is great exultation on the part of the soldiers, and excessive lamentation on the part of the Hobby-Horse and the Fool. After great exertion the latter invariably succeeds in healing the Earl of his wounds, and then the procession re-forms and marches onward once more. At every public-house there is also a stoppage for purposes of refreshment, and as there are many such houses in Combmartin the progress of the mummers is necessarily slow. Moreover, there are further innumerable delays, caused by the perpetual efforts of the performers to levy additional contributions from the visitors who throng the street. As a general rule small sums are given readily, for in case of refusal the Fool dips the besom which he carries in the nearest gutter and plentifully besprinkles the rash recusant and should not this hint be promptly taken the Hobby-Horse proceeds to lay hold of the victim's clothes with his 'mapper', and this detains his prisoner till the required blackmail is forthcoming. About night-fall the procession reaches the sea.[24]

Why was it banned? According to some commentators, this was basically due to an early outbreak of health and safety. The *Illustrated London News* tells us in 1856 that 'The custom was abolished a few years ago, in consequence of the melancholy death of the then (assumed) Earl, who, having partaken too liberally of the refreshment supplied him, rolled over some stone steps and lost his life.'[25]

This sounds all too probable, and the writer of *Olde Devon Customs* in 1957 even gives the man's name – a Mr Lovering – but the *North Devon Journal* in 1856 called it a 'fable' and perhaps it is.[26] This account is quite specific, however: 'This tragic event is supposed to have sobered the party up a trifle, and their visits to the remaining taverns were of a shorter duration out of respect to the dead man's relatives.'[27] Note that they still *went* to the pub ...

Writer J.L.W. Page states:

the rowdiness and drunkenness inseparable from such a function became unbearable. So the day came when the Earl was hunted for the last time, and in 1837 the show was suppressed. But suppressed not altogether to the satisfaction of the inhabitants. One old lady told me with what an awful joy she would give her halfpenny to escape the jaws of the 'mapper', a terrific wooden affair worked by the hobbyhorse, and which laid hold of any non-paying delinquent. She was really quite enthusiastic about this by-gone revel, and I shall never forget the unction with which the old creature finished her narration by exclaiming, in good old-fashioned Devonshire, 'My dear soul, I should like to have 'un again!'[28]

The *North Devon Journal*, also in 1856, additionally notes that 'On these occasions a sort of blackmail was levied upon the inhabitants, all of whom were bound to contribute something to the revellers, which was spent, as all such money generally is, in drink.'[29]

Kathleen Toms, in *Notes of Combe Martin* (1906), remarks, 'At every public house (and there were more even in those days than there are now), the party would stop for refreshment. It may be imagined therefore that the journey down the street occupied some time, and that when the sea was reached, the procession had waxed somewhat disorderly.'[30] The journal of the Devonshire Association backs this up in 1917, with an anonymous commentator who had interviewed three very old men in the village: George Dendle, aged 95; Ezekiel Lovering, aged 86; and William Chugg, aged 85. These old gents had taken part in the last hunting of the Earl of Rone in 1837:

From conversations I have had with these three old men from time to time, I learn that this strange old local festival – altogether unlike any other in the whole of North Devon – during the last few years of its existence was gradually losing much of the historical importance it may have possessed, owing to the introduction of a good deal of rough horse-play and drinking habits. There were at that time nine public-houses, and it is said that a rather prolonged halt for 'refreshments' was made at each.

On the last occasion upon which it was held (1837) it would appear from my informants that there was so much mirth and wild conviviality during the strange procession from 'Lady's Wood' at the very head of the town to the seaside (1½ miles nearly) that most of the principal 'actors' were pretty well 'done for' by the time they had left the third public-house downwards; also, that there were hundreds of people, not only from this place, but also from surrounding parishes, all dressed in gay holiday attire, following the noisy procession.[31]

Toms also suggests that the custom is a survival of the old morality plays, which were often performed around Whitsun, so the subtext would be that the Earl of Rone is something of an excuse, an almost allegorical figure around which to base the festivities, whether he really had anything to do with Combe Martin or not. Certainly the Hunting of the Earl of Rone seems to have echoes of the mystery/morality plays, with the presence of the Fool.

So this custom has, like the bonfire festivities and many others, diminished in part due to public objections to rowdiness and drunkenness. Donations to the proceedings (such as for buying rounds in the pub) were solicited and if a person refused, the Fool would sprinkle them with water from the gutters. If they were still reluctant to put their hands in their pockets, the Hobby Horse would step in. The Grenadiers were armed with firelocks, lending an air of menace to the proceedings. Several of these above accounts, which are collated on the Earl of Rone website, suggest that the custom deteriorated over the years; while never exactly solemn, the festivity gradually degenerated until it was no more than an excuse for an increasingly rowdy pub crawl, possible culminating in a tragic accident. In this, it does, as I've noted, bear a resemblance to the bonfire nights.

While the revived festivity does, I am sure, feature local pubs, it's a lot less rowdy these days and surplus money is donated to various good causes in the village. It commemorates the death that put paid to it, by walking in silence past Lynton Cottage, on the steps of which the tragedy is said to have occurred. If you live, were born or were educated in the village and the surrounding parishes of Berrynarbor, Kentisbury and Trentishoe, you have a right to take part, and visitors are welcome, although they aren't allowed to dress up as members of the Senior Party (some individuals from overseas apparently are, if they were instrumental in reviving the custom – in some cases their grandchildren have a right to take part). However, visitors can dress up generally – the Earl of Rone website says that the costume is 'vaguely' nineteenth-century peasant, which gives you quite a large margin of error. Trainers, Crocs and Wellington boots are frowned upon; ditto baseball caps and hoodies.

Mummers and the Law

We've looked at mumming and mystery plays with regard to subversion, and we've noted that this tradition still continues to some degree. But mumming and other traditions have come under the spotlight recently in the form of another kind of transgression, an inadvertent one involving the ostensibly boring subject of insurance.

It will not have escaped the attention of the reader that many of the customs we describe in this book are not without an element of risk. Morris dancing, for example, might seem a relatively sedate activity – not so, as Morris dancer Ron Shuttleworth notes:

> Many years ago, Coventry Mummers were booked to do a show in a College Students' Union bar. We were crowded onto a minuscule stage in one corner and to perform his 'vaunt' our Turkish Knight stepped onto one of the many low tables in the room. Whilst brandishing his large metal scimitar he caught one of the students a glancing blow on the head, which needed a couple of stitches. We apologized and bought the man a drink and thought no more about it UNTIL quite a while later I, as Bagman, got a letter from his solicitor claiming that the blow had caused him to fail his exams, and hinting at heavy damages.
>
> Fortunately we were members of the Morris Ring which rules that all Members and Associates must be part of their Public Liability Insurance scheme, so I just bundled the papers up and sent them to the Ring. We

heard nothing further about it, but I learned much later that the lad had been paid out. You might think that nothing could happen to you, but consider the chain of accidents that could arise from the flying tip of a broken wooden sword.[32]

Good for the Coventry Mummers in their prudent membership of an association that has PLI. This is an illustration of why it's necessary – but it can prove expensive. Various British traditions have come under threat as a result of the cost of insurance. The customs that we're describing in this book are not big business, profit-driven enterprises. They are organized and practised by volunteers and enthusiasts who are not in it for the money; they keep these customs going out of love and they're probably ploughing money into the custom rather than drawing it out.

At the moment, under British law, in addition to insurance policies, if you have more than two performers in any venue, you need an entertainment licence. This was highlighted in 2002, when the Wessex Morris dancers turned up at their usual venue, the Red Lion pub (now the Giant Inn) in Cerne Abbas near the famous giant, and found the licensing officer of West Dorset District Council awaiting them. Had they gone ahead with their performance, the landlord of the Red Lion would have been fined. The side performed in the street instead.

Several articles were written in the press; Dr Kim Howells of the UK Department of Culture, Media and Sport held a meeting with representatives from the English Folk Dance and Song Society (EFDSS) and the Morris Federation, among other Morris dancing organizations. The EFDSS and the three national Morris organizations (the Morris Ring, the Morris Federation and Open Morris) lobbied for the redrafting of the law and held a mass demonstration by Morris dancers in Trafalgar Square, London, in May 2003.

As a result of this, Lord Redesdale tabled an amendment in the House of Lords to try to exempt Morris dancing from the Act. David Cameron (at this point the MP for Whitney, not yet the prime minister) supported the exemption in the Commons; we may note that his Cotswold constituency includes a number of places where Morris dancing remains enthusiastically practised. Unfortunately, folk drama, such as the mumming plays, did not survive last-minute drafts and were thus not exempt, although Morris dancing is. A campaign spearheaded by Wiltshire Morris side the Potterne Boys, which ran from 2006 to 2009, managed to get folk plays included, otherwise pub landlords faced shelling out up to £600 and possibly more to apply for a licence. Since many of these groups collect money for charity, this was obviously unsustainable but fortunately, the campaign was successful.

Thus, despite this contretemps, the Wessex Morris side survived. They are still dancing twenty years later, and performing their version of the St George and the Dragon play in the Giant Inn. We have met them in this book before – they are the current owners of the remodelled Dorset Ooser.

Crossbones Cemetery and the Southwark Mysteries

The Southwark district of London has had a long association with the esoteric world, as the home of twentieth-century occultist Austin Osman Spare and (before the fire that ravaged it) the Cuming Museum, which housed the Lovett Collection of magical artefacts from London. More recently, another of its hidden gems has become the focus of a small but dedicated following among British Pagans, occultists and indeed Christians and members of other religious groups. This is an example of several events and gatherings that are not part of any organized inter-faith movement in the UK, but that have developed organically across Pagan, Christian and other forms of worship and are becoming examples of contemporary folk practices. The rites at Crossbones are transgressive not in their performance (they are profound but orderly events) but in whom they honour.

The cemetery of Crossbones dates from the medieval period. It is a graveyard for the outcast dead – mainly the medieval prostitutes of Southwark who were known as the 'Winchester geese' (because they were licensed by the Bishop of Winchester) and who worked in the area known as the Mint, one of Southwark's worst slums. They were licensed to work in the Liberty of the Clink, which lay beyond the law of the City of London.

Crossbones closed in 1853 and still houses the bones of an estimated 15,000 people. In the 1990s, the graveyard was disturbed as a result of the establishment of the Jubilee railway line. Poet and writer John Constable experienced a vision in 1996, in which the spirit of the outcast women, an entity known as 'the Goose', came to him and inspired his epic cycle of south London lore, *The Southwark Mysteries*. This series of poems, plays and esoterica was performed at Shakespeare's Globe Theatre and Southwark Cathedral, and John is still involved with Crossbones today although he now lives in Glastonbury. The cemetery has become something of a shrine, its gates decorated with ribbons dedicated to the dead, and there is an event there every month to honour the people whose bones lie in the graveyard. This is a non-denominational event, but UK pagans are closely involved and many attend the monthly ceremony. John Constable, writing under the name of his alter ego John Crow, says:

> Friends of Crossbones has always recognised that Crossbones was an unconsecrated burial ground, without gravestones or other markers, which for centuries was ravaged by body-snatchers and hit-and-run developers. We've consistently worked to remember and honour the 'outcast dead', along with living outsiders, in creative acts that celebrate their lives and their value to society. Rather than attempt to recreate a conventional cemetery, we've emphasised the wild garden and the folk art: the flowers growing through cracks in the tarmac, the rubble used to create garden beds, the throw-away objects transformed into DIY shrines and artworks, the deliberately primitive map, the shrine at the gates. All this reflects the spirit of Crossbones as a place of transformation which challenges the values of the dominant culture. The Dean of Southwark Cathedral recognized all this, choosing to perform an 'Act of Regret' rather than seeking to reconsecrate the site or to introduce crosses or gravestones.[33]

The cemetery has recently become host to several art initiatives, with concerns that these should not turn into an example of the corporate art world co-opting local events and informal practice. A recent sonic installation caused some controversy, since it apparently blacked out some of the DIY features that have been placed there by local visitors to the garden. There is an awareness that there may need to be some resistance to the big artistic organizations of the capital 'claiming' Crossbones as a 'sad, forgotten place', when it has been a vibrant focus for celebration by a variety of spiritualities for many years. The cemetery guardians need to be cautious of events and installations that 'exemplify "top down" attempts to appropriate the power of people (and specifically the power of the powerless)'.[34]

However, these concerns aside, it is clear that the monthly events at Crossbones have become a focus for everyone who is sensitive to the geographical magic of London to gather and honour the dead. Hedgepriestess Jacqueline Durban says:

> Crossbones is an absolute wonder in my mind and she has a way of looking after herself. After all, who would have thought that a tiny group of relative edge-people could end up persuading TFL [Transport for London] to allow a garden on a site that's worth millions to them? And now it's there and full of butterflies, bees and dragonflies. I doubt that the geese ever saw anything so beautiful and now they are buried in it. Who could ever have dreamed that such a thing could happen? And that is magic, whatever path you happen to follow. Crossbones is an absolute beacon of hope on a world that often feels beyond redemption.[35]

John Constable's *Southwark Mysteries* was first produced in the Globe in 2000. It was then staged in Southwark Cathedral on Easter Sunday in 2000 (and again in 2010), generating substantial controversy in the fundamentalist Christian community over its perceived pagan elements. However, the Dean of Southwark Cathedral has acknowledged that even though the Crossbones rituals may appear pagan, they are nonetheless part of Southwark's cultural identity. The spirit of the mystery play thus lives on, in some surprising, but very contemporary forms.

Audiences Behaving Badly

As a side note, bad behaviour at the theatre is obviously nothing new – but unfortunately it still goes on. An article in *The Guardian* in 2023 noted that there are contemporary performances in which audiences tend to behave poorly. Theatre staff apparently dread renditions of the *Rocky Horror Show* (in which audience members are encouraged to dress up as characters). *Dirty Dancing*, *Motown the Musical*, *Mamma Mia* and *Grease* also have bad reputations for disruptive audiences.

> More recently I worked as a front-of-house assistant at a festival and one its biggest-selling shows was *The Choir of Man*, a feelgood, jukebox musical. It's a great show – I know it almost off by heart (one of the side-effects of front-of-house work) – but the audience behaviour during the run was outrageous. Customers would arrive drunk and continue to drink throughout the performance (the show does unfortunately encourage it), sing over the top of the performers and argue with and insult other audience members and staff.
>
> Some patrons attempted to get on to the stage, make their way into dressing rooms and follow performers back to their accommodation. The managers' response?

They told us to 'monitor' disruptive customers and act like security guards. My final straw was when a rude and aggressive customer was flagged as disruptive throughout the show, refused to leave when it was over, and we were given no support by the duty manager. I handed in my notice.[36]

North was responding to the plea made by Colin Marr, director of the Edinburgh Playhouse, in the same month. He says that audience behaviour has become significantly worse after the COVID-19 lockdowns, and called for audiences to respect theatres and their staff by behaving appropriately. Like other theatre managers, he is working with the UK's largest theatre operator, Ambassador Theatre Group, to tone down advertising campaigns that suggest the performance is going to be a riot – and that audiences should join in. Marr told the press:

One of the main things we are trying to do is around messaging and working closely with producers. We are talking to them about marketing. So, when we market shows let's not have phrases such as 'best party in town' or 'dancing in the aisles' – the show has something much stronger than that to sell.[37]

Marr's comments came after a performance of *Jersey Boys* was interrupted when the police had to be called after a fight broke out in the audience. This is a phenomenon with which our theatregoing ancestors would have been familiar, unfortunately. Some of Marr's staff were spat at and one was punched. North, during her first performance of *Rocky Horror*, wasn't assaulted, but a young woman did throw up all over her. Alcohol is a primary culprit. North remarks to *The Guardian* that too many theatre managers won't take action and throw people out of the theatre, but this more passive culture may be changing. Marr says:

> This is becoming far too regular an occurrence – not just in our theatre but in venues across the UK. There is a very small minority of people who come to our theatre and choose to sing, dance and talk throughout the show in a manner that disturbs others. They either don't know, or don't care, how much this spoils their fellow audience members' experience.[38]

Recently, in 2023, there have been reports of people throwing things as gifts onto the stage – not just flowers or the women's underwear that used to be a feature of Tom Jones's performance, but more startling items. American rock singer Pink was 'gifted' with a flung wheel of cheese.

Interview with Ben Jeapes, Abingdon Passion Play

Passion Plays traditionally happen around Easter and tell the story of the last few days of Jesus's life, usually from the entry into Jerusalem, then encompassing the Last Supper and his betrayal, trial, crucifixion and resurrection. They tend to be community affairs, and the tradition goes back at least to medieval times.

The Abingdon offering has historic roots going all the way back to December 2012, when a group of friends from different churches were out on a walk together. They all concluded that as Abingdon is one of the oldest continually settled locations in the British Isles, with a rich tradition of church involvement in the community and once boasting an abbey the size of Wells Cathedral – and even producing an Archbishop of Canterbury (Edmund Rich, a saint to boot) – it really should have a Passion Play. Twelve short weeks later, in March 2013, it did. It was chaotic, exhilarating and borderline deadly – but also great fun.

After that, the play settled down into a three-yearly pattern, so was held again in 2016 and 2019. The script in 2013 was essentially John's gospel without all the he said/ she said bits getting in the way of the dialogue; I had to do a lot of work to streamline it and make it flow. It also had existing songs levered in at various points. Scripts and songs for 2016 and 2019 were written by local, semi-professional talent, and all the productions have involved the community to a large extent. Then along came COVID to muck everything up, though tentative plans are now for the next performance in 2024.

What do you enjoy about them?

I find myself in full agreement with the founders. Abingdon has other traditions, after all. The Morris Men of the town annually elect a Mayor for Ock Street (any inhabitant of Ock Street is eligible to vote), and the same street boasts Europe's longest street fair every October – a legacy of the apprentice hiring fair held there every year since medieval times. Until the 1970s we were the county town of Berkshire. I live in the kind of town that *should* have a Passion Play and it's a pleasure to be part of the team providing one. I enjoy the feeling of camaraderie among the cast and crew, and the goodwill within the community that it seems to generate.

In the 2013 production I enjoyed being co-opted as script editor for the first draft of the script, and designer, typesetter and editor of the programme – all the kinds of things I know I'm good at. I also found myself playing the part of the Centurion, which taught me to my surprise that I quite enjoy acting and am tolerably good at it (though I haven't indulged since). Even pretend authority has a way of going to your head, or maybe it was the uniform; as Jesus progressed to Golgotha, stumbling under his load, the crowd of watchers and tourists was in danger of obstructing him so I could improvise an order to the legionaries to clear the rabble out of the way.

I also found that production extremely wearying on the nerves, so for the next two I stuck to being part of the choir – which, like acting, taught me that I can sing quite well and enjoy doing that too. I was in the choir at school but hadn't sung in a group and in public since, but this was much more fun.

What do other people think of your involvement? Do they approve, or do you get criticized for it?

There is a body of opinion opposed to any kind of public display of religiosity, so there has been a lot of online sniping about the plays, not just their existence per se (though there was a lot of that) but the inconvenience to the town of shutting off streets etc. Never mind that the shops all did record trade off the crowd during the performances. However, there was absolutely no protest in public, despite the many opportunities for someone with a real grudge to be seriously disruptive, if they so chose. The events themselves always had a real atmosphere of community and goodwill. The crowds were so large that I seriously doubt they were all churchgoers! I think the nicest moment was when – again, online – someone grumbled along the lines of 'huh, Christians should be helping the poor, not wasting time putting on shows like this!' The chairman of Abingdon's largest social charity, a secular organization, left a return comment to say just how much help his organization got from the churches of Abingdon, and it was precisely events like this that energize them.

What role do you think these customs play in the modern world? Do you think they are still important (or just a bit of fun), and if so, why?

I find it impossible to discern exactly, but I do think establishing this 'tradition' *ex nihilo* somehow tapped into something far older in our community, and that can only be good. A visiting church historian a couple of years ago pointed out something to me that I had missed despite living here since 1991. The abbey disappeared after the dissolution – its grounds are now a public park – but the original gate into the abbey grounds is still here, just across the road from the marketplace. The town centre has been so remodelled in recent years that it's hard to see, unless you look at it from above, but five major routes still radiate out from that gate. One of them is now a pedestrian mall, but they are ancient ways, they are still there and they start at the entrance to the abbey. The church had one heck of an impact on the formation of this town, with tentacles reaching into every area of life. Large parts of Abingdon are still owned by an entity called Christ's Hospital, which now is a registered charity but was originally the public corporation set up to take over the abbey's secular interests in town after the dissolution. It's all easily forgotten now, of course, but I feel like the Passion Play has dug a new well reaching down to an ancient stream.

Is your chosen folk custom important to your identity?

Not in itself, as I'm involved in several other church activities. But it is an expression of my Christian identity that I value. That said, I still haven't decided if I'll take part in the 2024 production. If someone asked me outright why I do it, my answer would probably be more that I enjoy it than for any especial spiritual reasons.

How has your chosen custom changed during your engagement with it? Has it become more diverse, for instance?

Abingdon itself is not the most diverse of towns. It's not 100 per cent white but it is predominantly so, and I think the plays themselves have been pretty much white in terms of cast and crew. The most notable exception is our very first Jesus, who was Black! (An exceptionally talented young actor called Kit Young, who was then only eighteen but stole the show. To no one's surprise he went on to RADA, has acted on stage with some big names and is now carving out a screen career too.)

One area it has changed is in management and professionalism. See below for some description of the chaos of the 2013 production. Thereafter it swiftly professionalized, becoming a registered charity with a committee running it.

There was also the decision that each show should be different, so it's never the same old same old. The first was a promenade play around different locations, with the crucifixion on the same spot where the high altar of the abbey would once have stood – dead symbolic! In 2016 we'd learnt the lesson of shepherding a crowd of 1,000+ strong around town, and had a more controlled production on a stage in the town centre. 2019 was back to the abbey grounds – again the high altar spot – but with just a community choir and three professional actors playing Mary Magdalene, Simon Peter and the Centurion. Not even a Jesus! They cleverly produced the impression of a Jesus by talking about him and acting around where he would be, so you actually came away with a memory that Jesus had been there even though he hadn't been. That production came at the end of an all-afternoon pageant held in the abbey grounds.

Do you think interest in your folk custom is diminishing or growing?

Hard to say. As I say, I'm not even sure if I'll be in the 2024 production – if only because it's apparently going to be held in June, which isn't exactly Passiontide. But as much as I can, I will certainly support it.

Is there a transgressive element to your chosen custom?

I still cringe at the health and safety implications of the 2013 production, which is the kind of society norm you really should not be breaking. Due to freezing weather, a last-minute rearrangement meant that everything from the Last Supper to the Trial before Pilate took place in the nice, warm, indoors Guildhall, before heading outside again for the Crucifixion and Resurrection. Which was lovely, but absolutely no provision had been made for regulating the number of people coming into the building. Nor had we realized quite how large the crowd would be. Because there was no mechanism for counting them in up to a certain limit and then shutting the doors, they just kept coming and coming and coming, and I honestly thought we might have a mini-Hillsborough scenario on our hands. Also, because I was dressed conspicuously as the Centurion, that somehow made me an authority figure that people turned to. One lady said she was feeling faint, so I escorted her out of the building – one of the advantages of being a bulky 6-foot-plus. Then I went and cowered backstage until my bit came up. Oberammergau it was not.

Otherwise, we did our best to avoid being transgressive, though see the above point about online comments indicating dissatisfaction. More to the point, with the best will in the world it's possible to get an antisemitic message from the Passion story. Concerns were expressed to the producer for the 2013 production and the script got a last-minute rewrite to make it ABSOLUTELY CLEAR it was the Romans who crucified Jesus, not the Jews. (Even if it was done at the behest of the Jewish leaders, but there's not much you can do about that.) They have remembered this lesson for subsequent productions as well. At least, I would say so from my non-Jewish perspective.

It's certainly unusual, and I think that's enough to make people sit up and take notice. Most years, the only observable Easter activity is a blink-and-you-miss-it procession through the town centre. An event every three years in which the town centre stops and everyone has a great time as well definitely stirs things up.

SEVEN

Bonfire Night: Gunpowder, Treason and Plot

O ne of the biggest festivals in the British calendar is Bonfire Night, often just called 'November the Fifth' or 'The Fifth of November'. It is an annual occasion that is unique to Britain; it isn't celebrated anywhere else in the world – although there are obviously anniversaries that involve fireworks, such as the Fourth of July. (Bonfire Night was originally exported to the USA with British settlers, where it was known as 'Pope Day', but this died out with the advent of the American Revolutionary War.) As every British person knows, Bonfire Night commemorates the Gunpowder Plot, and every year, memes swoop around social media remembering Guy Fawkes as 'the only man to enter Parliament with honest intentions'. But was he? What were those 'honest intentions'? And how did an act of terrorism come to be one of the most beloved celebrations in the British calendar, while still managing to be fraught with controversy of different kinds even today?

The Gunpowder Plot was an attempt to blow up King James I and the English Parliament, reaching its culmination on 5 November in 1605. The ringleader was not Guy Fawkes himself, but one Robert Catesby, and his aim was to replace a Protestant kingship with a Catholic one and to put an end to the persecution of Catholics in England. James I had initially seemed sympathetic to that particular faith group, but this did not last. The king gave a speech in which he explained that he 'detested' the faith and ordered all Catholic priests and Jesuits out of the country. Catesby intended to kidnap James's daughter, the nine-year-old Princess Elizabeth, and establish her on the throne as a puppet monarch.

The plot, which began in 1604, failed. Lord Monteagle, the brother-in-law of Francis Tresham, one of the conspirators, was warned not to attend Parliament on 5 November via an anonymous letter. Monteagle alerted the authorities, taking the letter to James' first minister Robert Cecil, the Earl of Salisbury, and he initiated an investigation. One of Catesby's fellow conspirators, Guy Fawkes, was discovered by a justice of the peace, Sir Thomas Knyvet, in the cellars of the Houses of Parliament along with a number of barrels of gunpowder (the conspirators had managed to rent the cellar, rather than tunnelling beneath it, which had been the original plan). Since the plotters had been informed of the existence of the letter, this was a high-risk strategy and it did not pay off. Caught red-handed, Fawkes gave a false name and said that he was an employee of Thomas Percy – also not the wisest move, since Percy was known to have Catholic sympathies. Fawkes himself was a convert to Catholicism, born in York in 1570.

Fawkes was arrested and tortured, confessing the names of his colleagues. The rest of the plotters were rounded up, and were either killed during the process of apprehension or were captured and executed, although Fawkes pre-empted this by throwing himself from the ladder that led to the gallows and breaking his neck. In addition to Catesby and Fawkes, the conspirators were Thomas Wintour, Jack Wright and Thomas Percy, but the group had expanded to include Robert Keyes, Robert

Wintour, John Grant, Kit Wright, Thomas Bates, Ambrose Rookwood, Francis Tresham and Sir Everard Digby. Today, for some reason, it is Fawkes who has passed into popular legend as the ringleader of the plot and it is his name that has become most closely associated with it.

Two longstanding traditions emerged from this near disaster for the English Parliament. Bonfire Night, originally known as Gunpowder Treason Day, was established in 1606 as an anniversary of thanksgiving for this near-miss (*not* as a celebration of the actual plot!). Even today, before the annual State Opening of Parliament, the Yeomen of the Guard undertake a ceremonial investigation of the cellars under the Houses of Parliament just in case anyone else has had the same idea. We no longer have to undergo mandatory church attendance on the fifth to give thanks for the deliverance of Parliament, but this was a part of the original Act. The bonfires themselves stem from the grassroots: people lit them after the failure of the plot to give thanks and this practice was allowed by the authorities to continue as long as it proceeded, in an early concern about health and safety, 'without danger or disorder'.[1] The cynical reader might consider this unlikely, especially given that actual gunpowder was given to civic authorities such as Canterbury, sometimes in quite large quantities, for commemorative 'explosions'. The diarist Samuel Pepys watched boys flinging crackers about the streets in the 1660s.

Bonfire Night has thus always had a rather anarchic aspect, and this has continued throughout its history. In the early days, Puritans used it as an opportunity to speak out against Catholicism in treatises such as Francis Herring's *Pietas Pontifica*, John Rhodes's *A Brief Summe of the Treason intended against the*

King & State and Thomas Taylor's *A Mappe of Rome.*[2] When James I's son Charles (who would become Charles I) married a Catholic, Henrietta of France, in 1625, anti-Catholic sentiment was given a new lease of life and effigies of the Pope and of the Devil were burned – a custom that gradually mutated into effigies of Guy Fawkes himself and, among some Bonfire societies today, representations of the *villain du jour*, mainly politicians. The years leading up to the Civil War saw an increase in partisan 5 November celebrations, with the Pope being compared to the god Pluto, who rules the underworld in Roman mythology, and Papist plots being 'uncovered' left, right and centre. Conspiracy theories flourished. The Houses of Parliament were said once more to be under threat, along with people's actual homes, from tunnelling Papists.

Once the Interregnum got under way, the new government let Bonfire Night go ahead, with its fires and explosions, and this continued into the reign of Charles II. One particularly awful manifestation in 1677 included the burning of an effigy of the Pope filled with live cats, and in 1682 the celebration became so unruly and violent that the London militia were called in and fireworks were banned. This ban was greeted with as much public enthusiasm as you would expect and, in 1688, when William of Orange landed in England on 5 November, the day after his birthday, the anniversary became fixed as a celebration of freedom and thanksgiving.

Guy Fawkes was not forgotten, however. In 1790 *The Times* carried a report of children 'begging for money for Guy Faux' and in 1802 a group of men with an effigy were imprisoned for begging.[3] Violence and lawlessness continued to mark the occasion in towns that are still known for their Bonfire celebrations, such as Lewes in Sussex, where yearly rioting and the running of lit tar barrels through the streets were a feature (the tar barrels still are; the rioting not so much). The passing of the Catholic Relief Act in 1829, which accorded increased legal rights to that religious group, sparked renewed waves of anti-Catholic sentiment. London was illuminated every November by the fires and an annual fight around one at Clare Market was held by the local butchers.

Young Exeter

Bishop Henry Phillpotts, a High Church Anglican opposed to Parliamentary reform, was burned in effigy during a bonfire celebration in Exeter in 1831, and was joined twenty years later (thankfully also in effigy and in Exeter) by the burning of the figures of the twelve new Catholic bishops, an event triggered by the Papal restoration of the English Catholic hierarchy. Exeter seems to have been a particular hotspot of civic unrest around this time of year, culminating with riots in the 1860s for which the infantry had to be called in. Again, tar barrels were run through the streets and fireworks were thrown, and the windows around the cathedral green had to be boarded up in case they were smashed. Cathedral authorities lived in fear of the West Front being damaged and tried to encourage revellers to build their enormous bonfire away from that side of the building, with limited success.

Much of the earlier unrest was caused by a group called 'Young Exeter', led by John Eyre Kingdon. They adopted a costume, which included sou'westers, white jackets and trousers. Eventually an agreement with the authorities was reached in the 1850s, in which the big bonfire was placed elsewhere than the cathedral green, and it was agreed that effigies should be confined to representations of the Pope and the Devil.

In 1879 the Riot Act was read and some revellers were jailed, after which the Bonfire celebrations became significantly more muted. In 1882, there was a bonfire but no injuries or rioting, and Young Exeter issued their own calming proclamation:

For be it known beloved each beloved son
Of Fair Exonia, who joins this glorious fun,
With frisky fireworks to commemorate
The thwarting of a crime, to seal the fate
Of Liberty; shall muster as of yore,
With lighted bonfire, and while cannon roar,
In my Cathedral Yard, let each one try
To preserve the peace and keep his powder dry.[4]

By the 1890s, there were no more bonfires lit in the cathedral yard. This may have been due in large part to the legal crackdowns, but may also be a result of the passing of a particular generation – how young 'Young Exeter' were at this point is difficult to assess. (Kingdon himself was dead by this stage.)

We should note that Exeter already had a reputation for riots and rough justice. Skimington riding, which we will look at later on, was a commonplace practice in and around the city, and Bonfire Night seems to have taken up any slack; we've just seen that prior to the ban, effigies of unpopular locals were burned on 5 November along with the Pope and the Devil, or were hanged on mock gallows, as in a case in 1849 that involved an effigy of the Reverend Charles Rookes and the servant whom he had seduced, Mary Brookes. This is a classic case of public shaming, but the Bonfire Night celebrations led, not infrequently, to injuries and deaths. In 1865, ten people were treated in the local infirmary for severe burns, and in one case the loss of an eye (this was regarded as an average year).

Clerics, such as the vicar of St Sidwell, complained that Exeter was subject to mob rule and that great political commentator Beatrix Potter, no less, noted that the 'rabble was notorious' in the city.[5] This was not confined to Skimington rides and Bonfire Night; there was unrest in the late nineteenth century over efforts to tighten up the alcohol licensing laws. The Bishop of Exeter was targeted and public displeasure was exhibited in a variety of ways, including the use of asafoetida stink bombs, red pepper throwing and violence against property. The Salvation Army was also targeted, owing to their temperance stance. According to Dr Todd Gray, in his book on the history of bad behaviour in Exeter,

Perhaps the last Exeter mob of any size formed in 1907 in support of a man who came home early to discover his wife was in the midst of eloping, possibly to Canada, with a young male lodger. Apparently the story spread like wildfire, and it didn't take long for a mob to gather nearby who were sympathetic to the husband. Eventually the lodger was evicted and he was followed by more than a thousand women and some men through the streets. The lodger fled and found his paramour but their subsequent history has not been found.[6]

One observer said in 1843: 'the people of Exeter were the veriest ruffians upon earth – even the Eskimos and the Hottentots, and all other nondescript people under the sun, were held up to greater admiration than the people of Exeter.'[7] Gray says:

> The evidence suggests Exonians were more likely to join in mobs than residents of other towns and cities, and occasions such as Guy Fawkes Night provided the perfect excuse. The mobs seem to have been there for entertainment and a crude attempt at moral judgement.[8]

Quite why Exeter should have been the scene of such lawlessness is questionable; perhaps it was just an issue of interpersonal dynamics. There seems, however, to have been a lot of it about. The *Devon Live* newspaper describes Dr Gray's books as telling

> the story of 146 individuals who were singled out in Exeter for being different – heretics, traitors, murderers, sportsmen, arsonists, witches, deviants, heroes, adulterers, prostitutes, celebrities, spies, grave robbers, cannibals, insane, fifth columnists, slanderers, royals, Bolsheviks, eccentrics, suffragettes, rioters, reformers, lepers, aliens, arsonists, zealots, and spies.[9]

Whether this is an unusually high number of malefactors remains to be seen. You could probably do the same for most urban centres of any size throughout Britain. It certainly wasn't confined to Exeter; similar scenes were enacted in Guildford in Surrey, not normally seen as a hotbed of social revolt.

The Guildford Guys

The Guildford Guys seem to have been the equivalent to Young Exeter:

> as the years rolled on they became increasingly boisterous and mischievous. By the 1850s the events can only be described as blatant hooliganism, on a scale that today would see police officers in full riot gear and full coverage by the media.[10]

In 1852, Bonfire Night in Guildford involved a mob that was several hundred strong and carrying bludgeons. They proceeded to rampage through the streets, damaging property. Afterwards, two Guildford clergymen wrote to the town council to complain, demanding compensation for damages to their properties, which, they said, were caused by the mob. The council refused to pay up and the case went to the Home Office, who asked William Taylor, the Mayor of Guildford, for an explanation. The authorities in Guildford were ordered to sort the town out, but they lacked policemen and volunteers were short in supply, not wanting to confront the violent mob of around 45 people, who, like others before them, dressed in tin foil and women's clothing, with their faces blacked. They demanded money from passersby and became aggressive when people refused. In the 1850s, a policeman lost an eye when a stone was thrown at him and people were naturally wary of putting themselves in a position where they would have to confront a large, unruly mob. The Riot Act was read (literally) but nothing came of it; legislation is useless unless it can be enforced.

The Times became involved, trumpeting that Guildford must do something about the violence. From the barracks in nearby Aldershot, 150 men from the 37th Foot and 50 from the 1st Royal Dragoons were sent under the command of one Lt Col Grey. The mayor was replaced and his successor was successful in recruiting a number of special constables. After a fight between the law and the Guys, a new police superintendent armed his men with cutlasses and after this, unsurprisingly, the violence abated. The authorities continued to crack down on any outbreaks and some of the Guys were arrested and sentenced to hard labour. Eventually the violence petered out.

So what sort of people were the Guys of Guildford? In general, all were young men, in their twenties, and employed; the Bonfire disarray seems to feature the employed working class rather than the unemployed or significantly disaffected. Two were painters, one was a cooper and one was a coachsmith's employee. In this, members of these crews bear a resemblance to young men who engage in football hooliganism, who are often not the unemployed 'benefit scroungers' depicted by the *Daily Mail*, but members of professions (at least one football hooligan in the heyday of such violence was revealed to be an estate agent).

In 2012, it became apparent that memories of the violence in Guildford were still raw. A sculpture featuring a chair surrounded by flames – the seat of an effigy – was proposed for a local roundabout, but was met with objections from one resident, Bernard Parke, whose great-grandfather had been a policeman during the riots in the nineteenth century. Mr Parke told the BBC:

How can you celebrate a riot? Would you dream of celebrating the Birmingham riots?

This was a time of distress, sheer vandalism, when they had burning barrels of tar running down the high street ... On one occasion they actually threw a policeman on a bonfire. How can you celebrate something in that way? I'm not a romantic. I don't think riots are art at all.[11]

His objections were countered by local historian David Rose, who commented that 'This sculpture is not only commemorating acts of violence but the fact that the town got on top of it and managed to quell the rioters.'[12]

In any event, the sculpture was turned down by the council for the roundabout. An alternative location was suggested, but in the end the sculpture was chosen to feature in an exhibition at the offices of KPMG in Canary Wharf, rather than Guildford itself. Ironically, one of the objections came from chief inspector Matt Goodridge of Surrey Police, who suggested that the sculpture might encourage further antisocial behaviour, since Guildford police were still having trouble with young people in the city centre in the present day:

It is unusual that we should wish to oppose a sculpture, I would not dream of casting any doubt on its artistic benefits ... When I saw this particular installation my immediate reaction was, it is a fantastic opportunity to try and climb the installation and nothing has changed my mind. Five metres is a long way up to fall to solid ground and it could be fatal. If not, then it would cause serious injury. From my perspective and the perspective of Surrey Police, the temptation around public disorder could cause problems in the future.[13]

In 1859 the Observance of 5th of November Act was repealed in an effort to cut down on some of the violence that attended Bonfire Night.

Bonfire Night Today

We have been speaking of Bonfire Night violence in the past tense, but should we be doing so? When I was a child growing up in the 1960s and '70s, many people held small firework parties in their back gardens but there were community events, too, in parks and recreation areas. These were generally peaceful occasions, although the newspapers would be full of horror stories the following day of injuries sustained through not treating fireworks responsibly. Now, after COVID-19, large community events are probably becoming more commonplace, outweighing individual celebrations – such as Burnham-on-Sea, where a fireworks event is held on the beach, marking the start of the Somerset carnival season. This, too, is a jolly, community-centred event.

However, a report in *The Guardian* from 2022 suggests that any optimism we hold that Bonfire lawlessness is a thing of the past might be sadly misplaced. In the Niddrie area of Edinburgh on Bonfire Night that year, a Molotov cocktail was thrown at a police car and police videos showed a gang of motorcyclists racing through the city, with fireworks and petrol bombs being flung at terrified motorists. Parts of the city were put into lockdown, with police asking locals to remain inside their houses. Police social media referred explicitly to this as 'youth related' violence.[14] City council leader Cammy Day said that this behaviour was 'disgraceful and disgusting', and added that those responsible would 'feel the full force of the law'.[15]

Meanwhile, further south in Leeds, police were attacked with missiles and fireworks, and the riot police were called in. A flare was thrown in a club hosting a Kasabian gig. Bradford Moor, Liverpool, Manchester (where rockets were fired at passing motorists) and Salford also saw incidents in which, for example, fireworks were hurled at fire crews attempting to extinguish an unlicensed bonfire, and in Halifax a teenage boy, seventeen-year-old Qais Muhammad Ratyal, died. Fireworks had been thrown by a group of boys, including Ratyal, and the police were called. While climbing a fence in his efforts to evade the law, Ratyal fell through a greenhouse and despite treatment in hospital, subsequently died from his injuries. Janazah Announcements, a bereavement notification service for Muslims in South Yorkshire, put up a post which said:

> A young man who had his whole future ahead of him has sadly lost his life. In the past few days I've been highlighting the same issue for youths not to attack members of the public and emergency services with fireworks. Kids think it's a laugh to throw fireworks at emergency services. It ain't a joke no more.[16]

Ratyal died in Halifax but apparently came from Bradford. Locals in the former town had been complaining of groups of youths from Bradford descending on the area. Residents in

Leeds said that it was like being in a 'war zone'. Student Sally-Anne Brayshaw, nineteen, said: 'I live in one of the houses. My housemate and I were watching through my window. Some of the fireworks almost hit us square in the face. If the window wasn't in the way or open, we would have been scalded to hell.'[17]

Nowadays, riot gear, drones and the National Police Air Service are deployed, rather than constables with cutlasses, but we might argue that the principle remains the same. In an unpleasant echo of the earlier violence, two police officers were taken to Edinburgh's Royal Infirmary in November 2022 and treated for a head injury and glass in one eye. In total, 483 calls were made to police in Scotland concerning firework-related offences, but this is a drop from 2021, when around six hundred were made in Scotland alone. Manchester authorities have created a #BangOutOfOrder campaign, supported by the fire services and the RSPCA, 'aimed at preventing, tackling and protecting against antisocial behaviour, criminal damage and other harm during the Halloween and Bonfire period'.[18]

Mr Maris, Gold Commander for Operation Moonbeam for Police Scotland, said:

> Our initial analysis of the incidents arising on Bonfire Night show that, for the overwhelming majority of the country, people enjoyed the occasion safely and responsibly.
>
> However, in some areas, particularly Edinburgh, various individuals have shown blatant disregard for the safety of the public and the emergency services and have actively targeted police officers and firefighters during the course of their duties.

This behaviour is completely unacceptable and will not be tolerated. I want to make it abundantly clear that considerable follow-up inquiry will be conducted in relation to all of these incidents, utilising all resources at our disposal to identify those responsible and bring them to justice. Do not think that just because you evaded police on the night, that we won't be knocking on your door in the near future.[19]

Operation Moonbeam was created in 2018 as part of a police initiative to deal with violence on and around Bonfire Night. This is a tri-service operation, specifically dealing with public disorder and antisocial behaviour. The numbers of people who actually engage in this kind of behaviour remains small, and probably were comparatively small in the past as well, but that behaviour is exacerbated by the presence of dangerous items: fireworks are, after all, explosives, and they can do a lot of damage, as images of burned-out cars after Bonfire Night in 2022 demonstrate.

Some of this antisocial behaviour in 2022 may be a legacy of an autumn of unrest across the Midlands and north of England, stemming from football-related violence between Muslim and Hindu youths, itself said to have been promulgated by right-wing factions (both white British, and in India and Pakistan). Violence broke out in Leicester in September 2022, in incidents where fireworks were also thrown.

Perhaps like earlier incidents, it is not something inherently lawless in Bonfire Night itself, despite its violent history and its inception in an act of terrorism, but more that some of these festivals and commemorations, involving fires and explosives as they do, form a trigger point for existing tensions and resentments. Groups of young men who may be seeking excitement and who are easily whipped up by social media resemble those groups in Exeter and Guildford, fuelled by pamphlets that called explicitly for violence.

Bonfire Societies

Bonfire Societies themselves have survived into the twenty-first century, yet unlike Young Exeter and the Guildford Guys, these are not lawless gangs, but well-organized longstanding organizations that take care to adhere to modern health and safety laws. Here, their expression has become one of tradition rather than grievance and resentment, and of support for various charities; all the Bonfire Societies raise money for various worthy causes. Such societies are found throughout a number of towns in the south and southwest of the UK. Historically, Bonfire Boys came mainly from the labouring ranks, divided in some towns into different trades (Maldon's 'boys' were shipwrights, for instance).

Lewes in Sussex is one of the best-known homes of Bonfire Societies, sometimes called 'the bonfire capital of the world'. Whereas other places in Sussex, such as Eastbourne, have just one society, the little town of Lewes currently has seven: Cliffe, Lewes Borough, Commercial Square, South Street, Waterloo, Southover and Nevill Juvenile. The celebration always takes place on 5 November (many bonfire nights elsewhere now tend to take place on the Saturday falling before the fifth, for instance, to correspond with modern working weeks), unless the fifth is a Sunday, in which case Bonfire Night is moved to the night of Saturday the fourth. After a parade through the main streets of Lewes, which is swelled by members of other Bonfire societies across Sussex and adjoining counties who also march, the Bonfire Societies then continue to their appointed spot and hold a display of fireworks. Standing on the Downs overlooking Lewes can be an awe-inspiring experience, as all of these displays (with the exception of Nevill, who hold their celebration a couple of weeks earlier) take place at more or less the same time.

This is a big event: the Bonfire Societies, along with the members of other bonfire organizations who join in the parade, amount to some 5,000 people and spectators can number around 80,000. For a small market town, this is a significant crowd. It is legendarily very difficult to get into and out of Lewes, at least by car, on 5 November. Many of the spectators come in from nearby Brighton and other towns on the train. Some years ago, I had to attend a funeral in Eastbourne on the afternoon of 5 November and asked some relatives in Lewes if they were going to be there, since they knew the deceased; they reminded me that they were essentially in lockdown as it would be impossible to get out of, or back into, the town on that particular date.

The Lewes Bonfire Celebrations website says, in relation to its history:

I am not going to get involved as to who was first or when, as this is not 100% clear as day follows night, but will say that there were other Lewes Bonfire Societ[ies] in the past and that they have now long gone, and that they were formed out of a need to be more 'user friendly' as before there would be riots, street fires etc and the bonfire night celebrations were in danger of being closed down altogether, so the bonfire boye was born with his Hooped Guernsey and blackened face.[20]

By now, the reader will be familiar with some of the anti-social behaviour that accompanied Bonfire Night, and in this case, it produced the inception of the Bonfire Societies to ensure that the celebration was allowed to continue. There are references in one of the Lewes Churchwarden's account books to payments given to bell ringers from 1661 onwards, on 5 November. One entry from 1723 states, 'Nov, ye 5th. Item: Pd. ye ringers being ye day of Deliverance from ye powder plot'.[21]

Lewes' celebrations were halted during the Interregnum but were reinstated during the reign of Charles II. In 1679, pic-tures of the Pope, Guy Fawkes and other 'enemies' of the state were carried in a parade by young men on poles (Cliffe still marches under a 'No Popery' banner). In this, Lewes reflects other Bonfire societies; the tsar featured on some bonfires at one point.

Gradually, the celebration then entered a period of decline, but was revived in Lewes in the nineteenth century, and this is where it seems to have begun to become troublesome. In 1806, eighteen Bonfire 'Boyes' were arrested, and in 1829 there was a riot after an altercation between some of the Bonfire Boyes and a local magistrate, Mr Whitfield, on Cliffe bridge. Local lore has it that there was more than one magistrate and that they were thrown bodily into the River Ouse. Lewes police prohibited the celebration a few years later in 1832 but their proclamations against it were ignored. The celebration was moved out of town and away from the High Street, but was subsequently allowed back. In 1847, things kicked off again and, as in other towns such as Guildford, the Riot Act was read and the police were drafted in. This caused some comment:

Remember, my boys, remember,
No run is allowed at 'The Jug';
And the private rooms, in December,
Are decidedly cool, though snug!
Whoever finds winter quarters there,
Will remember the 5th for the future, I'll swear;
On the 'tottle of the whole', Then,
Twere best to avoid the din'.
Let every one of the bold men,
Keep fast his doors within;
Lest he find too late when regrets of no use,
For the sake of a Fawkes he's been made a great
    goose.[22]

To keep the celebration going, the first two Bonfire Societies, Cliffe and Town (now Lewes Borough), were formed in 1853. Lewes feels strongly about the Gunpowder Plot, due in part to the burning of seventeen Protestant martyrs in the town in the 1550s, part of the Marian persecutions. A memorial, funded by public subscription, was built on Cliffe Hill in 1901 to commemorate them.

But forming organized societies did not entirely quell either the lawlessness or the rancour between Bonfire Societies and the authorities. In 1906, the police tried to prohibit both bonfires being made in the streets and tar barrels being run through the town. When this prohibition was violated, four Bonfire Boys

were arrested but subsequently acquitted (a celebratory bonfire was built outside the courtroom to welcome their release).
This tension continued into the 1990s: a secret meeting was
apparently held by police in 1992 to discuss policing the bonfire
celebrations, but as a result of protests about this, the Bonfire
Safety Council was formed and still exists today, consisting of all
parties with an interest in the celebration, including the police
and St John's Ambulance. In the 1930s, effigies of the Pope and
more extreme forms of anti-Catholic sentiment were toned
down, at the request of the then-mayor.

Feelings still run high:

> Even today as you read this, oppression is high on the list
> with the misinformed authorities afraid of the common
> man and his choice of enjoying himself. All a bonfire
> boye or belle wants is peace, tolerance, celebration, free-
> dom of choice, thought and remembrance of those that
> sacrificed their lives for our freedom, and remembering
> those that died for us.
>
> Sectarianism does not exist in the Lewes Bonfire
> Night Celebrations today, despite what you may read,
> hear or see from the media clowns or internet trolls. 'Ha',
> I hear you say, 'What About No Popery?' Popery was a
> catholic regime not a religion. Look it up.[23]

Why Lewes, though? We have noted that there were seventeen Protestant martyrs from the town, and Lewes certainly
takes religion seriously; there are a high number of churches
and chapels here. Seventeen blazing crosses are carried through
the town on Bonfire Night as a commemoration of the Marian

martyrs and a wreath is laid at the war memorial. In addition, the various societies dress in costume (we will take a more in-depth look at this later) and there is a women's and men's tar barrel race along Cliffe High Street, after which one of the barrels is hurled into the Ouse. Apparently this symbolizes the throwing of the magistrates into the river after they read the Riot Act to the Bonfire Boys. The fiery crosses are also thrown into the Ouse.

Effigies are pulled through the town and these have included Pope Paul v (1605) and Guy Fawkes, plus a number of unpopular figures of the relevant year: Liz Truss, Rishi Sunak and Vladimir Putin featured in 2022. Truss (and a lettuce) took pride of place, perhaps a reaction to the economic havoc caused by her mini-budget. Putin was portrayed as Satan. However, not all the effigies were negative: one was in celebration of Ukrainian President Volodymyr Zelenskyy. Lewes Borough Bonfire Society said:

> This year we salute the man who leads his nation in its brave stance against oppression and invasion and is carrying his country men and women to ensure they have the freedoms we in the west so cherish yet take for granted.[24]

In contrast to other urban centres, no arrests were made and no injuries were sustained at Lewes in 2022.

> There is always some bigotry from some Bonfire Society members towards other Bonfire Societies and the general public, but in my book, all the Bonfire Societies are equal

in the sense that they are all celebrating the freedom of/from oppression, speech, authoritarianism, etc and without them the Lewes Bonfire Celebrations would not be worthwhile or exist.[25]

Each Bonfire Society has particular costumes, usually of two different types. Suffragettes, smugglers, English Civil War soldiers, Romans and monks all feature. Cliffe, for instance, dress as French revolutionaries and Vikings, which is relatively uncontentious, but to a modern eye some of the choices are now regarded as outdated in terms of social progressiveness. Commercial Square, whose HQ is the Elephant and Castle pub, dress as American Civil War soldiers and as Indigenous Americans. While the latter choice was apparently inspired by a visit to the USA by earlier society members, who witnessed the difficulties faced by Indigenous communities, it sits badly with a generation who have become accustomed to concepts such as cultural appropriation. (It must be noted that Lewes has strong links with the USA: Thomas Paine lived in the town and John Harvard, who founded the world-famous university of the same name, married a woman from Lewes.)

Lewes Borough Society, which was one of the first Bonfire Societies, adopted Zulu and Tudor costumes after the Second World War. The Tudors are no longer around to complain but the Zulus are and, to an extent, they have. Rather like some Morris sides, the use of blackface has proved contentious in modern times and the (invited) presence of a Zulu dance troupe some years ago brought matters to public attention. Initially, Thandanani Gumede, who leads the musical and dance group Zulu Tradition, commented that he did not regard the costuming of Borough to be inherently racist. Gumede told *The Guardian* in 2017 that he

> would be offended by people showing up in a Ku Klux Klan uniform. So far, based on the information I have, I haven't [seen] anything racist. I was flattered to see there were people trying to look like me as opposed to saying it is wrong to look like me.[26]

A petition against the use of Zulu costuming by the Bonfire Societies was, however, signed by 1,300 people in the run-up to 5 November of that year. (It is not clear how many residents of Lewes itself were signatories.) It stated that the 'public display of caricatured, negative stereotypes of black Africans within our community is racist and serves only to increase tension and division within our diverse community'.[27] A counter-petition was formed, stating:

> We assert that nothing about the traditions of Bonfire encourages or incites these attitudes and defend the right of each society to self-determination. We further assert that an attack from outside Bonfire on any element of a Society is an attack on that society and that an attack on one society is an attack on all societies.[28]

Borough asserted that the costuming was to commemorate the loss of the Zulus, rather than being disparaging. Diversity Lewes, a local charity, became involved with the difficult task of mediating between the two groups. Chair Tony Kalume, who is himself Black, told the press, 'If you see a white man blacking up it's like a mockery. There's all the years of slavery and white supremacy. It's the idea that we don't care if you like it or not.'[29]

Obviously, an ethnic or racial group is not a monolithic block when it comes to opinions, and Gumede initially disagreed, saying that initially the pictures he saw resembled an actual Zulu and that some care had evidently been taken to reproduce the costumes accurately. For example, the costume included a leopard skin umqhele, a 'crown' similar to his own, and appropriate body paint. He remarked that if someone had blacked their face and dressed in a Tarzan costume, he would have regarded that as racist. Subsequently, however, Gumede was introduced to costumes that were considerably less accurate and he did raise objections to those:

> I was really disappointed . . . bones through the noses, dead monkeys, skulls, horns, huge feathered head-dresses. They looked barbaric, like a cross between a Viking and a showgirl. It was incredibly offensive. Nothing about those outfits resembled a Zulu warrior.[30]

He did not feel that the costumes, however, were intended to cause deliberate offence. Since a lot of the Lewes costumes are quite old – a hundred years in some cases – it is likely that some of these dated from an earlier time in which stereotypes were more rife and public awareness of racism was more limited. While researching Padstow's Darkie Day, I came across a number of comments that said that 'no offence was intended'. This may well be the case, but it fails to take into consideration the fact that social climates change over time and what might have passed without comment or even notice in the nineteenth century might be regarded differently through a twenty-first-century lens. The right-wing press is fond of the adjective 'oversensitive', but this is subjective; it could as easily be argued that previous ages were 'undersensitive'.

Borough's Mick Symes said, 'We lost our way a bit, but we are delighted to welcome Zulu Tradition to what will be a most wonderful night.'[31] He went on to say that from 2018 onwards, society members in Zulu costume would no longer lead the society. Unfortunately, further controversy took place that year when a small child belonging to a Borough member was blacked up. Activist group Bonfire against Racism told *The Guardian* that blacking up a child was manipulative and felt deliberately provocative.[32]

Zulu Tradition's agent, Jacey Bedford, told me that a woman had also adopted brownface, which is regarded by many people of colour as equally objectionable. Mick Symes apologized and stated that quite robust changes had been made and would be reinforced. However, Gumede withdrew Zulu Tradition from the Lewes celebrations:

> Online I saw people defending it and saying he was just carrying on a tradition. The reason I am upset is that as a Black person I face a lot of racism. My greatest fear is that people get away with it and nothing is done. I didn't expect I would be in a position where I would have to deal with blackface again.[33]

The issue still hasn't really been resolved. The philosopher Thomas Kuhn, writing about paradigm shifts, pointed out that paradigms don't wholly change until the people who most strongly cling to them have died.[34] These are often generational shifts. Contemporary society, and its ideas of what's right and what's wrong, is moving quite fast and it may be some time before people move away entirely from practices that they've known for the entirety of their lives. Ideas can take a while to disseminate, while those who bear the brunt of them can feel that this dissemination is taking place all too slowly.

> Bonfire is so locally entrenched that people who on any other day would say blackface is unacceptable are prepared to make an exception and say it is not racist, even though their Black neighbours are saying it is offensive. There's an expression in the bonfire societies, 'We wun't be druv' [We will not be driven] and it is happening again now.[35]

This last comment was made to *The Guardian* by an anonymous resident of Lewes, who said that he had been attacked the previous year for speaking out.

In subsequent years, however, some of the more contentious costuming has been dropped, due to local and international opposition, including Lewes District Council. Councillor Zoe Nicholson commented in the wake of George Floyd's murder in the USA:

> My thoughts also turned to bonfire in Lewes Town and the offence caused by a minority in the procession with 'blacked-up faces'. I know the vast majority of bonfire society members find this practice as objectionable as I do, so I am sure we can draw a line under this together.

We license the fire sites that are hired from us by most of the bonfire societies and we have zero tolerance to 'black face' in any event on our sites. We will strengthen our licence agreements to prevent this practice.[36]

Writing in *Varsity* magazine in 2021, Francesca Fairhead, who grew up in Lewes, expresses a level of cognitive dissonance that is not uncommon to Lewes residents:

Bonfire is for the people who have lived in Lewes all their lives, who fundraise year-round going door-to-door dressed as pirates or smugglers, spending whole days of October making torches one by one. Bonfire tradition is so deeply entrenched that there forms a strange disconnect between every day, where the majority of those who march would never dream of wearing such elaborate costumes, and Bonfire, when allowances are made.

Attempts to alter costumes are met, to quote *The Guardian*, with 'diehard bonfire enthusiasts' claiming that campaigners 'are trying to wreck their traditions':

I am not saying that Lewes Bonfire is acceptable as it is, and I certainly don't want to make excuses for it. The extent of the racism and intolerance ingrained in its history and still present today is truly sickening. However, to ban Bonfire entirely would remove a huge part of what it means to be from Lewes and would change the identity of the town forever. It would also do a disservice to the people who are trying to make change.[37]

Fairhead, who also touches on the anti-Catholic sentiment of the whole event, suggests that Lewes examines its past with a rather more careful eye, commenting that there is no need to cancel Bonfire Night altogether, and that traditions can be altered without affecting their authenticity (rather as Morris sides, as we've seen, have adopted green- or blueface rather than blacking up).

A note on 'we wunt be druv' – this in the vernacular ('we won't be driven') is the unofficial motto of the county of Sussex and pretty much does what it says on the tin. It describes an attitude of determination and independence at best, stubborn intransigence at worst. It's also the motto of the Bonfire Societies and of Harvey's Brewery, which is based in Lewes. The motto itself probably originates in the Weald and is noted in the late 1800s. The peasants of the Weald have indeed been revolting; once in the Peasants' Revolt in 1381, under Wat Tyler, and again in the rebellion led by Jack Cade in 1450. A rhyme to celebrate 'we won't be druv' goes as follows:

Sussex Won't Be Druv

Some folks as come to Sussex,
They reckons as they know –
A durn sight better what to do
Than simple folks, like me and you,
Could possibly suppose.

But them as comes to Sussex,
They mustn't push and shove,
For Sussex will be Sussex,
And Sussex won't be druv!

Mus Wilfred come to Sussex,
Us heaved a stone at he,
Because he reckoned he could teach
Our Sussex fishers how to reach
The fishes in the sea.

But when he dwelt among us,
Us gave un land and luv,
For Sussex will be Sussex,
And Sussex won't be druv!

All folks as come to Sussex
Must follow Sussex ways –
And when they've larned to know us well,
There's no place else they'll wish to dwell
In all their blessed days –

There ant no place like Sussex,
Until ye goos above,
For Sussex will be Sussex,
And Sussex won't be druv.[38]

Writer and folklore enthusiast Pete Ansell reports:

Back in the early 80s when I was teaching foreign students in Brighton I took a bunch of Italian and Spanish
students to the Lewes bonfire night to show them a
genuine bit of British folklore. All went well till we got
to the bit where there was an effigy of the Pope about
to be thrown on the fire and everyone started chanting

'Burn the Pope! Burn the Pope!' My students started to feel distinctly uncomfortable. 'Fascinating British folk traditions' suddenly felt a lot darker.[39]

Firle Bonfire Society

Lewes is not the only place in Sussex that hosts Bonfire celebrations; as mentioned, other villages do as well. One of these is Firle, not far away at the foot of the South Downs, whose Bonfire celebrations date from at least the 1870s – the vicar of Firle for more than twenty years, the Reverend Crawley, mentions going out to see the 5 November bonfire in 1879.[40] Firle also issued medals in the early 1900s to indicate a person's membership of a Bonfire Society. In 1905 there were what must to the reader be familiar objections, perhaps on a more national level, which were countered by the Lord Chancellor. His comments were printed by the *East Sussex News:*

> 'Why should we stop?' he asked. 'People who utter these cries say we endeavour to incite malice and hatred against the party who were the cause of the most diabolical plot, but this is not so. We simply celebrate the fifth in thankful providential frustration of a plot which, if it had succeeded, would have completely swept away our county, King and Parliament. Does not our celebration show our enemies that they have to deal with people who are, and ever intend to remain, loyal to their King, their country, and their church?'[41]

According to the Firle Bonfire Society website, a lot of the fireworks were homemade, including the 'Firle Rouser'. What could possibly go wrong?

However, despite the early endorsement of the Lord Chancellor, Firle Bonfire would not have survived the twentieth century had it not been revived; the society folded in the 1970s due to a lack of support. This, as we've seen, is characteristic of many folk customs, which tend to wane and wax, depending usually on a few enthusiastic personalities. In 1981, the Bonfire Society was revived and in 1997 became a limited company. It does not just support 5 November but also one-off events such as the queen's Jubilee, the Firle Festival and local commemorations associated with the aristocratic family in situ, the Gages.

Firle got into trouble in the early 1990s, when the main effigy burned in 2003 featured a caravan decorated with pictures of the Gypsy, Romany, Traveller (GRT) community with a numberplate reading PIKEY, a result of resentments and tensions with travelling groups. Feelings had been running high: two hundred pheasants belonging to the then-Viscount Gage had been killed and a travelling group was blamed. The group was evicted in September, leaving piles of rubbish behind. (I would note, however, that although this does happen, there is often an issue with refuse collection from traveller sites, who also find themselves banned from the local tip. Getting rid of rubbish isn't as simple a matter as it might sometimes seem. On the other hand, sometimes individual groups are just irresponsible.)

The local MP, Norman Baker, cited effigies as part of Bonfire celebrations. Both George Bush and the local chief of police had also been burned in effigy at Firle, which follows the practice along with Lewes. But a number of parents expressed concerns that this particular representation was too close to the bone, a villager of Romany heritage also complained, and the Commission for Racial Equality became involved. The then-chair of Firle Bonfire Society replied that 'It was primarily intended to criticise the local authorities whose lack of action had caused so much frustration locally.'[42]

However, that frustration presumably continued when the police arrested all twelve of the organizers. Assaults on the traveller community have been an issue in Sussex, among other places. Margaret Murphy, a member of the GRT community, had a narrow escape in Crawley in the same year when a firework soaked with petrol was lit next to her caravan. The vehicle went up in flames, killing her puppy, although fortunately her alarm went off in time to save the rest of the site. Having spoken to members of the GRT community in Somerset, I am aware that caravan burning is not unknown as an internecine measure of revenge within traveller communities themselves, but it is also often an act committed by hostile outsiders. Signs reading 'No travellers' in premises in both Lewes and Hove did not help an already tense situation. A spokesman for the Brighton-based Friends, Families and Travellers organization told *The Guardian*, 'Attitudes towards travellers remain comparable to those experienced by Black Americans in the 1950s.'[43]

We'll look again at the issues surrounding attitudes to the GRT community when we come to consider Appleby Horse Fair.

Sound and Fury

Bonfire Night will be referenced again when we look at carnivals in the West Country, but we will note a more recent objection to 5 November: the issue of noise. When I was a child, a few people complained about the bangs and explosions, and I remember some pets being averse to it, but with the advent of social media, complaints about the terrors suffered by animals probably outstrip references to celebrations themselves (at least on my Facebook feed). These complaints have substance: not only pets, but wild and farm animals can be panicked by the sudden and unpredictable noise.

There are a number of campaigns currently attempting to limit sales of fireworks to a particular period (for instance, immediately around Bonfire Night itself) and to restrict the times of day at which fireworks can be let off. They also seek to reduce the maximum permitted noise level of fireworks for public sale from 120dB to 90dB. The RSPCA has been running its #BangOutOfOrder campaign since 2019 and says that 25 out of 175 unitary councils have signed up. This is becoming easier to track, police and manage with the increasing popularity of large organized displays as opposed to the back garden Bonfire Nights that were more common in the 1970s and '80s.

Guy Fawkes and Anonymous

As previously noted, Guy Fawkes himself has been adopted by many as a kind of folk hero, with a prominence that he didn't really possess during the original plot. His iconic, stylized face, with a pointed black beard and big hat, has recently appeared all over the place, as though he's been cloned. At one point, wearing paper or cardboard masks for Bonfire Night was common; comics gave them away free to children and in 1843, *The Lancet* published a stern warning in the form of 'Notes of a Case of

Death from Fright', in which the case of a person scared to death by a kid in a Guy Fawkes mask is investigated. Gradually, wearing masks for 5 November became less common and was overtaken by mask wearing at Hallowe'en.

However, a Guy Fawkes mask was then used in the popular graphic novel *V for Vendetta*, written by Alan Moore and illustrated by David Lloyd. The story is set in a dystopian future in the UK in which the anarchist protagonist V, hidden behind a Guy Fawkes mask, seeks to overthrow a brutal government. The mask was mass-produced by Warner Bros when a film was made of the story, and these masks were adopted by hacktivist group Anonymous, spreading out into the wider protest sphere. The association with the Gunpowder Plot and *V for Vendetta* proved irresistible and the mask, in a modified form, then made its way back into the movie sphere in the film *Mr Robot*, which depicts a fictionalized version of Anonymous. Moore said in 2008:

> I was also quite heartened the other day when watching the news to see that there were demonstrations outside the Scientology headquarters over here, and that they suddenly flashed to a clip showing all these demonstrators wearing *V for Vendetta* Guy Fawkes masks. That pleased me. That gave me a warm little glow.[44]

David Lloyd, the creator of the mask, remarked:

> The Guy Fawkes mask has now become a common brand and a convenient placard to use in protest against tyranny – and I'm happy with people using it, it seems quite unique, an icon of popular culture being used this

way. My feeling is the Anonymous group needed an all-purpose image to hide their identity and also symbolise that they stand for individualism – *V for Vendetta* is a story about one person against the system. We knew that V was going to be an escapee from a concentration camp where he had been subjected to medical experiments but then I had the idea that in his craziness he would decide to adopt the persona and mission of Guy Fawkes – our great historical revolutionary.[45]

Moore himself told *The Guardian*:

when I was writing V for Vendetta I would in my secret heart of hearts have thought: wouldn't it be great if these ideas actually made an impact? So when you start to see that idle fantasy intrude on the regular world . . . It's peculiar. It feels like a character I created 30 years ago has somehow escaped the realm of fiction.[46]

The mask has, indeed, taken on a life of its own, spreading across the world in the context of a variety of protest movements. It has, for instance, been banned in Saudi Arabia, where it is seen as an incitement to revolt. What Guy Fawkes himself would think of these historical echoes must remain within the realm of speculation.

EIGHT

All the Fun of the Fair?

Fairs and festivals are a part of the British landscape. I drove through our local street market this morning, there will be a fair coming to town later in the summer and no one who lives in Somerset, as I do, can ignore the mighty juggernaut that is the Glastonbury Festival, which descends on us almost every June. Some of the fairs and festivals that we'll be looking at in this book are ancient, such as the fairs set up by Royal Charter in the medieval period, and some are very modern, such as the Stonehenge Free Festival of the 1970s. New festivals are emerging all the time, like the celebrations of arts and culture of Montol in Cornwall or the Winter Solstice festival of the Burning of the Clocks in Brighton. These are not transgressive practices – unless one takes a very stretched view of transgression and interprets these as expressions of support for the arts in a political climate that seeks to strip funding right down to the bone. But both fairs and festivals have a chequered history when it comes to illegality, violence and crime – some of it perpetrated by the police, as we shall see.

Fairs, as we've just noted, go back a long way in Britain. There is evidence – from the amount of charred bone fragments and broken pots in places such as the stone circle of Stanton Drew near Bristol – that our tribal ancestors often gathered together, to trade cattle and other products, exchange news and feast. Later, Britain became home to the 'charter fairs' – gatherings licensed by Royal Charter, which probably emerged from street markets or the *vigilia*, gatherings that began in Roman times and were adopted by the early Christian Church to mark, for instance, the commemoration of a particular church, perhaps on the day of the saint to which the church was dedicated. Even in a pious realm, it is natural for people to want to buy something to eat once they've paid their devotions, not to mention having a drink, and stalls would be set up around the churchyard by enterprising traders to cater to these needs. These *vigilia*, or 'wakes', form the origins of the later chartered fairs. There are records of them in the ninth century on the continent, but one of the first was granted by William the Conqueror to the borough of Yaxley.

Today, we see fairs as primarily entertainment-based, focusing on rides and candyfloss, and often rather rowdy. Like today, markets were held regularly (perhaps once a week, like the one in Glastonbury that I mention above) whereas fairs were occasional but regular, tied into a season and, usually, a religious festival – such as Michaelmas. Animals and produce were sold, but many of these events were also hiring fairs, in which agricultural labourers would be taken on for a season.

Winchester, for instance, had a large fair every September, followed by other cities and towns throughout the year such as Nottingham and Stamford, with smaller chartered fairs at other regional centres in between. The Great Fair at St Ives, Cambridgeshire, every Easter, dating from its charter granted to the Abbey of Ramsey in 1110, was truly international, running for an entire month and hosting merchants from across the continent. Along with some of the other large fairs, it even had

its own court and law enforcement: a piepowder court, established purely to govern conduct at a particular fair and overseen
by the local mayor and bailiffs, or in the case of charters granted
to abbeys, the Bishop's justiciars. Sergeants-at-mace applied the
law at St Bartholomew's Fair in London.

Piepowder Courts

The name 'piepowder' (spellings vary widely, sometimes within
the same document) has nothing to do with pies or powder, but
comes from the French pieds poudrés, or 'dusty feet', referring to
travellers and later applied to members of the court who would
be walking around the fair (which would, in most cases, itself
be a dusty or muddy environment, depending on the weather
– again, think of the Glastonbury Festival). A mention in the
records from Southampton in 1623 mentions that the poor court
officers had no option but to walk about dispensing justice, since
the stage at the Town Hall where they normally sat had been
taken over by a bunch of actors in order to stage a play.

> The lowest, and at the same time the most expeditious,
> court of justice known to the law of England, is the court
> of piepoudre, curia pedis pulverizati; so called from the
> dusty feet of the suitors; or, according to Sir Edward
> Coke, because justice is there done as speedily as dust
> can fall from the foot.[1]

Breaches of contract, debt and trespass (for example, nicking
someone else's spot) were the most common complaints. The
plaintiff had the burden of proof, and most complaints were

decided then and there with a penalty such as a fine imposed, although for more serious crimes, the pillory was sometimes brought into play. Really serious crimes, such as those involving someone's death, would be investigated by the Royal Justices, being deemed too important for these little local courts. Matters had to be settled within a day and a half – critical for a relatively short-term event with a large transient population. Anyone committing a crime at a fair and then skipping town would be hard to retrieve in medieval England. If the case involved debt, the offending party's goods could be seized. In Colchester in the mid-fifteenth century, the piepowder court heard the following case:

> Piepowder court held at the moot-hall before the bailiffing to the custom of the town beyond memory, and by the market held all day, on Friday before the feast of the of the Holy Cross, at the eighth hour in the forenoon of that day.
>
> To this court came Thomas Smith, who complained that Cristina van Bondelyng was indebted to him for £60 10s. 10d found pledges to prosecute his suit; and the sergeant was ordered to summon her before the court at the ninth hour.
>
> At the ninth hour, plaintiff being present, but defendant not appearing, precept was issued to the sergeant to attach her goods and chattels so that she should appear at the tenth hour.
>
> At the tenth hour, defendant not appearing, the sergeant certified that he had attached twenty-three woollen cloths belonging to her. An order was made

to record a first default and to summon her for the eleventh hour.

Again at the eleventh hour, no defendant appearing, a second default was recorded, and a summons issued for her appearance at the first hour after noon.

At that hour, defendant being still contumacious, a third default was recorded. Plaintiff was permitted to prove his debt, and appraisers were sworn to inspect and value the goods seized. Judgment was recorded for plaintiff for his debt and 26s. 8d. damages.

At the fourth hour after noon the appraisers returned the value of the goods at £61 4s., which were delivered to the plaintiff; and he found pledges to answer defendant in the same court, should she plead in a year and a day [i.e., on the fair day in the following year].[2]

The powers of such courts had been largely absorbed into the mainstream legal system by the seventeenth century, but some of them persisted, if in name only. The last one to be abolished, at the Stag and Hounds pub in Bristol, met its end in 1971, although it hadn't actually sat in session since the late nineteenth century. This does show, however, how some of these old law enforcement structures lingered into our own day and age.

Charter Fairs

Charter fairs were different from fairs today, emphasizing trade and hiring rather than entertainment, but they would have had their fun side nonetheless – and also their political side, too. They peaked in the thirteenth century, with more than 2,000 charters granted to fairs between 1200 and 1270, when the economy was starting to become a little more sophisticated; woollen goods were imported and exported from Britain and, as ever, the hub of this trade was in London. However, merchants in other coastal cities saw the old chartered fairs as an opportunity to bypass greedy London merchants. Customers also regarded the fairs as an opportunity to buy fewer commonplace goods, such as spices or wax, at a lower cost – just as in our own day, when people often attend street markets to buy things at a lower price, since stallholders don't have to pay the same rates and other overheads as permanent shop premises. Churches or local nobility were also able to profit from hosting the fair.

A number of these old fairs are still going, although their forms may have changed. Chichester's Sloe Fair, for instance, is around nine hundred years old; its charter was granted by King Henry 1 to the Bishop of Chichester, Ralph de Luffa, in 1107. Henry left the decision as to when the fair should be held to the bishop himself, and de Luffa decided that it should start at the Feast of St Faith the Virgin (6 October) and run through to the feast of St Edward eight days later. This changed in 1752 with the shift in calendar and the fair then ran from 20 October onwards, in a reduced form. De Luffa was able to set up a piepowder court to police it – the fair clearly needed it, as accounts of drunken behaviour at such gatherings are common and in the nineteenth century one constable was charged with being drunk while actually policing the fair.

Ruth Bagnall, writing in the Chichester Local History Society's journal, described the fair in the twentieth century as 'a couple of days of real enjoyment for young people with roundabouts, swings, coconut shires, the big dipper, shooting ranges and hoop-la's' but the fair had already had several incarnations by then, from the cattle sales of its early days to the peak of its existence in the nineteenth and twentieth centuries, featuring lion tamers, conjurors, fortune tellers, acrobats and, as a kind of pièce de resistance, in 1904, a steam-driven railway.[3]

Fairs are often unpopular due to the antisocial behaviour that can accompany them, and in addition to the piepowder courts regular attempts were made to abolish them. I recall similar discussions between the Town Council and various groups in Glastonbury in recent times. The Glastonbury Tor Charter Fair is the second oldest in the country and was originally held on the Tor itself (probably on the lower slopes). It was granted a charter by Henry I in 1127 but pre-dates this; the charter was to allow the continuation of the fair as long as it was held on its traditional site, a suggestion that the fair had been going some time before royal approval was conferred upon it. It is now purely an entertainment-type fair with rides, but up until the 1960s it was focused on livestock.

In 2017, the fair was moved into town, into St John's car park behind Glastonbury's primary hotel, the George and Pilgrim, garnering fierce opposition:

> A petition was delivered to the town council at the time, signed by 105 local people with a letter highlighting the worry, indignation and outrage many of us feel at this unwarranted, underhand and patriarchal imposition on local residents.[4]

'Patriarchal' might be a newer cause for complaint, but the sentiments behind the objections are as old as the fairs themselves. Due to this local protest, Glastonbury's fair is likely to be moved in future to a new, purpose-built site on the outskirts of the town. Chichester's Sloe Fair met similar opposition earlier in its history. Unpopular with the town council, the local Board of Guardians tried in 1904 to extend the workhouse onto the site of the fair. However, despite its reputation among the town's worthies, the fair remained popular with the citizens of Chichester, who petitioned to save it. They succeeded: it is still going strong today. A blog post relating to the fair asked for reminiscences, some of which were somewhat eyebrow raising:

> I did enjoy the fair but it was also a sad time as I was a child that worried about all the poor fish that were prizes, also I didn't like the boxing ring as my Dad always had a go as he had been a bare knuckle fighter in Glasgow and he considered it easy money. One year when I was seven I tried to stop him climbing into the ring by hanging onto his legs but a man grabbed me from behind and pulled me off then threw me down onto the mud, I was not happy.[5]

However, this pales in comparison to the Epping Forest Stag Hunt, which started as an actual hunt by local worthies to re-assert ancient hunting rights, but by the nineteenth century had degenerated into an occasion in which numerous urban Cockneys pursued an old stag. It was banned in 1847.

Carnival

When we hear the word 'carnival', we tend to think of Notting Hill, which we will come to shortly, but there are carnivals across the UK, particularly in the West Country, and they differ greatly from one another. In Somerset, the term instantly conjures up images of enormous illuminated carts pulled on low-loaders by tractors, processing through the streets of local towns in the dark nights of November. The wattage that these events put out is so great that, one year, returning over the Mendip hills from Bristol, I fleetingly thought that Wells had suffered from some localized nuclear event. The carnival belonging to the little town of Bridgwater is the largest illuminated carnival in Europe.

When did this start? Our ancestors had horse-drawn carts but would have relied on candlelight or rush lights for illumination until relatively late in the day. The history of carnival, however, begins in relation to a custom we've already looked at in some detail: the Gunpowder Plot. Robert Parsons, the Jesuit priest who was one of the instigators of the plot, came from Nether Stowey, not far from Bridgwater. Like Lewes, this local element lit the fuse for future celebrations; the strongly Protestant nature of the West Country means that the nature of the celebration was to commemorate the failure of the Gunpowder Plot.

Bridgwater carnival began as a massive bonfire in the Cornhill. Initially based on a wooden boat filled with tar barrels, this method was abandoned relatively swiftly due to running out of boats and, in an excess of enthusiasm, newer boats being commandeered. This was, obviously, not very popular among the local fishing community. However, the parading of 'guys' to the bonfire did survive, borne by participants known as Masqueraders or Features, terms that are still used today. Lamps were deployed in the nineteenth century and the carnival became electrified in 1913.

The carnival has been held ever since, with breaks for the Second World War (when a participant walked the route with a group known as 'Kilties' in order to keep the tradition going in spirit if not in actuality) and during COVID-19 and its aftermath, returning in 2022. At Bridgwater, each carnival ends with the practice of 'squibbing', in which a squibber stands with a tall pole with a firework (the squib) attached; these are then lit, to spectacular effect, although today's squibs are soundless.

Originally, as an offshoot of Bonfire Night, the Bridgwater carnival was held on 5 November. This was then moved in 1919 to a fixed date, the first Thursday in November (Thursday being Bridgwater's early closing day). Bridgwater became the first night in the carnival circuit, with carnivals subsequently being held in other local towns nearby. The council then suggested fixing the date to the weekend – not a popular move, on the grounds that it disrupted 'Black Friday', which is when Bridgwater celebrated another successful carnival, usually with some heavy drinking. However, carnival was finally moved to the weekend after the turn of the millennium. The circuit today starts in Bridgwater, moves to North Petherton, Burnham-on-Sea, Shepton, Wells and Glastonbury, finishing in Weston-super-Mare. Other counties, such as Devon, have their own circuit, and there is also a Wessex and a South Somerset circuit. My first experience of carnival was at Castle Cary, and there is an unofficial one at Midsomer Norton as well.

Today, the purpose of carnival (as well as having fun) is that of charity: donations are taken over the course of each evening and go towards designated charities, as well as to the maintenance of the event itself. Like many British traditions, events to fund the carnival are held throughout the year.

Carnival in the West Country is less contentious than Lewes and some of the Sussex Bonfire Nights. Rather than satirical effigies forming the focus of the evening, the carts concentrate on aspects of popular culture. I remember a *Pirates of the Caribbean* cart, and Disney themes remain a perennial favourite. Antisocial behaviour is comparatively rare at these events, too, so, since our remit is transgression, we shall move on.

Notting Hill Carnival

Carnival is not, of course, confined to the West Country. As we mention above, if you were to ask Britons what the word 'carnival' means to them, the minds of many people would go immediately to Notting Hill. This is one of the main events in the British, and certainly in London's, calendar. But unlike the carnivals of the West Country, Notting Hill is not an old festival, dating as it does back to 1966. However, its roots are solidly embedded in activism and in the search for justice. Broadcaster and writer Darcus Howe says: 'If there weren't race riots in Notting Hill I don't believe that we would have had the Notting Hill Carnival. If it wasn't for the murder of Kelso Cochrane, Carnival wouldn't have happened.'[6]

A carpenter of Antiguan origin who was hoping to go into the legal profession, Cochrane died in 1959 in Notting Hill after a racially motivated attack. Anger and fear within the

Black community ran high, and around 1,200 people attended Cochrane's funeral. Alarm had spread to the government as well: Home Secretary Rab Butler set up a public inquiry, but criticisms were made of the governmental response and of the fact that senior police officers had denied that the violence was racially motivated. Admittedly, some of it stemmed from class as well as racial tensions within the community; working-class Teddy Boys were fuelled by far-right agitation on the part of people like Oswald Mosley, founder of the British Union of Fascists, and Colin Jordan of the White Defence League. Property belonging to local Caribbean residents was vandalized and in August 1958, clashes between Teddy Boys and Caribbean youths, which had already seen a number of West Indian men assaulted in a spate of separate incidents in London and other cities, peaked in the Notting Hill Riots, which broke out at the end of the month. An estimated four hundred white youths were involved, using weapons such as petrol bombs, butcher's knives and iron bars. One hundred and forty people were arrested, most of them white.

Cochrane's murderers were not named until 2011. In 2021, his family set up a petition calling for a further investigation into his murder and the Met are currently apparently re-examining the case. In 2009 a blue plaque was placed to commemorate Cochrane. Whether the police had tried to play down the violence as non-racially motivated in order to try to calm community tensions or whether their denials were simply another facet of racist motivations (institutional or individual), or both, is not clear. The police insisted that the riots were the work of 'hooligans'. In the words of Detective Sergeant Walters of Notting Hill police:

Whereas there certainly was some ill feeling between white and coloured residents in this area, it is abundantly clear much of the trouble was caused by ruffians, both coloured and white, who seized on this opportunity to indulge in hooliganism.[7]

Whatever the motivations of the police, it has since become clear that they were aware of the racist component of the rioting. Several thousand people were at one point attempting to locate West Indian homes and break into them, and assaulting anyone who was Black. The rioters were blatant in their defiance of the police. Sentencing was, however, relatively heavy: nine of the original ten white youths who had gone out in search of trouble were jailed for four years apiece.

But attempts to de-escalate racial tensions in the neighbourhood were already ongoing. Community activist Raune Laslett set up a small children's fair in Notting Hill, in part to address local tensions. She noted:

We felt that although West Indians, Africans, Irish and many other nationalities all live in a very congested area, there is very little communication between us. If we can infect them with a desire to participate, then this can only have good results.[8]

The event, inspired by the London Free School system, was unconnected with that held in 1959, organized by Claudia Jones, a Trinidadian activist. This was an indoor 'Caribbean Carnival' in St Pancras Town Hall, and the event was recorded and broadcast by the BBC. It featured a number of artists, including singer Cleo

Laine. Jones also founded the *West Indian Gazette* and, teaming up a husband-and-wife pair of booking agents, began to promote the idea of carnival throughout London. In 1966 the first Notting Hill street carnival was organized, with a steel band parading through the streets. Vincent George Forbes, aka Duke Vin, is credited with bringing the first sound system to the carnival.

This was initially quite a small affair, but the seeds of what is now Europe's largest street festival and the second largest carnival in the world (after Brazil's Rio Carnival) were set. Aswad and Eddie Grant appeared at early carnivals and the event became a significant launching platform for Black British musicians. This continues today – although bands such as Busta Rhymes and Major Lazer have appeared at more recent carnivals, the establishment of the Wilf Walker Community Stage in Emslie Horniman's Pleasance park is designed to give a platform to launch local community musical talent. The event now draws somewhere in the region of 2 million attendees.

Notting Hill has not been without its challenges. Like many of the events that we have featured in this book, it has been marred by violence and rioting, disruption that stems from tensions experienced by the Black community in London. Caribbean youths engaged in pitched battles with the police in 1976, an outbreak of violence that heralded the Brixton and Toxteth riots of the 1980s and that stemmed primarily from the Black community's frustration at police harassment, particularly at the 'sus' laws, which meant that anyone could be stopped and searched on sight. Around a hundred policemen were hospitalized in total. Dotun Adebayo, now a BBC London radio presenter, was in the area at the time as a sixteen-year-old. He later told the BBC:

Within seconds the whole place erupted and I realized I was in the middle of a serious disturbance. I had never seen policemen running away from a situation before. I don't know where all the rocks came from but they were raining down on the fleeing cops. One or two police vehicles . . . tried to make it up the road but were turned back with a shower of missiles. I saw a lot of terrified faces in 1976 and 1977. Faces of young kids and parents who didn't know where to turn to safety. I hope I never see that again.[9]

After the event, only two youths were charged. There were calls for the carnival to be cancelled. Professor Chris Mullard, chair of the carnival committee, told the BBC that 'Carnival was always seen by the state and the establishment as something that they wanted to stop, because they saw it for what it was – a form of cultural resistance.'[10]

The carnival was not banned, however, and relations with the police gradually improved. Dotun Adebayo considers it to be one of the most peaceful carnivals in the world.[11] The riots are considered to have been critical in the implementation of the Race Relations Act in 1976, set up to outlaw racial discrimination.

Notting Hill Carnival is not free from problems today, or from crime. Logistically and statistically, you're not going to have a short event in a public neighbourhood of a major city attended by more than a million people without some element of law-breaking. The police do have problems in controlling the event, due partly to manpower and partly to the sheer scale of the carnival. In 2022 two female police officers were sexually harassed and a young rapper was stabbed to death, which led to calls for the event to be held elsewhere, presumably on a site outside the city, as Glastonbury is situated, or a fenced-off area in somewhere like Hyde Park that would then be ticketed, again like most music festivals. The Chief Superintendent of the Met, Rob Shepherd, commented on Twitter:

> Ticket it, put it in Hyde Park, get the organisers to pay for the policing, don't change our tolerance towards abuse or crime from what we would allow on any other street on any other day. 74 injured officers is not acceptable for what is meant to be a positive community event.[12]

Ken Marsh, chairman of the Met Police Federation, reported that several hundred fights had been broken up over the weekend and police had seized a number of knives. But to put this into context, the event experienced a lower level of violence and crime than both the Reading and Leeds music festivals and also less than the European Championship football finals in 2020. The number of arrests was also significantly lower than in 2019, when more than three hundred people were arrested. Most of these were for possession of drugs, but 37 were for assaults on police officers. Commander Dave Musker, in charge of carnival policing for 2019, imposed a Section 60 Criminal Justice and Public Order authority across the Notting Hill Carnival area and areas of Harrow Road in that year.

> We don't have the resources to deal with it. This is tens of millions of pounds of public money that is spent on policing this. We are left ultimately responsible for it,

whatever goes wrong . . . and the mayor will be down our throats quicker than you can blink if something terrible goes wrong.[13]

In total, 209 arrests were made during the carnival in 2022 and of these, 33 were with reference to possession of offensive weapons. However, Marsh was clear that 98 per cent of people attend carnival just to have a good time, not seeking violence.

The most serious incident in 2022 was the murder of Takayo Nembhard, a 21-year-old rapper from Bristol who was stabbed during the event. He was found in Ladbroke Grove and died in hospital. Following an appeal by police, an eighteen-year-old man handed himself in to police in Bristol in December and was charged with murder. Four other people have also been implicated. But six other people were also stabbed at the event in 2022.

Devotees of Notting Hill Carnival have continually commented on negative media coverage, and in this, they are in company with organizers and participants of many other events, including Lewes Bonfire Night and the Appleby Horse Fair. They have a point: the press does tend to focus on the sensational and the controversial, because stoking outrage sells newspapers. Commentators noted the difference in coverage between Reading festival – where a sixteen-year-old died from taking an ecstasy tab, fifty people were ejected for 'serious disorder' and tents were set on fire – and Notting Hill. The coverage of Reading was more favourable, but that event has a primarily white audience. Commentators also suggested that a white youth caught in possession of drugs is more likely than a Black youth to receive a caution rather than arrest. Critics of this media coverage say that making the Notting Hill Carnival appear dangerous is an annual media event in its own right and point out that the number of arrests is fractional – around 0.015 per cent of total attendees.

There is, by the way, a truism that at Glastonbury Festival there will be one death and one birth every year, and this too seems to have been born out at Notting Hill, with someone going into labour (though it isn't clear whether she was actually attending the Carnival or was simply a resident!).

The carnival does have a cost: it requires about £7 million to put it on, but this is put into perspective by the estimated £93 million that it brings into the London economy.

Appleby Horse Fair

The position of Gypsy, Romany, Traveller (GRT) groups in the UK is a difficult one: consistently ostracized throughout British history, these communities sometimes react against it and may have internal tensions of their own that manifest adversely. My current boss and various friends come from the Roma community and say that whenever a member of that community does something antisocial, it's spread across the newspapers, which never seem to report on the positive things that the community do, thus reinforcing negative stereotypes. In 2023, the Evidence for Equality National Survey revealed that 62 per cent of Gypsy or Traveller people living in the UK had experienced racially motivated assault, exceeding the levels of assault on members of all other ethnic groups. Forty-seven per cent of Roma had experienced racist attacks, with 35 per cent experiencing physical assault. Access to health and social care is also low and, correspondingly, members of these groups have poor health in comparison to the rest of the UK population. Life expectancy for GRT members is 10–25 years below that of the general population – this is a figure that is below life expectancy in some developing nations. Around 51 per cent of GRT members have had little formal education.[14]

Like every other ethnic group, this is not, however, a monolithic block of people. Irish travellers have been resident in the UK since at least the early nineteenth century, and the traveller movement says that Gypsies (the word coming from 'Egyptian', which they were commonly held to be – the general consensus now is that they originate in northern India) have been in the UK since around 1515. However, there are also indigenous people of nomadic heritage here in Britain who have married into Roma and Irish families. All of these groups have distinct languages and customs, and are clearly identifiable from one another although they are often lumped together in the mainstream cultural eye.

The custom that gets the most attention in the UK press, often negatively, is Appleby Horse Fair. This is an annual GRT gathering in Appleby in Cumbria, held from the first Thursday to the second Wednesday in June. It is the largest GRT fair in Europe, attracting several thousand people and, obviously, since this is its purpose, a large number of horses, which are washed in the river Eden and then ridden up and down to display them. In previous times, Appleby was one of many horse fairs. It is not known when it began; it was granted a charter from King James II in 1685 but this charter was cancelled before it was enrolled, so the original date of the fair remains moot. Appleby had a medieval borough fair at Whitsuntide, which stopped trading in 1885, and the current gathering is a legacy of the 'new fair', which started as a drovers' market in 1775. It has been a primarily GRT occasion since 1911, when Lord Lowther gave Fair Hill to Appleby Town Council as common land. The council shut Fair Hill, but the fair went ahead anyway for around the next sixty years before the area was once more opened up. It is currently partially licensed and ticketed, but has a working group chaired by Eden District Council, plus representatives of the Gypsy and Traveller community, Cumbria Constabulary, South Lakeland District Council, Cumbria County Council, the RSPCA, the Environment Agency and others. A Shera Rom (head Romani) operates as liaison between the police, other organizations and the various traveller groups. This is set up at Fair Hill under licence from the town council. There is currently a move in place to look at the legal viability of making the fair an organized, fully licensed event, but this might not happen – in part because the council structure is changing, and the new local authority will take the form of Westmoreland and Furness Council from 2023 onwards. Organizing fairs is not one of the core functions of a council, although there are exceptions. The *Travellers' Times* notes that the closest event to the Appleby fair in terms of licensing and legislation is the Notting Hill Carnival.[15]

The fair is popularly associated in the tabloid press with antisocial behaviour. However, the figures do not bear this out. At the 2021 fair, thirteen people were arrested, but prior to that numbers of arrests have been decreasing and the local police say that arrests made are in proportion to other large gatherings; the horse fair is not anomalous in terms of crime or arrests. In 2022, eighteen people were arrested out of a crowd of 40,000

– compare this with the Grand National, which in 2023 saw 118 arrests out of a crowd of between 65,000 to 70,000. (This, actually, was somewhat anomalous for racing as well and came about due to the presence of animal rights activists at the event, but it does put the arrest figures into perspective.) There are on average about three arrests per 10,000 people at Glastonbury Festival. In 2022 some arrests were made on the basis that police had had information that a group had been planning to come to the fair armed with bladed weapons and bats, in order to cause trouble. Comparing Notting Hill to the Appleby fair, the *Travellers' Times* says that the number of arrests at the latter are higher than Notting Hill, but arrests at the carnival tend to be for more serious offences (including murder). They also note, however, that analogies between the two events can only go so far, since Notting Hill takes place in a capital city and the horse fair in a very small rural town.[16]

The Multi-Agency Strategic Co-ordinating Group (MACSG) say that Gypsy and Traveller Representatives have no sympathy with offenders, and that they fully support police, Trading Standards and HMRC decisions in regulating issues (such as lack of vehicle tax). The RSPCA pay close attention to the fair, but report that the majority of horses involved are in good condition and are looked after well.

The press – particularly the *Daily Mail* – is prone to posting lurid photos of the staggering amounts of litter that appear after the fair (they do this with Glastonbury Festival as well) but usually don't report on subsequent events, which is that there is a mass clean-up, conducted by travellers and their families. Les Clark from Eden District Council, who is Chair of the Appleby Horse Fair MASCG, commented in the summer of 2022:

I'd particularly like to note that, this year, we have had a tremendous amount of good feedback about the work of our clean-up crews who have been working long hours to try and ensure Appleby and the surrounding area is kept clean. We have received hundreds of comments about their work which has started early each morning with litter picking and continues throughout the day, clearing rubbish and cleaning toilets, followed by cleaning the Sands area each evening.[17]

The *Travellers' Times* points out that

the Appleby 'communities' do not all hold the same view. Some local residents support the fair, some put up with it, and some are against it and want it banned or the management of it drastically changed.[18]

Appleby Town Council note that Bill Welch, who is a Romany Gypsy and the present licence holder, currently pays for the clean-up after the event and that this is not subsidized by local taxpayers.

From 2022 onwards, the local church will be offering sanctuary to GRT members, following increased powers granted to the police to seize travellers' homes. Reverend Nicky Chater, who is chaplain to the community, told *The Guardian*:

We will be asking churches to look favourably on allowing Travellers to park on suitable land like meadows and car parks, which have access from the road, and to talk to local authorities about providing facilities, perhaps toilets and rubbish collection. There is a long tradition of Travellers finding sanctuary on church land and we want to revive that shared history.[19]

In the nearby town, Kirkby Stephen's Councillor Dews adds, 'The fair isn't unique in attracting violence, littering and anti-social behaviour – so it's wrong to stigmatise the whole GRT community. They are not sufficient justification for banning the event.'[20]

In many ways Appleby is closer to the old medieval fairs, with its emphasis on livestock: an aspect of the fair that has long since died out, unless one counts cattle markets or agricultural shows such as the Bath and West.

Festivals

Festivals are a big component of the UK's summer calendar. Most of these are based around music, and many have been running for decades. The most famous is Glastonbury – now the UK's biggest (and definitely not free) festival, which is still very much alive and kicking, having started in 1970 as the Pop, Blues and Folk Festival held at Worthy Farm, at Pilton in Somerset. Although it's named after the little town with the Tor and is held in sight of that famous landmark, it's not in Glastonbury itself, something that has confused generations of tourists.

Some 210,000 people attended the 2022 festival, along with more than 3,000 artists performing on more than a hundred stages. Paul McCartney headlined, joined by Bruce Springsteen and the Foo Fighters' Dave Grohl. Live content from the festival was streamed 23 million times on the BBC throughout that year. Organizers say that there was 85 per cent less crime at the 2022 festival compared to 2019 levels. Two hundred and ten thousand are estimated to have attended Glastonbury in 2023. It has come a long way in fifty years from the original Pilton Pop, which was inspired by the Isle of Wight music festival and Woodstock, and saw 1,500 people (not in fact an unrespectable number for a small festival today) paying £1 per head in 1970. The headliner then was Marc Bolan with T. Rex, already a major star, who is said to have been passing the site on his way to Butlin's in a velvet-covered limousine just as organizer Michael Eavis had discovered that The Kinks had pulled out. Bolan was promptly drafted in. So Glastonbury hit the ground running from its inception and has not looked back. Its origins lie in the music movement, partly in the protest movement (it has championed environmental campaigners Greenpeace and also CND), and in the hippy spiritualism of the 1960s; its main stage remains a pyramid and is allegedly sited on a ley line. It has seen attendances by a number of politicians and notable people, such as the Dalai Lama in 2015. (When told about this, my elderly mother asked diffidently, 'will he sing?' – sadly the Tibetan sage did not, thus depriving us forever of, perhaps, his cover version of 'The House of the Rising Sun'.)

The festival has faced, and continues to face, its own battles, mainly over the granting of a music licence. It is not universally popular in the district, although, as a Glastonbury resident of nearly twenty years, I can report anecdotally that most people recognize that it's put our little town on the global map and years' worth of simmering opposition has been substantially reduced now that the festival has sorted out the terrible traffic problems that used to beset this part of Somerset in June. Michael and Jean Eavis faced down four prosecutions in 1984 alone. The festival faces criticism these days not so much for its political content or its countercultural stance, but in relation to what many alternative types regard as its rampant consumerism: the festival states that it had a post-tax profit of £1.43 million in 2018, cash reserves of £10.6 million and charitable donations of £2.1 million. This was, however, pre-lockdown and COVID-19 has impacted the festival's reserves, along with much else. However, in the 2023 Honours list, Eavis was awarded one of the nation's supreme accolades for contributions to music and charity, and is now Sir Michael.

Glastonbury might top the bill, but the UK has a number of other headlining music festivals as well: Reading, Boomtown and Boardmasters among them. Overall, there are more than nine hundred festivals taking place in the UK each year, and some people make their living travelling the festival circuit, as food vendors or clothing traders or in one of the many sidelines that are a feature of these events.

Safer spaces

The Association of Independent Festivals' (AIF) Safer Spaces At Festivals campaign has signed up 103 festivals at the time of writing. The aim of the campaign is to reduce sexual assault and violence at festivals, with links both to local authorities and advice on bystander prevention (how to intervene in a crisis rather than how to prevent bystanders – we are not, here, a million miles away from the piepowder courts). Rape Crisis England and Wales, Good Night Out, Safe Gigs for Women,

Girls Against and UN Women have all had input into the campaign. But how common is assault at festivals?

In the AIF's latest audience survey post-2019, 98.7 per cent of 2,283 respondents, 68.83 per cent of which identified as female, answered 'No' to the question 'Did you experience sexual assault or harassment at any festival this year?'[21] The organization goes on to point out that women often don't report rape, which is true, but which makes it very difficult to assess the extent of the problem.

Wallyvision

Here we digress, but only slightly, to look at the Wally movement, as this was a crucial part of the free festivals that are the direct ancestor of many events today. The Wallies are a phenomenon that keeps bubbling up from the grassroots and fringes of modern British protest culture. A 'wally' is an old piece of slang meaning someone who is a bit of an idiot; not harmful, just clueless. Readers of a certain age will remember the children's picture book *Where's Wally?*, with the signature character and his stripy hat hiding amid various crowds.

But Wally has another meaning in British fringe culture, too. It functions a bit like Spartacus: if all are named Wally, Wally cannot easily be found. The late Jake Stratton-Kent – occultist, writer, punk anarchist and a Wally himself – claimed once that it stood for the Wessex Anarchist Libertarian League of Youth, or was Gaelic for 'elite warrior' (it isn't – Jake had an element of the trickster about him). Wallies are mischievous, though, especially with regard to their origins. The general consensus is that the name comes from the originator of the Stonehenge

Free Festival, Wally Hope – rather ironically, since this was itself a pseudonym for Philip Alexander Grahame Russell, a young Trustafarian. Living in Notting Hill, Hope encountered a kind of London-based version of the yippies, a prankster-style movement called the Dwarves, and set up his own version, called the Wallies. The name apparently derives from a lost dog at the Isle of Wight folk festival that turned into a countercultural in-joke.

After the festival at Stonehenge, the Wallies set up a makeshift commune in a field near the stones, referring to themselves as 'the Wallies of Wessex'. This was also known as 'Fort Wally, c/o God, Jesus and Buddha, Garden of Allah, Stonehenge Monument, Salisbury, Wiltshire' – an address that probably didn't go down very well with the local authorities. Neither did the pseudonyms ('Wally Raleigh') or Hope's appearance in court dressed as an officer of the Cyprus National Guard. The encampment also had a motto: 'Every Body is Wally, Every Day is Sun Day'. Everyone took on the name 'Wally' as an adjunct to their forenames or made up a combination of names entirely (this was to prevent charges being brought by the Environment Agency). A beaming Hope appears at the time in a photo, accompanied by an equally smiley senior policeman; relationships with the local cops were clearly not terrible, but the group were nonetheless evicted. The Wallies were composed of all manner of people, including one member of the Tartan Army, a sort of prototype Scots IRA (*not* the same as the football fans who adopt the same name), and a local squaddie based at Tidworth.

It was an open camp, inspired by a diversity of wild ideas, but with the common purpose of discovering the relevance of this ancient mysterious place by the physical experience of spending a lot of time there.[22]

The judge commented that he felt that they were all good folk but made the camp move on regardless; it shifted a few yards away onto the Drove, which was owned by the Highways Department rather than the Department of the Environment.

Hope himself was from a wealthy background – he was due to inherit £39,000 on his thirtieth birthday – but he was effectively orphaned at the age of twelve when his father died. His mother, who was Danish, was still alive but lived out of the country. He had spent time in the Mediterranean, including on Ibiza. He believed that he had encountered a reincarnated Christ in Cyprus and carried a copy of *The Shroud of Turin* everywhere he went ever since. His interests included the Matter of Britain, the freeing of Albion and particularly sun worship. He told people that God had ordained his presence at Stonehenge (quite how the local farmer to whom Hope communicated this in a letter responded is lost to history, but one can't imagine that it was entirely positive). Jake Stratton-Kent, writer and fellow Wally, commented of him:

> he was no anarchist, he was a hero, a sun god, a king. He had charisma, he had vision. He also had an Achilles heel, like all sun gods he had to be crucified ... He was a very bright star that burnt out the quicker for being bright. He was a brilliant flame that died for lack of tinder.[23]

Hope had also been in prison in the 1960s on drugs charges, and attended the Aldermaston anti-nuclear march. He also attended the anti-Vietnam demo in Grosvenor Square, gradually becoming politicized, and developed a love of jazz. Around 1970 he moved to Glastonbury, which he credited with having changed him in a permanent shamanic way.

Many of his friends attributed almost mystical qualities to him, as we can see above. LSD, which he saw as a sacrament, probably contributed to this. There are photos of Hope clad in a shirt (made by his grandmother) emblazoned with an eye of Horus. Hope's friend Jeremy Ratter, aka Penny Rimbaud, said of him:

> One day in our garden, it was early summer, he conjured up a snowstorm, huge white flakes falling amongst the daisies on the lawn. Another time he created a multi-rainbowed sky – it was as if he had cut up a rainbow and thrown the pieces into the air where they hung in strange random patterns. Looking back on it now it seems unbelievable but, all the same, I can remember both occasions vividly.[24]

Hope was living at Dial House, a commune near his guardians in Essex, and this allowed him to use the premises in order to organise the Stonehenge festival, covered by Radio Caroline. Hope wanted to set up a communal, caring festival without violence. (At Windsor a hot dog van had been set on fire, which Hope considered to be entirely antithetical to the true festival spirit.) He invited pretty much everyone to the first Stonehenge festival, including the Beatles, the Dalai Lama and the entire female aircrew of British Airways, since he apparently considered the airline stewardess – smiling, feminine, caring, beautiful

– to be the Platonic archetype of the female ideal. (It was a time before feminism had gained a great deal of traction within the counterculture.)

Stratton-Kent wrote of Hope:

He and I discussed the magical aspect of the Wally ideal. I was lauding the moon and even denying the physical fact that her light is derived from the Sun. Wally Hope was still a walking Apollo, but there was division between us all, the cities were winning.[25]

After his court appearance, Hope told the press:

These legal arguments are like a cannon ball bouncing backwards and forwards in blancmange. We won, because we hold Stonehenge in our hearts. We are not squatters, we are men of God. We want to plant a Garden of Eden with apricots and cherries, where there will be guitars instead of guns and the sun will be our nuclear bomb.[26]

In 1975, on his way to Stonehenge and following his arrest for possession of a small quantity of LSD, Hope was sectioned under the Mental Health Act and at length put in a psychiatric hospital, the Old Manor, in Salisbury, thus missing the festival. The police had raided his camp on the pretext of looking for an army deserter, but there is a view that they were targeting Hope. In the prison hospital, prior to his placement in the Old Manor, he was diagnosed with schizophrenia, on the flimsy grounds that he was operating under two names.

Eventually Hope was released. He returned to Rimbaud's commune, but was in significant ill health, which his friends attributed to his stay in the hospital and the medication that he had been given there. Stratton-Kent says that he was put on Largactil, a heavy-duty anti-psychotic: 'He got fed more downers than both the Kray twins put together.'[27] He went back onto the festival circuit, but sadly died a few days after leaving the Watchfield Festival, on 3 September 1975, and returning to his guardians in Ongar. He was 28. The official verdict was suicide via a barbiturate overdose, although this was disputed by the GP who found Hope and who applied to the British Medical Association for clarification; they suggested that his death resulted from prescribed psychiatric drugs. Before the third inquest, however, Hope was cremated.

Conspiracy theories abounded after this – that Hope had been bumped off by secret services, for instance. The police were at this point gearing up for Operation Julie, one of the biggest LSD busts in British history. He returned to the next Stonehenge festival nonetheless, in the form of his ashes, which Penny Rimbaud took with him and which were scattered at his beloved stones.

An American schoolboy, Garry Denke, wrote up the initial court case for his school paper:

A strange hippie cult calling themselves 'Wallies' claim God told them to camp at Stonehenge. The Wallies of Wiltshire turned up in force at the High Court today. There was Kris Wally, Alan Wally, Fritz Wally, Sir Walter Wally, Wally Egypt and a few other wandering Wallys. The sober calm of the High Court was shattered as the

Wallies of Stonehenge sought justice. A lady Wally called Egypt with bare feet and bells on her ankles blew soap bubbles in the rarefied legal air and knelt to meditate. Sir Walter Wally wore a theatrical Elizabethan doublet with blue jeans and spoke of peace and equality and hot dogs. Kevin Wally chain-smoked through a grotesque mask and gave the victory sign to embarrassed pin-striped lawyers. And tartan-blanketed Kris Wally – 'My mates built Stonehenge' – climbed a lamp-post in the Strand outside the Law Courts and stopped bemused tourists in their tracks. The Wallies (motto 'Everyone's a Wally: Every Day's a Sun Day') – made the pilgrimage to the High Court to defend what was their squatter right to camp on Stonehenge . . . the Department of the Environment is bringing an action in the High Court to evict the Wallies from the meadow, a quarter of a mile from the sarsen circle of standing stones, which is held by the National Trust on behalf of the nation. The document, delivered by the Department to the camp, is a masterpiece of po-faced humour, addressed to 'one known as Arthur Wally, another known as Philip Wally, another known as Ron Wally and four others each known as Wally'. For instance, paragraph seven begins resound-ingly: 'There were four male adults in the tent and I asked each one in turn his name. Each replied "I'm Wally."' There are a soft core of about two dozen, peace-loving, sun worshipping Wallies – including Wally Woof the mongrel dog. Hitch-hikers thumbing their way through Wiltshire from Israel, North America, France, Germany and Scotland have swollen their numbers. Egypt Wally wouldn't say exactly where she was from – only that she was born 12,870 years ago in the cosmic sun and had a certain affinity with white negative. Last night they were squatting on the grass and meditating on the news.[28]

Accounts of the British counterculture display a tension, or perhaps a synergy, between a mystical hedonism that at its best is reminiscent of William Blake, and a push for social and political change. Attempts to depict this as a uniform movement with sinister antecedents have never been massively successful. Although quite a lot of activism is organized, the Wallies somehow typify the British counterculture between the 1960s and the early 1990s: disorganized, spontaneous, impromptu and essentially socially if not politically anarchic. It is a mindset that is not popular with the British establishment, to say the least, as later events were to show.

Battle of the Beanfield

Many of today's festivals are big-business affairs focusing on the international music industry, but many have their origins in the spirit of the old charter fairs. It is not only the historical fairs, seasonally held, that have been subject to outbreaks of violence and disorders. The problem continues into the present day, where – it is to be hoped – we have more structural legislation against it than the ancient piepowder courts. Whether the law is more effective remains to be seen – remember that the intention behind the piepowder courts was that they acted swiftly due to the transient and temporary nature of the event and its population.

Rather more drawn out was the infamous Battle of the Beanfield, in June 1985 – a day that has gone down as one of the more shameful events in recent British social history. To understand how this arose, we need to look a little further into the history of Wally Hope's Stonehenge Free Festival.

The Stonehenge Free Festival involved modern Druids but was not set up by them. Emma Restall Orr, who writes extensively on Druidry, notes:

I never went to the Stonehenge free festival of the 1970s and 1980s; I've never much enjoyed being in the midst of a crowd. Having said that, I've heard wonderful things about it from people I respect. I've heard horrendous things about it, from others I respect equally. It's a personal thing, I guess, whether or not you like these muddy, damp, noisy, crowded, exhilarating events. But like it or not, in the end, with the counterculture aggression spurred on by Maggie Thatcher and all she was doing, the free festival erupted into violence and both the festival and temple were closed. Druids who were involved back then kept the pressure on English Heritage to reopen the site, but as they were a part of the festival culture it wasn't until others joined the negotiations, representative from the larger Orders of the mainstream Druid faith community, that English Heritage and the police began to listen. In the past year or two, the talks having reached a state of sanity with sound relationships made, we opened up the meetings, inviting other Druid Orders, Pagan organizations, and interest groups from the local, New Age and other faith communities to join.[29]

The Free Festival ran from 1974 until 1984, as close to the summer solstice as possible. It was, in a sense, born out of violence, emerging after the demise of the Windsor Free Festival, held in Windsor Great Park from 1972 until 1974 by a number of London-based commune dwellers such as Sid Rawle and Ubi Dwyer, who was in fact a middle-aged clerk in Her Majesty's Stationery Office (presumably not remaining in this post for long after he was jailed as a result of his involvement in Windsor). It was anti-monarchist (hence the choice of location, basically squatting in the queen's back garden) and politically motivated. Photographer John Hopkins notes:

> The[se events] were about participating, rather than just sitting waiting for things to happen. To an extent, it grew out of squatting. Historically all these Crown Lands have been ripped off from the people. So the idea of putting Windsor Great Park to constructive use seemed very interesting.[30]

Free LSD was also offered to anyone who couldn't afford it. Drugs information organization Release ran an aid tent that, its own medic admitted, came to resemble a scene from a Hieronymus Bosch painting.

By 1973 the short existence of the Windsor Free Festival had garnered an audience of 8,000 people. In 1974, when some 15,000 people attended, there were around three hundred arrests even before the Festival was raided by the police on its sixth day and summarily dispersed with the aid of truncheons. Women and children were assaulted, a response that caused the Home Secretary to demand an explanation from the Thames

Valley Chief Constable David Holdsworth. A number of participants successfully sued Thames Valley. Seven national newspapers, including the *Daily Telegraph*, joined in with calls for an enquiry into the incident. Journalist Mark Hudson, who attended the 1974 Windsor Free Festival but left before it was dispersed, described it to the *Daily Telegraph* thirty years later:

> in the glade beyond was gathered a great Babel of bizarre alternative groups – from ultra-Leftist White Panthers to the Divine Light Mission and the notorious Children of God – everyone there with the intention of creating a perfect society, right there, spontaneously, illegally. And nobody was in control.[31]

Describing Windsor as the 'last stand of the psychedelic underground', Hudson's report goes on:

> Arriving in Windsor on the Sunday evening, I was confronted by the bizarre spectacle of an English small town apparently under martial law – the streets deserted except for screeching police vans, the verges around the park heaped with cars taken to pieces in drug searches.[32]

The Free Festival itself never recovered, but the energy of Windsor moved on to Stonehenge, which, as we've noted above, was started in 1974 by Hope and that continued the countercultural spirit. It was somewhat lawless: my late partner attended the first one with a friend, who was in fact a drug dealer but everyone else suspected him of being an undercover policeman as a result of his choice of shoes (they had some trouble with this public perception). Restrictions on access were gradually imposed and in 1977 the monument itself was fenced off. (We should note that with regard to Stonehenge, it is not just the stones themselves that are endangered by people climbing all over them, but also the seventy-plus species of lichen that grow on the stones, some of which are extremely rare and some of which only otherwise grow in maritime areas.)

By 1984 the festival was attracting tens of thousands of people – at least 30,000 were held to have attended that year's gathering. Although attendees were depicted in the press as 'hippies', a significant number came from the so-called Peace Convoy, a post-punk travelling group now more commonly called New Age Travellers or, more derogatively, 'crusties'. (A Glastonbury friend described them to me in 1990 as 'clad in various shades of filth', although my own experience of them has varied from some absolutely stellar individuals to people who were very much not – much as one might expect of any social group, really.) The Peace Convoy was so-called due to its association with CND and the anti-nuclear peace camps.

Five of you – £60 each, forget about the Tax and Insurance (fascist claptrap), let's just chuck a few mattresses in the back of the Bella Vega and head for the nearest festival where we will be welcomed with open arms and be swallowed up into the new age traveller family bosom – and what a beautiful, bountiful and jolly socially diverse bosom it was; anarchists, venusians, pikies, pixies, conspiracy fugitives, Kray associates, old school, new school, never been to fucking school

– wheeler, dealers, medicine spielers – tryers, flyers, out
and out liars – saints, sinners, all of them winners – all
of them strangers in their own very strange land.[33]

The Peace Convoy was composed of around 150 vehicles
by this stage and becoming a serious concern to the police,
combined with its visitations to other countercultural sites
of interest to the authorities such as Greenham Common, to
which the Convoy drove after Stonehenge in 1982. It was not
only a concern to the police, but to politicians, too: 'we are
only too delighted to do anything we can to make life difficult
for such things as hippie convoys.'[34] Home Secretary Douglas
Hurd called the Travellers 'nothing more than a band of medieval brigands who have no respect for the law or the rights
of others'.[35]

Violence on the picket line in South Yorkshire had already
broken out earlier in the year, in the so-called Battle of Orgreave
between striking miners and the police. It has been called one of
the worst manifestations of industrial violence in British history,
and the zeitgeist in which this took place eventually culmin-
ated in an outbreak of police-driven aggression and the largest
number of civilian arrests (five hundred travellers were arrested)
since the Second World War: the Battle of the Beanfield.

In 1985, the Thatcher government banned the Stonehenge
Festival, a result of a last-minute injunction by English
Heritage, who own the site, and on 1 June the Peace Convoy
was intercepted on its way to Salisbury Plain. In an effort to
avoid police roadblocks, the Peace Convoy detoured into a
field of broad beans and tried to negotiate with the police, who
responded with violence and who also seem to have illegally

covered up their ID badges. Images of pregnant women being clubbed over the head rapidly made their way into the media and the movement earned a slightly unlikely ally in the form of the Earl of Cardigan, David Brudenell-Bruce, secretary of the Marlborough Conservative Association, who had also been heading for Stonehenge.

He first got wind of the convoy via a phone call from the police, who asked him to 'shut down' Savernake Forest. The earl (one imagines, patiently) explained that this wasn't possible, since an entire forest could not simply be barricaded off. On heading into Marlborough for a meeting, he was startled to encounter the convoy itself, plus a large number of Ford Transits on its tail, containing the police. The convoy made its way to a campsite at the edge of Savernake, the earl's own land, for the night. Somewhat alarmed, the earl paid a visit to the police the next day and was told by an officer that the intention was to arrest every person in the convoy by the following night. A helicopter would be used, and the arrests would be carried out on open ground rather than in the forest itself, so that people could not flee into the trees.

Even more alarmed, the next day the earl followed the convoy, keeping close to an HTV film crew. The convoy, he noted, contained a small number of actual anarchists but was mainly composed, in his view, of families living in buses with their children.

Police rushed out on foot, from behind their barricades. Clutching drawn truncheons and riot shields, they ran round to the driver's door of each vehicle, slamming their truncheons into the bodywork to make a deafening noise, and shouting at every driver, 'get out, get out, hand over your keys, get out.'[36]

This was not an impromptu move. The police said that the operation 'had been planned for several months and lessons in rapid deployment learned from the miners' strike were implemented'.[37]

However, planned or not, the police realized that they needed reinforcements and called in members of the Police Support Unit, who had been trained in public order and riot control. The police maintained that travellers had tried to break through the roadblock and that they had retaliated. The Earl of Cardigan was a witness to subsequent events (from his viewpoint, a police transit van had collided with a large coach heading into the beanfield) and for his pains was dubbed a 'class traitor' by the *Daily Telegraph* – which he sued, along with *The Times*, the *Daily Mail*, the *Daily Express* and the *Daily Mirror*. He won his case and bought a BMW with the proceeds. Much was made of the fact that his ancestor had led the charge of the Light Brigade, as evidence that the earl was somehow genetically bonkers. He pointed out to *The Independent*, on the thirtieth anniversary of the Battle of the Beanfield, that while there was problematic behaviour on both sides, and he observed a 'lawless element' within the convoy, his principal condemnation was for the police: 'You do not expect to see numerous uniformed police officers simply lose their temper and commit criminal acts like smashing the dashboards of abandoned vehicles with hammers.'[38]

The earl told the *Marlborough Times*,

From behind the barricade came around two dozen policemen with their truncheons drawn. They smashed through the first vehicle's windscreen, hauled out the occupant and then hauled him off to custody. The second vehicle was a converted ambulance with a lone girl in it. I was standing on the roadside bank right beside that vehicle, so I could see them smash up her windscreen. I saw four or five policemen climb in and they dragged her out through a broken window by her hair, right over the broken glass.[39]

The earl also saw a pregnant woman being clubbed to the ground by police officers, which formed part of his testimony at the forthcoming lawsuit. There is a body of opinion that holds (in my view correctly) that if the earl had not been present at the beanfield, and willing to testify in court, the event would have been swept under the carpet.

Various members of the convoy apparently attempted to negotiate with the police, but this was spasmodic and eventually had little effect. The Earl of Cardigan, who managed to listen in on some of these negotiations, reported that the attitude of the police was that everyone concerned was as good as under arrest from the get-go. At around 7 p.m., it became clear that the police were making a move and those from the convoy who were able then took a classic 'wagon train' approach and began circling with their vehicles, very slowly. The response of the police to this was simple: throw missiles, including truncheons, lumps of flint and even helmets, to smash in the windscreens and then arrest everyone in the vehicle when it came to a stop. Finally, all vehicles came to a halt except the brightly coloured

Rasta bus, which was chased around the field by a commandeered bus like something out of a very slow Steve McQueen movie. The Earl of Cardigan reported that the police, having finally managed to halt the Rasta bus, then took their frustration out on the occupants. A woman and a baby were covered with broken glass. Others were hit.

Nobody died, but eight police officers and sixteen members of the convoy were hospitalized that night. Arrested convoy members were dispersed throughout police stations across the south of England and there were subsequently complaints that children and adults had been separated. Most were charged with 'unlawful assembly', although a large number of these charges were subsequently dropped.

Some of the remaining convoy limped back to Savernake forest, where the earl was again approached by the Chief Constable, who asked for his permission to evict them.

> They said they wanted to go into the campsite 'suitably equipped' and 'finish unfinished business'. Make of that phrase what you will, says Cardigan. 'I said to them that if it was my permission they were after, they did not have it. I did not want a repeat of the grotesque events that I'd seen the day before.[40]

The site was eventually evicted through normal court channels.

Cathy Augustine, co-vice chair of the Labour Representation Committee, writes:

> This is part of the same shameful thread that runs through local British history with key events including the

Peasants' Revolt, the betrayal and execution of Leveller leaders, crushing of Luddite protests, the Peterloo Massacre, the Swing Riots, transportation of the Tolpuddle Martyrs, Orgreave, Battle of the Beanfield, the aftermath of Hillsborough, the naked power of the state unleashed against the many – again and again and again. This is the naked face of state violence when the mask slips – or when the establishment decides it's powerful enough to remove the mask and show the full ugliness of what lies underneath.[41]

The Beanfield did not come entirely out of the blue. A member of Wiltshire constabulary later told *The Independent* that bad blood between the police and the travelling community had been building up for years.[42] Rose Brash, who was involved in the Beanfield and was aged twenty at the time, told *The Guardian* in 2016,

it wasn't a battle, because we offered no resistance. Until she was about five, Kaya sobbed whenever she saw anyone in police uniform. The memory must have remained from being a baby . . . Whatever they tried to do us 30 years ago, it didn't work; it made us stronger. After 1985, there was no free festival at Stonehenge again, but we returned to the field later that year and picked beans to make hippy stew.[43]

The legal ramifications of this echoed into the 1990s. Lord Gifford QC represented 24 of the travellers at the Beanfield trial in 1991. He did eventually manage to arrange a settlement, but any monies awarded to the plaintiffs were swallowed up by legal costs.

Did any of the Convoy eventually make it to Stonehenge, their original destination? Remarkably, some of them did, two weeks after the 'battle'. They parked up some distance from the stones, accompanied by a large number of police in armoured carriers, cops in military trenches and a helicopter.

At this point, even the most conservative reader must be wondering whether this reaction was justified over what was an admittedly large number of vehicles, but occupied by people who were neither terrorists nor hardcore criminals. Images of women being thrown to the ground or clubbed over the head did not sit well with a lot of people. Yet there was no inquiry. ITN reporter Kim Sabido made an emotional commentary over his footage, which was then removed and replaced with a more dispassionate account. Sabido also claimed that some of the more unpleasant footage had gone missing. Some of this has since reappeared as a bootleg and was shown on the Channel 4 documentary *Operation Solstice*.

Those members of the convoy who were involved say that the Battle of the Beanfield permanently changed people. Many may not have been hippies per se, but there does seem to have been an attitude of positivity among the community, much of which did not survive the events of that summer.

The Chief Constable did, at least, call for an inquiry into the activities of one Les Vaughan, who ran a business in Salisbury serving papers for local solicitors. As well as organizing security patrols for local farmers around Stonehenge, he is also said to have approached members of the convoy and, after a preliminary conversation about pheasant shooting, offered to sell them a number of self-loading rifles for £45. The convoy, suspecting a set-up, refused. Vaughan was later exposed as a member of the paramilitary Column 88 and, among other far-right organizations, the British Nazi Party. Anti-fascist magazine *Searchlight* knew all about him. Had the convoy accepted his offer, the Battle of the Beanfield could have been significantly worse.

NINE

Cheese Rolling

From a highly politicized aspect of British culture, we now turn to one that is simply eccentric – but even this has had its controversial aspects. If you asked a foreigner to draw up a list of popular British pastimes, it is likely that rolling a gigantic cheese down a very steep hill, with a concomitant number of trips to A&E, might not feature in the top ten. However, cheese rolling, which takes place annually on Cooper's Hill in Gloucestershire, has fought off opposition for generations – mainly those in favour of basic health and safety. Why do people do it? Why is it so popular?

The official name of this event is the Cooper's Hill Cheese-Rolling and Wake, and it is held on the Spring Bank Holiday every year (originally on Whit Monday). It is thus related to the Wakes Weeks that we looked at in a previous chapter. The cheese rolling is not complicated. It involves a 7–9 lb Double Gloucester cheese, sometimes replaced by a foam replica. The cheese gets a one second head start and everyone else chases after it downhill. The first person to cross the finish line wins the cheese, and there are a number of races throughout the day, including separate ones for men and women.

Cooper's Hill is steep almost to the point of being vertical. The cheese itself, if a real cheese is used and not a replica, is solid and can reach speeds of up to 70 mph, so the possibility of it taking out a spectator is not unrealistic. Fractures among the chasers are not uncommon; fifteen people were seriously injured in 1993. One participant suffered spinal injuries but nonetheless returned in a future year. Brockworth Rugby Club gather at the bottom of the hill to ensure that people can actually stop.

Buns and sweets are distributed at the top of the hill by the Master of Ceremonies. The current cheese rolling is somewhat scaled down compared to the event in the 1800s, when it was accompanied by wrestling, gurning competitions and a shin-kicking contest. However, once confined to inhabitants of nearby Brockworth, cheese rolling now has an international dimension, with participants coming from as far afield as Canada and Japan.

When did this start? The first textual evidence of cheese rolling comes in a communication to the local town crier in 1826 but the event is generally considered to be a lot older, perhaps up to six hundred years old. However, hypotheses that it comes from an ancient Celtic rite – the wheel representing the sun, the thrown buns distributed for fertility and so on – must, like much else in this book, remain in the realms of speculation, as must theories that it dates from Phoenician traders in ancient times (the Phoenicians not being known for rolling cheeses downhill). Rolling food down hills is not confined to cheese: egg rolling was widespread in many parts of the country around Easter but has now more or less been replaced by Easter egg hunts.

The event has proved contentious, rather obviously, due to its risky nature and the high injury rate. In 2009 it was cancelled altogether, causing a local furore, but in 2010 residents of Brockworth flung a smaller cheese down the hill, as a matter of principle, and in 2011 there was a Save the Cheese Roll campaign.

In 2022, Brockworth resident and former soldier Chris Anderson, 'King of the Hill', won his 23rd cheese but intends to retire; since he has apparently suffered from a broken ankle, concussion, a torn calf muscle and other injuries, this is probably an example of quitting while he's ahead. He has auctioned at least one of the cheeses for charity after his infant nephew was diagnosed with nonketotic hyperglycinemia. 'Never ever again. I was so scared this year. It's the most nervous I've ever been. No more. I'm going to stick to the crowd and enjoy it now. I wanted to win this year for my daughter.'[1]

The 2022 women's race was won by North Carolina's Abby Lampe, who reported that 'I took a lot of tumbles but I'm feeling good. Did I lose any teeth? I was worried I was going to lose my teeth or break an ankle so all good. I can't believe I won.'[2]

However, although I have mentioned health and safety concerns above, we should be clear that those concerns do not, surprisingly, relate to breaking your leg because you're running after an enormous cheese. Rather, they have to do with site capacity. Organizers reported in the 2000s:

> The attendance at the event has far outgrown the location where it has traditionally been held for several hundred years: last year, more than 15,000 people tried to attend, which is more than three times the capacity of the site.[3]

The Guardian reported that Robin Hammond, of the Really Exciting Adventure Club, said:

I do understand the issues about the crowd, but wish that the local authorities had worked harder to ensure that we don't lose another part of our English culture to issues of crowd health and safety. Admittedly, last year had a record turnout to the event, which only goes to show how great this event is, with it being watched and talked about worldwide. I am sure that the local area benefits from the custom the crowds bring, so surely the local authorities have had time enough to consider the health and safety of this event.[4]

Participant Mike Smith told *The Guardian*, when confronted with cancellation, that he was 'dreadfully disappointed with the news. As a cheese-roller of many years, I look forward to the chance to really injure myself each year. I have no idea how I'll hurt myself this year now.'[5]

Jean Jeffries, a long-term resident of the area, says that her family history traces cheese rolling back to the 1700s.

I think maybe it was a 'rite of passage' for local lads who practised all year and treated the hill with some respect, knowing the route to take. It has only been a throw-yourself-off-the-top event in more recent history.[6]

In 2023 cheese rolling once more appeared in the news, beset by concerns from vegans. PETA have asked the event to use a vegan cheese. PETA's vice-president of Vegan Corporate Projects, Dawn Carr, protested that the hunted cheese is 'made by expelling fluid from the underside of an unwilling Gloucester cow'.[7]

There had at the time of writing been no response from the organizers, other than to tell the press that they were too busy organizing the event to respond to PETA's plea. But the cheese rolling was then in the news again in late May 2023 due to the lack of police and paramedics to cover the event. This has apparently resulted from 'no formal plans' being submitted to the local constabulary by the organizers. It rather appears that those who run the event have decided to duck under any considerations of health and safety legislation by ignoring them. However, I wrote this the day before the 2023 Cheese Roll, and the next day it went ahead, with at least some medical assistance, since the woman who won it, Canadian Delaney Irving, only realized she had won when she woke up in the medical tent, having been knocked out during the chase itself. She told *The Guardian* that the race was 'good . . . now that I remember it.'

Twenty-eight-year-old Mancunian Matt Crolla won the first race, commenting that 'I don't think you can train for it, can you? It's just being an idiot.'[8] *The Guardian* also asked Japanese contestant Ryoya Minami why he'd entered and he replied, 'Because I like cheese,' which isn't an entirely satisfactory explanation to my mind.

Thus, at the time of writing, the cheese roll is still going strong, despite concerns about its safety – surely one of the most eccentric customs in the British folk calendar.

Interview with Nimue Brown, Spaniel in the Works

The folk customs I am going to mention are mini versions of major customs. I run a theatre company – Spaniel in the

Works – and as part of the 2012 Olympics celebration I worked with Gloucestershire Archives to tour libraries and other venues performing Forgotten Sporting Heroes of Gloucestershire, as well as a workshop with mini versions of traditional Gloucestershire sports, some of which were in the Cotswold Olympics. These included Spurring the Barre – Gloucestershire answer to tossing the caber – and mini cheese rolling.

The main thing with these was to engage children and families with traditions in Gloucestershire. The mini cheese rolling involves a good scale model of Coopers Hill and rolling Babybel cheeses down the hill to see who could get it the furthest. We could often see which libraries were the cleanest from the amount of dirt the cheese collected.

Spurring the Barre involved tossing the inside cardboard roll from a carpet – again to see how far it could go.

I think the point of these events was to entertain, educate and inform about Gloucestershire traditions which might be disappearing. So yes they are important to the identity of the county. As are the folk tales we perform in our show *Dark Tales of Gloucestershire.*

How has your chosen custom changed during your engagement with it? Has it become more diverse, for instance?

Diversity with the initial library tour was very clear, with a wide range of children and families from different ethnic and socio-economic groups taking part.

Do you think interest in your folk custom is diminishing or growing?

I'd like to think that doing the mini versions increases interest in folk customs from the county.

Is there a transgressive element to your chosen custom?

When I moved to Stroud sixteen years ago, we went to see the cheese rolling, but it was cancelled because the mountain rescue team who had to be there for health and safety were called away to an earthquake in Mexico!!

While competitors might be risk-averse, the event organizers take the risks seriously.

TEN

Street Football

Today, we tend to think of football as a sport that is carried out either professionally, with big league players earning enormous sums of money, or at an amateur level on local playing fields, with a bunch of mates kicking a ball around on a Saturday morning. But historically, the beautiful game is rather wider than this, with local town or village-based football matches forming a significant part of the customs of the year.

Shrovetide is the traditional time to hold a local football match, dating back to the twelfth century, and this is still the case today in some areas, such as Ashbourne in Derbyshire. Why Shrovetide? And why football?

Just as cheese rolling is said to be an ancient Phoenician custom, there are some wilder theories about the origins of football, not least that it is a vestige of a custom in which a human head was lobbed into the crowd and kicked about. While our tribal ancestors could – at least according to Roman accounts – be pretty savage, there's no evidence for this. Unfortunately, some valuable evidence was lost in the 1890s when a fire wiped out records at the Royal Shrovetide Committee Office. However, suggestions that this early kind of football, sometimes known as 'hugball' (which sounds more like rugby), were related to an event called the Winchelsea Streete

Game hold rather more water, even if the Game does involve an object called the Frenchman's Head.

The Winchelsea Streete Game is not a Shrovetide custom but is held on Boxing Day in Castle Street in Winchelsea, East Sussex. The aim is for three teams, rather than the customary two, to gain control of the Frenchman's Head, aka the ball, and send it into a goal, namely a barrel at the end of the street. Like many of these football-based customs, the composition of the teams is loose, especially by professional football standards; passing hikers are hardly invited to play at Arsenal, for instance, but at Winchelsea they are welcome. A typical game is fast and furious, lasting about twenty minutes, and does not have much in the way of rules; the barrel (lately, a large green bin) is moveable, held by a marshal, and the only main rule is that the ball has to reach the goal.

The Game started several hundred years ago, possibly in the fourteenth century, and was an expression of defiance against the French during the Hundred Years War. Winchelsea as one of the prime south coast ports at that time, and had been besieged by the French navy.

This particular custom has been suppressed in previous decades because of, you've guessed it, antisocial behaviour, and there is video footage, for example from 2017, showing how violent this can get. Commentary on the YouTube video remarks that it's 'a bit like a civilised English street fight'. One person lost a tooth and someone else was tackled and went down on the pavement, although no one seems to have been actually hospitalized, which is more than one can say about the cheese rolling. In another year, the goal was stolen, and in 2010 there was an ongoing row about the score.

There are mentions of football in the fourteenth century. An Oxford student, one Thomas of Salisbury, found his brother Adam lying dead, apparently as a result of an assault from some Irish students when he was playing ball in the street. Early football hooliganism was clearly a thing. In 1314, football was banned by decree of the king, Edward II. The Lord Mayor of the City of London issued a declaration on his behalf:

> Forasmuch as there is great noise in the city caused by hustling over large foot balls in the fields of the public from which many evils might arise which God forbid: we command and forbid on behalf of the king, on pain of imprisonment, such game to be used in the city in the future.[1]

The French followed suite in 1331, banning the game known as La Soule. Later, in 1363 in England, Edward III also banned football, along with handball. Some authorities have suggested that this points to the emergence of basic rules. (Obviously, in modern football, the ball is never handled, unlike rugby or American football, but as we shall see, this isn't a regulation in most street football games.)

In the 1400s football is mentioned as part of a baptism (in case you're imagining the baby being booted about the church, one assumes that this took place as a friendly match after the christening itself). In 1410, however, Henry IV, following the line set by his predecessors, issued a statement setting fines on the authorities in towns in which football took place, further indication of the disapprobation in which the game continued to be held. It was banned again in 1548 by Edward VI on the grounds that it provoked riots. In 1583 Puritan pamphleteer Philip Stubbs referred to it crossly as a 'devilish pastime ... a bloody and murderous practice'.[2] Even from early times, therefore, football has had an association with grassroots violence.

> Bruised muscles and broken bones
> Discordant strife and futile blows
> Lamed in old age, then cripled withal
> These are the beauties of football.[3]

The 'beautiful game' indeed! But records show that organizations such as the Worshipful Company of Brewers were hiring out premises to groups that played football, so it's questionable how effective these royal bans actually were. Gradually, football became more acceptable. Cromwell was known to play, and the retinue of Mary, Queen of Scots, is also on record as holding a friendly match at one point.

At this time, however, we perhaps need to differentiate between street football that is tied to a particular time of the year, such as Shrovetide or Christmas, and football that consists of just kicking a ball around randomly.

In Ashbourne, Shrovetide football probably dates to the seventeenth century. Charles Cotton's poem 'Burlesque upon the Great Frost', written in 1683, mentions it:

> Two towns, that long that war had raged
> Being at football now engaged
> For honour, as both sides pretend,
> Left the brave trial to be ended
> Till the next thaw for they were frozen

On either part at least a dozen,
With a good handsome space between 'em
Like Rollerich stones, if you've seen 'em
And could no more run, kick, or trip ye
Than I can quaff off Aganippe.[4]

A game was held in nearby Derby, too, but it was banned in 1846. It's possible – ironically, given the origins of the Winchelsea Streete Game – that there may be links between the Ashbourne football match and a similar custom in Picardy. French folk historian Laurent Fournier has drawn some connections between the two, and believes that it may derive from the presence of the Cockayne family, who arrived with the Norman conquest and whose seat is at Ashbourne. But these types of ball games are very old: Nennius mentions them in his ninth-century *Historia Brittonum*, and the Roman game Harpastum is similar to some of the Shrovetide matches. Hurling is also a possible ancestor, played throughout the Celtic regions of the country. William Fitzstephen, writing in the 1100s, commented:

every year on the day called Shrove-Tuesday – the boys of the respective schools bring to the masters each one his fighting cock, and they are indulged all the morning with seeing their cocks fight in the school room. After dinner all the young men of the city go into the fields in the suburbs and address themselves to the famous game of foot-ball. The scholars of each school have their own peculiar ball: and the particular trades have most of them theirs. The elders of the city, the fathers of the parties, and the rich and wealthy, come to the field on horseback, in order to behold the exercises of the youth.[5]

Again, however, parallel development is not the same as linear descent, and we don't know which one is going on here – although the street football that we are looking at in this chapter is genuinely old. From the thirteenth to the fifteenth century, street ball games had become common, not only at Shrovetide but at other major Christian festivals such as Easter and Christmas (you'll note that the Winchelsea game is held on Boxing Day). Sometimes called 'mob football', technically some of these events are not football at all, since the ball can be thrown and may not even be a ball at all – for instance, as in the leather tube used in Haxey Hood or a leather bottle. The Atherstone and Sedgefield Ball Games are examples of these local competitions, as is La Soule, a similar custom in northern France. These can sometimes be grandiose, as in the magnificently titled Shrove Tuesday Football Ceremony of the Purbeck Marblers, which is part of a sequence of apprentice rites, initiating apprentice stonecutters into the profession.

In Ashbourne, where one of the most well-known Shrovetide matches is held, an early regulation forbids murder or manslaughter – perhaps this should have gone without saying, but there is a rule of thumb that you don't generally have a rule against something unless it's at least a possibility. And it is not for the faint-hearted. Participant Mark Harrison comments:

> I've got friends who are Up'ards, sure, but I'd think nothing of belting them, whether it's my butcher or

my brother-in-law. If someone comes toward me with
the ball, I don't see the point in tussling with them for
it. It's easier to just hit him and take it.[6]

A more modern rule is that the ball should not be trans-
ferred in a car. The dividing line is the Henmore Brook and
the two teams are known as the Up'ards, from north of the
brook who are said to perform best in wide fields, and the
Down'ards, from the south, said to perform better in narrow
spaces. The game starts at 2 p.m. and if a goal is scored before
5 p.m. the match is restarted, otherwise it ends when a goal is
scored after 5 p.m. with a final deadline of 10 p.m. It follows
the same format over two days: Shrove Tuesday itself and Ash
Wednesday. *Men's Health* magazine sent a journalist along in
2016, who described the Down'ards rallying speech, delivered
by team captain Brendan Harwood, as 'Churchillian':

> Over these two days we are a band of brothers. We may
> not have the numbers they've got, but we have the heart.
> We'll smash them through the car parks, we'll smash
> them through the fields and we'll smash them through
> the rivers. Plus, we haven't won in six years, so let's smash
> the smiles off those Up'ards' faces![7]

Played since 1667, nowadays the match starts in a supermarket car park and then progresses all across the town, its streets
and alleyways ('jittles'), parks and a pond. The teams have different goals – Sturston Mill for the northern team and Clifton
Mill for the southern team – which are about 3 miles apart.
These were actual water mills at one point, and the winning

team would originally have to enter the mill house and tap the ball against the mill wheel, but since the mills have gone now, a plinth on each site stands in for the wheel. The ball is carried, often in a 'hug' consisting of a large number of participants so that, as per Mr Harrison's comments above, it is hard to extract without some degree of force. Players train for the match and eat for it, too: one participant told the press that he had consumed sausage meat wrapped in bacon, a naan bread and a stir fry plus some cheese on the morning of the match (one has to admire his sheer fortitude in still being able to run around Ashbourne after all that).

The Shrovetide game has a reputation for rowdiness and violence: shops tend to board up their windows, and the game is banned from places such as the graveyard and the Memorial Gardens (also from private property, which is probably a relief to Ashbourne's more timid citizens), but not from the river, where one of the goal plinths is situated. A degree of heavy drinking is said to take place before the 'turning up' at the start. If you're planning on attending this event, you'd better have a liking for crowds, since Ashbourne football can involve several thousand people spectating and at least a hundred actual participants, and you will also need to take a robust attitude to physical injury. The beautifully painted ball itself contains cork, so that if it should end up in the river it doesn't simply sink. Once it's goaled, the person who scored that goal gets to take it home. In a piece on the game, *Men's Health* notes:

> This is a game of blood, guts and inter-town rivalry, forged along the muddy paths of medieval Britain. An Easter egg hunt, with a single oversized cork football

the object of pursuit, the only prize a bloody nose and a pat on the back in the pub.[8]

This version of Shrovetide football often has a celebrity who starts the whole thing off: footballer Stanley Matthews and (the then) Prince Charles have both done the honours in the past. The Up'ards have been largely victorious in recent years, including the most recent game of 2024. That year, participant Nathan Harrison told the BBC:

> My family are quite thick with Shrovetide blood – it goes quite far back so I've always had that pressure over my head. It feels really good to join that line of ball scorers.
>
> We had a few skirmishes during the day – me and my cousin broke off with it [the ball] and hid on a roof with it. I thought something might come of that but it ended up not going that way and we had to throw it back off the roof and it was chaos again.[9]

Although most of the players are men (a lot are local football or rugby players), this is not a wholly male activity. Doris Mugglestone goaled for the Up'ards and Doris Sowter for the Down'ards on Ash Wednesday in 1943. One spectator wrote:

> A hug (rugby-like scrum) immediately formed and the muscled men started shouting, flailing their arms everywhere. I stood back from the hug a little to judge exactly how rough or violent it would be. During this time a chap politely passed in front of me repeatedly saying 'excuse me' to anyone in his way. It took a few

seconds for the crowd to realise it was actually this chap that had the ball.

He had managed to move a small distance from the plinth but then had several hundred men running after him. He didn't have the ball for long.

At any one time there would be at least 10 men holding the ball. If they managed to keep hold of it, the ball would move slowly – but if a competitor managed to take possession it would move very quickly before being bogged down by a pile of men again. Sometimes the ball would be thrown into the air causing pandemonium.[10]

Strategy is straightforward but, from the perspective of a regular football match, unorthodox. Down'ards say that getting the ball into the river early is essential and one of the best ways to do this is by taking it into the pub and over the back wall of the pub's beer garden. *Men's Health* was told by one participant, 'I nearly drowned some fucker in the river just now. It got fruity in that water. Now, where's my wife, she's got my bottle of whisky.'[11]

An (anonymous) writer notes, however, that they saw only one policeman, and there were fewer injuries than anticipated:

Nevertheless – the danger of the situation and lack of authority means everyone is looking out for each other. If you fall over – someone will pick you up, if you get squashed – someone will make space for you, and if you don't like it – then people will attempt to move aside to let you get away from the crowd.[12]

There has been only one death recorded in the game's history, and this was the result of a heart attack. A medieval image in the British Museum (not necessarily relating to Ashbourne) shows a number of men with a ball and one on the ground, possibly with a broken arm. An early health and safety warning about the dangers of street footy?

The mayor of Ashbourne in 2016, Ian Bates, was 83 years old and a participant in the game for 45 years:

> I cannot emphasise enough how important Shrovetide is to Ashbourne. I remember back in the '60s, a young Down'ard wanted to score so he could keep the ball, and decided it'd be easier to score an own goal. There were members of his family that died decades later still refusing to speak to him.[13]

An annual football game is also held at Alnwick, in Northumberland. This dates from 1762 and was held between the parishes of St Michael and St Paul. It's more formal than the Ashbourne game, and smaller. Although there are a hundred people or so in each team, the goals are only 365 metres (400 yd) apart. In the early days, the ball was sent over the barbican and, like Ashbourne, the game ranged over the whole town. This changed in the 1820s and the game was shifted to the fields beyond the castle. The teams are made up of both men and women, and the ball may be handled or kicked. The Duke of Northumberland traditionally starts the game by throwing the ball from the castle. Whoever scores two 'hales', or goals, wins the match but the ball is then thrown into the river Aln – if you want to keep it, you have to swim down and retrieve it!

Spectators have described the game to the BBC as 'an afternoon of enjoyable madness'.[14]

The Atherstone Ball Game, also held on Shrove Tuesday, in Atherstone, Warwickshire, commemorates the 'match of gold' between the two counties of Warwickshire and Leicestershire in 1109, with the significant incentive of a bag of gold as a ball. Warwickshire won. Like other football matches, it has few rules (as with Ashbourne, you're not allowed to kill anyone) and is held between 3 and 5 p.m. on the old Roman road now known as the Long Street. Whoever is holding the ball when the whistle is blown at 5 p.m. wins the match. This match is policed: it can become violent, although reports of a man's ear being ripped off in 2019, the 820th game, appear to be exaggerated. Chief marshal and chairman Rob Bernard says:

> I've seen the videos and they didn't look good, especially when it was at the start when all the guests, dignitaries and cameras are all looking down. All eyes are on the fighting. We discussed it as a committee that night and it's not on, it's hard to say what we can do about it, though. In the past, when things have got out of hand, we've put it out there that the future of the Ball Game is under threat and it calms down a bit the following year.
>
> I know some of the lads who were involved and I've spoken to them, they threaten the future of the Ball Game.
>
> But then it comes back again. It is the nature of it. It's nothing new, if you look on Pathé News to the 1950s and 60s, you will see what they were getting up to back then, it's always been there.

But what we've got now is everyone has phones, everything is crystal clear and they can chop together all the worst bits and that's all people see.[15]

However, the West Midlands Ambulance Service told the press that no injuries had been brought to their attention and the police reported that no arrests had been made. Bernard also told the press:

We have no idea where it came from about someone's ear being ripped off. There were images with blood all over the ball that didn't look great but it certainly wasn't anything to do with anyone's ear.[16]

The ball game organization seems to have a strong relationship with the police, with Sergeant Neal Pearsall having been liaison with the committee for around twenty years. He told the *Coventry Telegraph*:

I have policed the ball game on and off for nearly 20 years and due to its nature and traditional values there will always be a level of violence involved. The people who take part, spectate and the actual players are aware of this. However, if any violence does take place it will always be highlighted to the town council for review.

The ball game is unique and has been a part of Atherstone culture and tradition for over 800 years and is organized by the town council and local community, for the local community.[17]

Bernard is keen to emphasize that the game has a charitable component: the ball is paraded round pubs in the weeks leading up to the ball game and donations are taken for that year's selected charity or charities. He has lamented that the reputation of the game gets marred by occasional outbreaks of violence or 'score settling', which dominate the headlines. But one might speculate that these football games are in a way a means for communities to let off steam, for scores *to* be settled, even illicitly. That this catharsis is not popular with the authorities can be seen from the litany of royal bans across the ages that we outlined above, but this does not mean that they do not play a role in both resolving community issues and in binding communities together. Atherstone has been described by its committee as 'our Christmas Day' and like the cheese rolling and other grassroots events there is an evident popularity remaining for them in a culture that has become increasingly (and in many cases rightly) safety conscious.

Children are thrown sweets and a golden penny but are then taken away to safety. In Atherstone, the teams are mainly composed of adult men. The astute reader will note that the participants quoted are all male, but there are exceptions. Little Inverness (Midlothian) held a game in which the two sides were represented by married and unmarried women. Any suggestion that this was less bloodthirsty is probably optimistic.

Haxey Hood is, similarly, one of these community football matches, although in this case the 'ball' is a long leather tube known as the 'hood'. This stems from a piece of local folklore in which the fourteenth-century Lady de Mowbray was riding over the hill near Haxey when her long silk hood blew off. A group of farmworkers chased it over the fields and finally caught it, but the one who did so was too shy to give it back to Lady de Mowbray and gave it to another farmhand who returned it. Lady de Mowbray, greatly amused by the episode, gave 13 acres to the community on condition that the chase was re-enacted every year.

Historically, this is impossible to verify but if it was pinned to a particular Lord of the Manor, the custom would have started around 1359 and thus the Haxey Hood is one of the oldest of these football and chase customs in the country. It does not, however, have its origins in an ancient solar rite. Folklorist Venetia Newall put paid to this longstanding hypothesis in the 1980s and has demonstrated that it's a fairly typical Twelfthtide custom that has lasted into the present day.[18]

As a postscript to these accounts of street football, an honourable mention must go to the World Black Pudding Throwing Championships, currently held at the Royal Oak pub in Ramsbottom near Manchester. Participants are armed with three black puddings apiece with the aim of knocking Yorkshire puddings off a 7.6-metre-high plinth (readers of a certain age may remember the popular TV show *The Goodies*, featuring the mythical northern martial art of Ecky Thump, in which you are armed with black puddings). As *Northern Life Magazine* notes, 'The symbolism is less than subtle.'[19]

The origins of the competition are said to lie in the Wars of the Roses, in which, after a pitched battle, the combatants ran out of ammunition and had to resort to a food fight instead. This is almost certainly not true, but it does lend an amusing origin story to the current practice!

The Kirkwall Ba'

Street football is played in Scotland, too, also dating from medieval times. These Ba' (ball) games are found throughout the country, including Kirkwall and St Ola in Orkney, where the Ba' is the last of the Christmas football games that used to be played in many communities across the island. Here, the two sides are the Uppies and Doonies (Up the Gates and Doon the Gates), but people come from all over Orkney to play it. Doonies have to get the ball into the sea, whereas Uppies have to take it further up the town, round the Lang to the Catholic church.

The Boys Ba' has no age limit downwards – you have to be under fifteen to play, but kids as young as five have been known to take part. Around a hundred children take part. The aim is to grab the ball and take it to the goal, and there's no time limit. In 1985 the game lasted a mere four minutes but in 2019 it went on for six hours. The Men's Ba' takes place a little later in the day, from 1 p.m. onwards, and the numbers here can be up to 350 people. The game ranges through the narrow streets of Kirkwall and can last quite a while. Debate as to who actually scores, and therefore gets to keep the handmade, cork-filled Ba', can last for some time. Due to the lack of a time limit and flexibility in terms of how long it takes to score a goal, the Boys' Game and the Men's Game can end up running alongside one another.

The game found itself affected by modern medicine, as formerly you were designated an Uppie or Doonie according to your place of birth; Doonies were born north of the cathedral. But Kirkwall's new hospital in the 1950s gave a heavy bias to the Uppies. However, participation from non-Orkneyites is not encouraged, largely due to health and safety reasons – if you've grown up with the game you can be expected to understand its hazards, whereas if you're new to it you're more likely to get hurt. Broken ribs are not uncommon after scrums form and collapse, rather like rugby.

These are Christmas-tide games, played on Christmas Day and Hogmanay. The Ba' is at least three hundred years old and, as with all these events, there is plenty of folklore to explain its origins. It's said to be the re-enactment of the slaying of an evil Scots lord named Tusker by an Orcadian boy called Sigurd. Having slain Tusker, beheaded him and carried his head back to Kirkwall, one of the tyrant's teeth pierced the boy's leg as the head hung on the saddlebow. Sigurd made it to the Mercat Cross, threw the head into the crowd and then died. Enraged, the townspeople kicked Tusker's head through the streets of the city and eventually this became the Ba'.

This story is in turn said to have its origins in the *Orkneyinga Saga*, in which Orkney's first earl, Sigurd Eysteinsson, travels to Scotland and kills Earl Maelbrigte Tusk. The story about the tooth and the death of Sigurd from infection appears here, too. Orcadian folklorists have sometimes tied this up to accounts of severed heads in Celtic legend, such as Gawain and the Green Knight, but this remains purely speculative. They also connect it to more local lore, such as the equinoctial battles between sea spirits the Sea-Mither and Teran, who are half-yearly rulers, battling it out in March and September for governorship of winter and summer.

They also tie up the Ba' to Norse ball games, such as that in the Icelandic *Saga of Gisli the Outlaw*:

Now they began the game, and Thorgrim could not hold his own. Gisli threw him and bore away the ball. Again Gisli wished to catch the ball, but Thorgrim runs and holds him, and will not let him get near it. Then Gisli turned and threw Thorgrim such a fall on the slippery ice that he could scarce rise. The skin came off his knuckles, and the flesh off his knees, and the blood gushed from his nostrils. Thorgrim was very slow in rising. As he did so he looked to Vestein's house and chanted:

'Right through his ribs
My spearpoint went crashing; Why should I worry?
'Twas well worth this thrashing.'

Gisli caught the ball on the bound, and hurled it between Thorgrim's shoulders, so that he tumbled forward, and threw his heels up in the air, and Gisli chanted:

'Bump on the back
My big ball went dashing:
Why should I worry?
'Twas I gave the thrashing.'

Thorkel jumps up and says: 'Now we can see who is the strongest or the best player. Let us break off the game?' and so they did.'[20]

Journalist Srijandeep Das reports:

It breaks out twice a year at a time when peace and good-will might be expected to prevail, the warring armies engaging in close combat with a ferocity that precludes respect for person or property. Even the law has been known to stand impotent as combatants surged and counter-surged through the environs of the police station, and memory has hardly dimmed the occasion when the local manse was invaded and despoiled. Casualties are high – but who cares? Crushed ribs and broken limbs are never enough reasons for the enthusiastic participants to desist from this traditional orgy of Orcadian violence which not even a sheriff's edict could ban – the Kirkwall Ba' Game.[21]

The documented origins of the Ba' game, played in the eighteenth century, shows that it took place on a field and the ball was kicked, like modern football, and never picked up – the current Ba' seems to have gone backwards in form! By 1850, handling the ball had become common, possibly due to an increasing number of participants and more restricted space in the narrow confines of Kirkwall.

The Ba's themselves are made in the Orkneys and there is a new one for each game. They're filled with cork so that they float, and one Ba' maker estimated that each ball took around four days to put together.

ELEVEN

Up Helly Aa

In the last week of January, in Lerwick in Scotland, the streets are lit by one of the UK's main fire celebrations: Up Helly Aa, where a replica of a Viking galley is set aflame and pushed out to sea. This is very much a volunteer-led community event – you are allowed to watch, but you're not permitted to participate until you've lived in Shetland for five years. In order to become a Guizer Jarl – head of the committee – you will need to have served on the committee for sixteen years. There's also a Junior Jarl, since local schools are closely involved.

Surely any custom involving a Viking ship must be very old? According to the committee, not so; there seems to have been a day marked as Antonmas or Up Helly Night 24 days after Christmas, but this was in rural Shetland rather than Lerwick itself. These festivities, suggest the committee, date from since the Napoleonic War, when sailors began to flock into the town (and, one presumes, brought gunpowder with them). In 1824 a Methodist minister visiting Lerwick on Olde Christmas Eve noted:

> the whole town was in an uproar: from twelve o'clock last night until late this night blowing of horns, beating of drums, tinkling of old tin kettles, firing of guns, shouting, bawling, fiddling, fifeing, drinking, fighting.

This was the state of the town all night – the street was thronged with people as any fair I ever saw in England.[1]

The minister does not sound impressed to have had his sleep interrupted. He would have been horrified some years later, when blazing tar barrels were incorporated into the festivities, as had become common in Bonfire celebrations down south, described by one observer thus:

two tubs fastened to a great raft-like frame knocked together at the Docks, whence the combustibles were generally obtained. Two chains were fastened to the bogie supporting the capacious tub or tar-barrel . . . yoked to these were two strong ropes on which a motley mob, wearing masks for the most part, fastened. A party of about a dozen was told off to stir up the molten contents.[2]

The story from then on mirrors that of the Bonfire Societies. The proceedings are rowdy and dangerous; the streets of Lerwick are narrow. The more respectable members of the community complained. Special constables were brought in to police the event, with limited success. Unusually, however, change came from within in the 1870s when a group of young intellectuals in the town decided to dignify proceedings. They invented a name, Up Helly Aa (probably taken from 'Upholiday', an old name for Twelfth Day); a series of costumes ('guising'); and a more formal, less anarchic structure to the whole thing. Ronald Hutton points out that this was sponsored by the Total Abstinence Society in 1870s, in an effort to provide an alternative to the alcohol-fuelled revelry of Christmas and New Year.[3] Gradually, a Viking theme became incorporated. The ship itself was brought in during the 1880s and the Guizer Jarl was introduced in 1906.

This is therefore a relatively modern festival, a typical product of nineteenth-century folk revivalism and enthusiasm, and despite its intellectual origins, it became a decidedly working-class festival. The smug and respectable were mocked, via the Up Helly Aa bill. The festival thus qualifies for inclusion in our list of customs that have an element of social mockery, and it made Up Helly Aa unpopular with not a few people.

The bill continues today, rather in the same manner as the effigy burnings in places such as Lewes, but it can take some surprising forms. The festival was cancelled in 2022, as one of the many casualties of COVID-19, but the bill was still posted. It read:

Tho' wir annual dramatic performance is on the rocks again, there's signs that the reign of the villainous baddies Covido and Omicrono is at last on the wane, thanks to the magic of our heroes Pfizer, AstraZeneca and BioNTechio.

They were helped by many thousands of good fairies and elves, who jabbed their way through the masses to give us immunity and sent those nasty little buggers packing. This boast seems to be a passport to less testing times ahead – and remind us that every day, normal activity is a day nearer.'

It then went on to list the Marshal's instructions:

1. Strange to say perhaps, positive guizers must stay at home, while negative guizers are free to mingle.

(Don't shoot the messenger – we didn't make these
    rules!)

2. Positive guizers needn't feel disconsolate – they
    get a week at home!

3. Positive contact between partying guizers could
    result in a Peculiar testing experience – beware!

4. Relay [*sic*] desperate guizers unable to resist the
    urge to march are reminded forcibly that charity
    around the halls is a privilege not a right.

5. If you must go with the flow, 'Flow' before you go!

6. As is usual on the night 'Keep dee mask on!!'

Wir Grand Old Viking Festival Up Helly Aa's undone
Still dark the torch, un-formed da march, still mute
    da rollin drum
Yet sleep wir mighty memories – but surely day will come
Wir rave will yet roll on!
Stand fast Vikings, fuelled up on traditions cast,
Yet wir battle-songs'll thunder on da blast,
Wir wild festive foy'll ring oot as in times past,
We'll welcome it, Oh Boy!
Roll oot glorious new pages,
In wir saga through da ages,
When wir jobs da plague engages,
Be safe and sound as wel
Floats da vaccine safely o'er us,
Soon wir dragon ship will land;
Virus banished fae wir chorus!
When we raise da flaming brand!
Guizers all passported fully,

Ere they join wir vaccined throng;
Covid-free and boosted truly-
Clear to feast and dance all night long;
'Cos we'll all be full of antibods,
Roll on '23' wir song!
We Norsemen – home – miss days gone by
When we were marching free:
But pure tradition can't defy
Da plague fae ower-sea.
So let wis ne'er forget da crew
Wha bravely fought an strived
To bring wis jabs so's we could save
Wir festive spree – wir pride![4]

At the bottom of this is a stern note that says: 'DEFACERS OF THIS BILL WILL BE SEND [*sic*] FOR SOME STARTLING TREATMENT AT THE LODBERRY!

So the old custom of mockery continues, but the target is now a virus, rather than a person. Unlike the nineteenth century, the parade now has a quite strict health and safety policy. The parade is under the control of Police Scotland, and the press is also controlled and given designated photo opportunities. A very calmly stated instruction is that 'You should also refrain from distracting guizers when they are carrying burning torches.' Marshals are easily identified, as they are dressed as Vikings.

The day begins just after 8 a.m., when the Guizer Jarl and his team progress around the town, accompanied by pipe bands. Songs are sung at the Market Cross. Later there is a civic reception at the Town Hall and the parade then visits hospitals, schools and nursing homes. Evening proceedings start around 7 p.m.

Unlike street football, this is highly organized, and the routes are clearly marked and adhered to.

TWELVE

Trick or Treat

We've looked at the 'money with menaces' aspect of customs like Wassailing earlier, and it's now time to pay some attention to another controversial custom, that of 'trick or treating' at Hallowe'en. Whenever the national press run an article on this, someone invariably bemoans the prevalence of an 'American' custom contaminating wholesome British ways, but is trick or treat a purely U.S. phenomenon, or was it home-grown?

Samhain, the pagan equivalent of Hallowe'en, is the great festival of the dead and of honouring the ancestors. Its history is murky, like all festivals. Conventional wisdom has it that Christianity stole many of the old pagan holidays, but with Samhain, it's particularly difficult to make this claim. There's very little evidence that the ancient Celts regarded it as the start of the New Year, as modern Pagans do now. It seems to have been a festival based on the slaughter of cattle for the winter season. Sometimes tribes lit hilltop fires, sometimes not; it varied across Britain and Ireland. It seems likely that modern Pagans have taken many traditions and customs from the Christian festival of All Soul's, rather than the other way around.

Trick or treating itself has various forms. Usually, it involves going around the neighbourhood in costume and being given treats, for example sweets or a small sum of money (sweets are the most common reward these days), on 31 October. In modern times, householders sometimes indicate whether they're willing to participate by putting a light in the window, such as a pumpkin lit with a candle, or just leaving a bowl of sweets on the front porch (this is risky, since more unscrupulous kids can take the lot). The modern greeting, when the householder opens the door, is 'Trick or treat!' but this is the most recent part of an old custom.

Guising, as this used to be known, dates from the sixteenth century in Ireland and Scotland, where it had a very similar form; guisers would dress in costume and sometimes put on some form of performance. From the fifteenth century, in Ireland and England, people would exchange soul cakes for prayers for the dead, a custom known as 'souling'. In some regions, special songs were sung, analogously to Wassail or carolling. This example is from Cheshire in 1891:

A soul! a soul! a soul-cake!
Please good Missis, a soul-cake!
An apple, a pear, a plum, or a cherry,
Any good thing to make us all merry.
One for Peter, two for Paul,
Three for Him who made us all.

God bless the master of this house,
The mistress also,
And all the little children
That round your table grow.
Likewise young men and maidens,
Your cattle and your store;

And all that dwells within your gates,
We wish you ten times more.

Down into the cellar,
And see what you can find,
If the barrels are not empty,
We hope you will prove kind.
We hope you will prove kind,
With your apples and strong beer,
And we'll come no more a-souling
Till this time next year.

The lanes are very dirty,
My shoes are very thin,
I've got a little pocket
To put a penny in.
If you haven't got a penny,
A ha'penny will do;
If you haven't get a ha'penny,
It's God bless you.[1]

You might recognize this song as part of a Christmas carol: 'Christmas is coming, the geese are getting fat'.

The prayers were intended to help those souls who were still trapped in Purgatory, and it still goes on in some Catholic countries such as Portugal. The cakes themselves are usually spiced (for example, with nutmeg or cinnamon) and are decorated with a cross, rather like hot cross buns but with currants rather than white flour paste. (If you fancy making your own, there are lots of recipes to be found on the Internet.) As the custom of souling itself gradually died out, people continued to bake soul cakes and they could be kept to ensure good luck. Shakespeare makes reference to this in *Two Gentlemen of Verona*: the character Speed complains that his master is 'puling [whimpering or whining] like a beggar at Hallowmas'.

There are records of the practice in Ontario, Canada, dating from 1911. This was, of course, a country that had a large number of Scots and Irish immigrants. It's now common in North America, with first mentions of the practice dating from the 1930s, and has spread down to Mexico, too. Charles Schulz's popular cartoon *Peanuts* featured it in the early 1950s, so it must have been common enough then for readers of the strip to understand the reference, and it also appears in a *Donald Duck* cartoon.

This sort of practice is very old, although its manifestation in different countries is not always connected. Athenaeus of Naucratis, writing in *The Deipnosophists*, speaks of how small groups of children dressed up as swallows would go from house to house asking for treats on the island of Rhodes in exchange for a song. They would threaten to trick the householder if they weren't given anything.

In Scotland, guisers, or 'galoshans' as they were known in certain parts of the country, would carry with them lanterns made out of hollowed-out turnips – the origin of the Jack o'lanterns that in the modern day have become carved out of pumpkins. (If you have ever tried to hollow out a turnip, you'll understand why the pumpkin has overtaken it in popularity, although the realization that one can use an electric drill has led to a small resurgence in turnip-carving.) Some commentators believe that the lantern is to frighten off any evil spirits who might be abroad as the guisers progress around the community, but others suggest that the candle within represents a soul trapped in Purgatory. Lancashire had a custom known as 'lating the witches', in which a procession holding candles climbs a local hill, and in some areas bonfires were lit at this time of year. The dialect word possibly comes from the Saxon 'leoht', 'to light'.

In Ayr, Scotland, in 1890 children are described as wearing masks and carrying turnip lanterns: 'I had mind it was Halloween . . . the wee callans were at it already, rinning aboot wi' their fause-faces (false faces) on and their bits o' turnip lanthrons (lanterns) in their haun (hand).'[2]

In some parts of the world, guisers are still supposed to actually do something to win their 'treat', such as sing a song or recite a poem. 'In costume' is liberally interpreted; for the children in Canada, this sometimes seems to have just meant a large hat, for instance. There have been suggestions that it gained popularity in the USA as a way of controlling a practice that had become increasingly rowdy and aggressive.

In the UK, this particular Hallowe'en custom had more or less died out, at least in England. Growing up in the suburbs of Gloucester in the late 1960s and early '70s, I do not remember anyone trick or treating, although we did have carol singers at Christmas. We did celebrate Hallowe'en to some extent, though – I remember bobbing for apples with the aid of my mother's large jam-making pan. Nor did we practise another old custom, a mild form of spell in which a girl peels an apple and throws the peel over her shoulder; the discarded peel is said to form the initials of a future fiancé or husband. There have been some suggestions that trick or treating itself took off again in the UK after the film *ET* came out, since it's depicted in that movie.

In the nineteenth century, souling became linked to the Mari Lwyd/hooded animal phenomenon, though with a different name since this took place over the border in England. In Cheshire the horse figure is named Old Hob, and in the Cheshire village of Warburton it was known as Old Warb. As with the Maris, the group accompanying it would progress around the neighbourhood soliciting money or drink, but Cheshire also had souling plays, too, with themes of death and rebirth, which involved the central figure of a horse's skull: if two groups of soulers met, they were obliged to try to break the other group's skull. Villages in Cheshire still perform some of these plays, and still involve the horse; essentially, this is a form of mumming play. In Wales, the custom was also explicitly linked to death and resurrection, named *hel bwyd cennady meirw* – 'collecting the food of the messenger of the dead'. In this version of the custom, the person who knocks on the door is the messenger of death.

Some contemporary witches follow the custom of the Dumb Supper at this time of year, in which a place is laid at a dinner table for someone who has died during the previous year; the ensuing meal is carried out in silence and, particularly in the USA, is served backwards with the cutlery reversed (so that you start with dessert and then progress to the main course). This has morphed from a previous custom in which the Dumb Supper is a form of love spell; mainly carried out by women, in this version the empty place at the table will hopefully be occupied by a vision of a future husband. In contemporary Paganism, the love magic of Hallowe'en and the 'thin veil' ghost-ridden May Eve seem to be swapping roles. In southern states of the USA, mothers occasionally set up their sons to erupt in through the window of a Dumb Supper as a prank.

In some parts of the USA now, trick or treat has turned into 'trunk or treat', in which organizations will give out sweets from the boots (trunks) of cars in a local car park. This has the dual advantage of not having to traipse around the neighbourhood with your children and also dispenses with the 'trick' element of the custom. In Canada, kids used to ask for 'Hallowe'en apples' but there was a rash of scare stories in the press at one point about razor blades being concealed in them. It is likely that this was nothing more than an urban myth, but not unnaturally it put parents off. Stories about poisoned sweets are also almost certainly untrue as well, but they're an old urban legend, starting, some folklorists have suggested, during the Industrial Revolution. These myths contain all sorts of worries and concerns, as is common with most urban legends – fears about strangers, anxieties about contaminated or adulterated food, and anxiety about one's children. Horror movies have not helped. There is a risk to children at Hallowe'en, at least in the USA; it is the day on which, more than any other, small children are killed by cars.[3] There isn't any arcane explanation for this – obviously, it's the day of the year on which more children are out in their neighbourhoods after dark and possibly in bad weather with poor visibility. I don't know if the same applies in the UK, but I suspect Bonfire Night poses more of a threat; it's still more common in Britain for kids to walk to and from school, for a start, than it is in the USA.

Some of the deaths that have been attributed to poisoned Hallowe'en sweets in the USA turn out to have been from other causes: family members who have murdered children blaming poisoned candy, for instance, and one instance of a child who discovered his uncle's stash of heroin. Some deaths were due to natural causes. Statistically, this also makes sense, along with the road traffic accident stats. If your child has a heart defect and is out and about at the time of an exciting custom, it's not unreasonable to expect health issues. But in 1985 a *Washington Post* poll determined that 65 per cent of American parents were worried about their offspring falling victim to poisoned Hallowe'en candy.[4]

But fears run both ways – not only with regard to the safety of one's own children, but anxieties about what other people's children might do. My father was always a bit nervous about what kids might get up to, not at Hallowe'en per se (it being, as I have said, an era before trick or treating really took off), but at any time of the year. Broken windows and a firework through the letterbox were the main sources of concern (neither of these things ever actually happened to us, I should add). Today, I suggest that the main form of 'trick' is the dressing up; you might realize that the diminutive zombie on your front doorstep is not a real flesh-eating revenant, but the child is probably delighting in the possibility of scaring the living daylights out of an adult, especially if you utter a pretend scream. 'Mischief night' in places such as Liverpool, in which teenagers might glue up your car door's lock, for instance, is another example.

In Alberta, Canada, in the 1920s the local press took a stern view:

> Hallowe'en night was observed in the usual manner by the young 'bloods' in Penhold. 'Fun is fun, and tricks are tricks', but when such public buildings as school and Memorial Hall are molested with no option for 'Treat or Trick', we cannot see where either fun or trick is enjoyed by the participants.[5]

Some parts of the USA restrict the age of trick or treaters by law: you're not allowed to do it after the age of twelve. Since teenage behaviour can be rowdy and troublesome, particularly when undertaken by groups of young men, as we have seen extensively in this book, some people might regard this as a wise precaution. One American publication, from the 1930s, mentions 'soaping' – using a bar of soap to rub over people's windows and prevent them from seeing out – this is less a trick, perhaps, than a public cleaning service![6] In this, early guising vengeances at Easter or midwinter are echoed; in the past, this usually consisted of throwing stones at someone's house, stealing their gate, blocking the keyhole or leaving broken shards of crockery outside their door to denote a mean, miserly inhabitant. Hurling cabbages was also popular, as was blocking up people's chimneys. In 2022, *Hull Live* cautioned that 'While the phrase may well be "trick or treat", the unspoken rule is that "tricks" are off the table, unless you know your neighbour so well that it's an accepted part of the fun.'[7]

We have mentioned its manifestation in Mexico, but trick or treating is also found in other parts of the world at different times. In regions of Scandinavia, for example, it's conducted around Shrovetide, and children still dress up as witches and ghosts. In Germany and Denmark, it's the turn of New Year's Eve. The supernatural element of the year has shifted focus in the past few hundred years or so: May Eve in the UK was seen as equally numinous as Hallowe'en at one point in our history.

THIRTEEN

Skimmity Riding

Throughout the history of England, in parish annals and in its literary canon, we occasionally come across reference to the practice of 'skimmington' or 'skimmity' riding. This custom may be unfamiliar to the reader, but we'll take a look at it in some depth and note that skimmity rides – in a rather different context – still take place today. The word 'skimmington' may give us an initial clue as to the nature of this practice: it means a large wooden ladle, and wives were sometimes said to use such a kitchen implement to beat their husbands – resulting in the need, according to the social mores of the day, to bring that wife to heel.

The custom is probably most familiar to readers, if at all, from Thomas Hardy's novel *The Mayor of Casterbridge*, in which the resentful Joshua Jopp comes across letters written to his adversary Michael Henchard by Lucetta Le Sueur, who had undertaken an affair with Henchard on Jersey prior to her marriage to the new mayor of Casterbridge. This is taken by the people of Casterbridge as an excuse for a skimmity ride – a public shaming of a woman who has had an illicit affair, and her husband.

'I say, what a good foundation for a skimmity-ride', said Nance.

'True', said Mrs. Cuxsom, reflecting. ''Tis as good a ground for a skimmity-ride as ever I knowed; and it ought not to be wasted. The last one seen in Casterbridge must have been ten years ago, if a day.'

A visitor to the pub overhears the planning of the ride and asks the landlady what it is:

'O, sir!' said the landlady, swinging her long earrings with deprecating modesty; ''tis a' old foolish thing they do in these parts when a man's wife is – well, not too particularly his own. But as a respectable householder I don't encourage it.

'Still, are they going to do it shortly? It is a good sight to see, I suppose?'

'Well, sir!' she simpered. And then, bursting into naturalness, and glancing from the corner of her eye, ''Tis the funniest thing under the sun! And it costs money.'

'Ah! I remember hearing of some such thing. Now I shall be in Casterbridge for two or three weeks to come, and should not mind seeing the performance. Wait a moment.' He turned back, entered the sitting-room, and said, 'Here, good folks; I should like to see the old custom you are talking of, and I don't mind being something towards it – take that.' He threw a sovereign on the table and returned to the landlady at the door, of whom, having inquired the way into the town, he took his leave.

'There were more where that one came from', said Charl when the sovereign had been taken up and handed to the landlady for safe keeping. 'By George! we ought to have got a few more while we had him here.'

'No, no', answered the landlady. 'This is a respectable house, thank God! And I'll have nothing done but what's honourable.'

'Well', said Jopp; 'now we'll consider the business begun, and will soon get it in train.'

'We will!' said Nance. 'A good laugh warms my heart more than a cordial, and that's the truth on't.'

The ride is planned and eventually executed, with Jopp whipping up the townsfolk's enthusiasm. For them, it is a grand jape; for him, it is an act of revenge.

'They are coming up Corn Street after all! They sit back to back!'

'What – two of 'em – are there two figures?'

'Yes. Two images on a donkey, back to back, their elbows tied to one another's! She's facing the head, and he's facing the tail.'

'Is it meant for anybody in particular?'

'Well – it mid be. The man has got on a blue coat and kerseymere leggings; he has black whiskers, and a reddish face. 'Tis a stuffed figure, with a falseface.'

. . .

'What's the woman like? Just say, and I can tell in a moment if 'tis meant for one I've in mind.'

'My – why – 'tis dressed just as she dressed when she sat in the front seat at the time the play-actors came to the Town Hall!'

Lucetta started to her feet, and almost at the instant the door of the room was quickly and softly opened. Elizabeth-Jane advanced into the firelight.

'I have come to see you', she said breathlessly. 'I did not stop to knock – forgive me! I see you have not shut your shutters, and the window is open.'

Without waiting for Lucetta's reply she crossed quickly to the window and pulled out one of the shutters. Lucetta glided to her side. 'Let it be – hush!' she said peremptorily, in a dry voice, while she seized Elizabeth-Jane by the hand, and held up her finger. Their intercourse had been so low and hurried that not a word had been lost of the conversation without, which had thus proceeded: –

'Her neck is uncovered, and her hair in bands, and her backcomb in place; she's got on a puce silk, and white stockings, and coloured shoes.'

Again Elizabeth-Jane attempted to close the window, but Lucetta held her by main force.

''Tis me!' she said, with a face pale as death. 'A procession – a scandal – an effigy of me, and him!'

The look of Elizabeth betrayed that the latter knew it already.

'Let us shut it out', coaxed Elizabeth-Jane, noting that the rigid wildness of Lucetta's features was growing yet more rigid and wild with the meaning of the noise and laughter. 'Let us shut it out!'

'It is of no use!' she shrieked. 'He will see it, won't he? Donald will see it! He is just coming home – and it will break his heart – he will never love me anymore – and O, it will kill me – kill me!'

And it does:

> 'She's me – she's me – even to the parasol – my green
> parasol!' cried Lucetta with a wild laugh as she stepped
> in. She stood motionless for one second – then fell
> heavily to the floor.
>
> Almost at the instant of her fall the rude music of the
> skimmington ceased. The roars of sarcastic laughter went
> off in ripples, and the trampling died out like the rustle
> of a spent wind. Elizabeth was only indirectly conscious
> of this; she had rung the bell, and was bending over
> Lucetta, who remained convulsed on the carpet in the
> paroxysms of an epileptic seizure. She rang again and
> again, in vain; the probability being that the servants had
> all run out of the house to see more of the Daemonic
> Sabbath than they could see within.[1]

The doctor is summoned, but it is too late for poor Lucetta. Like
a number of Hardy's heroines, she is literally shamed to death.

Hardy speaks of the 'din of cleavers, tongs, tambourines,
kits, crouds, humstrums, serpents, rams'-horns, and other historical kinds of music'.[2] Henchard, intending to throw himself
into the river on the news of Lucetta's death, finds that someone has got there ahead of him; he is met by the skimmington
effigy of himself, floating in the water. Lucetta's effigy is discovered further up the river a little later; to avoid being blamed for
her death, the citizens of Casterbridge pretend that they know
nothing of the skimmington ride and have thrown the effigies
in the river to get rid of them. The mayor, though saddened and
angered by the loss of his wife, and ignorant of Jopp's wicked

machinations, puts her death down to an accident caused by the townspeople's desire to put those above them 'to the blush'.[3] He's also reluctant to draw attention to his wife's prior affair and thus lets the matter slide without further investigation. In this, Hardy's understanding of human nature and small rural communities really comes to the fore.

But Hardy's depiction of the skimmity ride was not invented. He would have taken it from real life, for skimmity rides actually took place in England, such as one that occurred in Wiltshire in 1867. (Hardy's novel was written in 1888.) The targets of this real-life skimmity ride were the landlady of the Wheat Sheaf pub and a baker from Lower Heyford.

> George Coggins, a baker from Lower Heyford, was caught committing adultery with Mrs Thomas, wife of the publican of the Wheat Sheaf in Steeple Aston. A railway guard, named Bartlett, spied the couple through a knot in the wooden partition of their train carriage and then looked through the window for a better view.[4]

The villagers of Lower Heyford and Steeple Ashton joined forces and, as in Hardy's novel, proceeded to make a racket 'and the rattle was most noisy: all the old tin and iron utensils I should think to be found in both villages were rattling.'[5] This was evidently a quickly organized shaming, as it took place almost immediately and caused Coggins to hide in the waiting room (we don't know what the landlady did). However, it did not end there. A proper skimmity ride was arranged for the next night, again involving villagers from both places. This time the ride took place outside Coggins' cottage, but the outrage and bullying still did not end and spilled over onto a third night.

> [This] was a most tremendously noisy lew-balling night again. They had effigies of Mrs Thomas and George Coggins – she with a large crinoline and bonnet, and he a stout fellow with his baking apron on.

The effigies were mounted on poles (called stangs) and were made to kiss each other every few minutes. 'The place was swarming, the noise to a high pitch.'

Diana Gardner, writing in the Steeple Ashton archive, notes that there was a witness from Lower Heyford, a law relieving officer named George James Dew, who mentions it in his diary in terms of high approbation: 'I enjoyed it very much because I never saw one carried out so well before!'[6] She goes on to say:

> Such activities were known as rough music, lew balling, riding the stag, stag hunting, ran-tanning or skimming-ton, but in Oxfordshire (as in Dorset) skimmity-riding was the expression used. It was the people's way of expressing their disapproval of any perceived moral laxity such as illegitimacy, wife beating, hen pecking of husbands, a man marrying too young a girl, a wife re-marrying too soon after her husband's death, etc. It became illegal in 1882 but continued none the less.[7]

William Hogarth did two sets of prints relating to such an event: *Hudibras Encounters the Skimmington* (c. 1720–25). This was inspired by an episode in the second part of Samuel

Butler's *Hudibras*, published in 1664, a poem that satirizes the hypocrisy of Puritans during the English Civil War and gives an indication as to how long skimmity riding had been going on for. One of these drawings was purchased by Queen Victoria. In it, you can see objects – apparently clothing – carried on a pole, one of which appears also to bear a pair of horns. In the north of England, this form of public shaming was sometimes called 'stang riding', a stang being a pole carried between two men on which a figure could be mounted. As well as the terms used by Gardner, above, the practice was also known as 'charivari' or 'shivaree', both of which come from French. However, the etymology of the word goes further back to Vulgar Latin: *caribaria*, plural of *caribarium*, which translates as the custom of rattling kitchenware with an iron rod. This may itself come from the Greek καρηβαρία (*karēbaría*), a 'heaviness in the head'.

Folklore writer George Roberts defines the causes of skimmity riding thus:

   (i) When a man and his wife quarrel and he gives up to her.

  (ii) When a woman is unfaithful to her husband, and he patiently submits without resenting her conduct.

 (iii) Any grossly licentious conduct on the part of married persons.[8]

As in Hardy's novel, effigies were made of the errant couple, and at the end of the skimmity ride these would be either burned or thrown in the nearest body of water. Hardy implies that this occurred in Casterbridge in order to hide the townsfolk's involvement in the Mayor's wife's death, but although this serves the plot to good effect, it seems to have been common practice anyway, in order to ritually drown the figures involved.

Making an effigy of someone unpopular is obviously not confined to skimmity riding. It occurs across the world, in all cultures, and in other parts of the UK in analogous but not identical contexts. Those who have attended a Bonfire Night will be familiar with the figure of the Guy; throughout many of our childhoods, the sight of small groups of children on street corners with a stuffed effigy in a wheelbarrow and a can in which to collect the 'penny for the Guy' is an iconic memory. The pennies were usually used for the purchase of fireworks. In Lewes, Sussex, and other places that celebrate Bonfire Night in a big way, as we have seen, the effigy can be large and elaborate and generally commemorates that year's villain: I think Tony Blair was burned in the last year that I went, but Saddam Hussein, Margaret Thatcher, Boris Johnson and other figures on the world stage have all succumbed to the flames, at least in Lewes. Suffice to say that burning someone in effigy – whether or not it represents some old fragment of folk magic and cursing – does have an atavistic satisfaction and a somewhat cathartic effect all of its own, although whether it should be encouraged is a moot point.

Skimmity riding was last practised in the early 1970s, in one of the Devonshire villages.[9] However, it has seen a much more recent revival in the spring of 2022, in the original Casterbridge: Dorchester. Here, a skimmity ride took place to protest Dorset's plan to put 4,000 houses above Dorchester's water meadows. Protestors (plus a very excited small dog) banged pots and pans and carried effigies of a developer and a planner back-to-back, with the Town Crier walking ahead to publicize their objections and demands. Historian Leonard Baker describes an electoral protest in the West Country thus:

> At Bridgwater in 1832 the West Country custom of 'skimmington riding' or 'rough music' was deployed to protest a Tory electoral victory. The disturbance began when John Bowen, a local magistrate and anti-Reformer, arrested a man for drunkenness during the post-election revelry. Subsequently:
>
> The crowd commenced by uttering cries of vengeance against Mr. Bowen and 'all the Blue party' . . . his premises being at that time surrounded by a mob consisting of not less than two hundred persons, most of whom were armed with large sticks, and many of them in disguise. Soon after Mr. Bowen had entered, cries were uttered by the mob: 'We will have him out or pull down the premises.'[10]

Baker, considering this custom of shaming in the context of eighteenth- and nineteenth-century rural politics in the West Country, points out that skimmity riding was a clear form of grassroots community protest, and one in which women and men could take equal part. Cross-dressing was also often a feature, either in mockery, as attempts at disguise or as a way of adopting what was perceived to be the moral virtues of women (in rural areas, women were held to be the moral judges of character). It was revealed in court that 'one of the mob had his face blackened' while another was 'wearing fake curls and a dress'. Their leader was playing a bugle while wearing a 'large great coat, with a cape that came all around his body'. Baker notes that the 'presence of blackface, discordant music and crossdressing embed this act within the ritual structures of "skimmington riding"'.[11]

'Skimmington riding' was thus a form of remonstrance against those who endangered the moral code of rural society. By performing such a ritual outside Bowen's home, the protestors were directly likening his political activities with gross sexual misdemeanours. John Bowen, and the entire Tory party, were degraded to the level of a henpecked husband or adulterous woman. Furthermore, 'skimmington riding' was also traditionally coupled with the removal of an offender from the local community. Bowen's political actions had exiled him from West Country society, much like the sexual crimes of the cuckold. The enforcement of this exile was attempted not only symbolically through this shaming ritual but also physically. Cries of 'Down with premises!' and 'Away with the Blues!' permeated the crowd and as the night progressed many of those gathered around Bowen's home, including an increasing number dressed as women, attempted to pull down his house.

Bowen's home became a bridge between local ritual and national politics. The corruption of the Tories had to be cleansed, and by destroying both Bowen and his home Bridgwater could be 'freed from their influences'.[12] Baker regards skimmity riding and other forms of rough music as an integral part of protest movements among communities that had limited power:

> Blackface, crossdressing and 'skimmington rides' were not impediments to national political protest but aids. Their appearance provided local protestors with protest

repertoires that allowed them to express their distaste for the current state of British politics.[13]

We've noted from Hardy's novel that cans and cooking pots were banged – the aim was clearly to make as much noise as possible. In addition to this and the effigies, rhymes were often added, sometimes specifically aimed at the alleged malefactors:

With a ran, tan, tan,
On my old tin can,
Mrs. _____ and her good man.
She bang'd him, she bang'd him,
For spending a penny when he stood in need.
She up with a three-footed stool;
She struck him so hard, and she cut so deep,
Till the blood run down like a new stuck sheep.[14]

In medieval times, the custom seems to have been aimed at men who failed to exert sufficient control over their wives; society has notoriously been censorious of male as well as female survivors of domestic violence and abuse. There is a frieze at Montacute House in Somerset that depicts this. As Hardy's novel and many people's diaries illustrate, it was also aimed at adulterers and those who offended the standards of public decency. But by the nineteenth century the custom had changed to include men who beat their wives.

Shaming is often the only weapon available to abuse survivors. A friend of mine related how her grandmother, in Hull, dealt with a local man who beat his wife with a switch. She and the wife cut up the switch when he was at work, then baked the hard woody fragments into a savoury-looking pie. The wife then served this up to her husband. On taking a mouthful, he not unnaturally spat it straight out again. My friend's grandmother leaped from behind the door, where she had been hiding, and exclaimed 'You don't like it in your dinner? Well, she doesn't like it across her back!' The story then did the rounds of the district and, responding to this rather milder form of public humiliation, the man never touched his wife again.

In South Stoke, in Oxfordshire, one of the rhymes mentioned above illustrates this changing tone:

> There is a man in our town
> Who often beats his wife,
> So if he does it any more,
> We'll put his nose right out before.
> Holler boys, holler boys,
> Make the bells ring,
> Holler boys, holler boys.
> God save the King. [15]

However, skimmity riding wasn't confined to sexual or domestic matters. Butchers occasionally undertook it against those of their number who refused to adhere to labour practices, and it was also undertaken against people who blocked up footpaths or who profiteered. In Jopp's case, in *The Mayor of Casterbridge*, Lucetta's previous affair is a pretext; Jopp's real grievance is against those who have failed to give him a job, and he whips the townsfolk up into a moral panic and an excuse for entertainment to disguise the real cause of his resentment against Lucetta and Henchard. One wonders how many examples of skimmity riding had this kind of personal grudge at their base, rather than any genuine concern for public morals. As an example of publicly licensed bullying, the skimmity ride is hard to beat.

A riding was also carried out in Wells in 1607 against John Hole, the little city's Puritan constable, who had tried to put a stop to Wells' May games. The aim of the games was to raise money for the repair of St Cuthbert's church and the city folk reacted badly to Hole's actions, mocking him in a series of ridings carried out in front of a sizeable audience. In this case, the skimmity riding is pointedly anti-authoritarian, as were other ridings directed against local magistrates. Here, as in the Western Rising, the rides are less an expression of social bullying than they are a response to power by people who themselves had very little of it.

The Western Rising

In 1626–32 a series of riots broke out in the West of England, running from the Forest of Dean to Gillingham Forest on the Wiltshire/Dorset border, protesting disafforestation, when the legal status of a forest is altered so that it can no longer be preserved as a forest. Participants in these riots were mainly artisans such as tailors, tanners, carpenters or weavers, or labourers, including miners in the Forest of Dean; these were not generally peasants but people living within the forests themselves. The establishment was convinced that local landowners were behind the riots but there was a significant degree of obfuscation on the part of participants; arrest warrants show that ringleaders were often identified as 'alias Skimmington', and 'Lady Skimmington' also puts in several appearances.

Cross-dressing was another feature of these riots. We need to be careful here: this is not necessarily evidence of trans-genderism or, indeed, any alterations to the contemporary concept of the gender itself. As with blacking up, it's important not to reduce this to a single issue – in the case of these riots, the socially transgressive behaviour concerned has its roots in social injustice, its attempted redress and disguise. As with the Rebecca Riots in south Wales in the nineteenth century, men dressed as women to conceal their identities and confuse their opponents.

The Rebecca Riots

The Rebecca Riots were a protest by farmers in Pembrokeshire, Carmarthenshire and Cardiganshire from 1839 to 1843, mounted against the cost of toll roads. The name chosen for themselves by the protestors, 'Merched Beca' or 'Rebecca's daughters', comes from the Bible, deriving from the story of Rebecca and her daughters: 'And they blessed Rebekah and said unto her, Thou art our sister, be thou the mother of thousands of millions, and let thy seed possess the gate of those which hate them' (Genesis xxiv, verse 60). Bear in mind that this took place in a day and age when familiarity with the Bible was widespread and commonplace.

The leader of the group (most, though not all, of whom dressed in women's clothing) would engage in a form of call and response before tearing down one of the hated turnpike gates:

Rebecca: 'What is this my children? There is something in my way. I cannot go on ...'

Rioters: 'What is it, mother Rebecca? Nothing should
  stand in your way.'
Rebecca: 'I do not know my children. I am old and
  cannot see well.'
Rioters: 'Shall we come and move it out of your way,
  mother Rebecca?'
Rebecca: 'Wait! It feels like a big gate put across the
  road to stop your old mother.'
Rioters: 'We will break it down, mother. Nothing
  stands in your way.'
Rebecca: 'Perhaps it will open . . . Oh my dear
  children, it is locked and bolted. What can
  be done?'
Rioters: 'It must be taken down, mother. You and your
  children must be able to pass.'
Rebecca: 'Off with it then, my children.'[16]

Protestors might also blacken up their faces or don masks, again
in the interests of disguising their identities.

The Ceffyl Pren

The Rebecca Riots bear a resemblance to another form of 'rough
music' carried out in Wales: the Ceffyl Pren. The name means
'the wooden horse', and the leader of the early Rebecca Riots,
Thomas Rees/Twm Carnabwth participated in both the riots
and the Ceffyl Pren – a local tale that he borrowed his female
attire from a particularly strapping old maid named Rebecca is
probably untrue. Rees was a pugilist, and his violent chosen profession seems to have affected his social and political activities

as well; he only slowed down when he lost an eye in a bar fight in the 1840s.

The Ceffyl Pren itself is very similar to skimmity riding: it is a form of rough justice, conducted against local alleged wrongdoers who cannot be taken to court through an absence of evidence, and it was on the rise throughout the 1830s. Infidelity or informing on one's neighbours are examples of behaviour that was targeted by one of these mock courts. Fathers of illegitimate children who took refuge behind the Poor Laws to avoid paying for their offspring were also targeted. Participants would blacken their faces and adopt female dress, then parade the alleged perpetrator of the offence, who would be tied to a wooden frame, around the town in a torchlit procession.

In Anglesey in 1878, the local prosecutor, Owen Owens, was subjected to the Ceffyl Pren because he lived separately from his wife. He was carried around the neighbourhood on a ladder. By this day and age, however, a more functional police force was in operation and his accusers were arrested, convicted, bound over to keep the peace and fined. There was an outbreak of the practice in Conwy in 1882, in which a man and a woman were similarly tied to a ladder and paraded by a group of young men.

The practice of the Ceffyl Pren gradually died out as the police force became more effective, and perhaps as a more tolerant social age began to dawn. Its final manifestation is entirely benign; it's the name of the first Welsh-language rock band to tour America.

Skimmington Abroad

We've mentioned charivari and its French etymological roots. Similar practices are found across the continent: in France itself, *scampanate* in Italy, *Haberfeldtreiben* and *Katzenmusik* in Germany, *cencerrada* in Spain, and as itself in the USA. In some of these countries, and more besides, there's an echo of it still in post-wedding ceremony customs. Anyone who has been in a French town on a Saturday and heard a sudden commotion of hooting car horns in celebration of someone's nuptials might be witnessing the less malicious descendent of the local version of skimmington; it is first noted in France as a form of wedding celebration among the upper classes, later spreading down the class system. Tying tin cans to the wedding car is another possible legacy. But in France, charivari metamorphosed into a form of public shaming against marriages that went against prevailing social mores, for instance widows who married before the acceptable period of mourning had been seen out.

The Church also became involved, but in attempts to limit charivari rather than promoting it. The Council of Tours in the early seventeenth century took a stern view of charivari as a form of social censure, prohibiting it and threatening that anyone who practised it should be excommunicated. Charivari was subversive, taking on the moral judgement that should rightly have belonged to the Church at a community level – that would not do, the Church felt. It may also have felt that the custom might get out of hand and cause social destabilization. Their attempts to get rid of it were mixed: it still continued in rural areas.

However, the name is used across Europe for practices and things that bear only a tangential relationship to the original charivari, whether nuptial or shaming. For instance, in Bavaria, the word has come to refer to the little ornaments that adorn lederhosen, whether silver (such as a miniature pair of scissors) or hunting game trophies such as a fox's tooth. It also refers to the sudden inrush of clowns and other performers at the start of the classical circus.

In France, as in Britain, the charivari often turned to violence. Unlike the pot and pan banging in Britain, it sometimes took the form of an actual hunt, with the disapproving mob depicting themselves as hounds and the targets of the charivari as 'stags' (whether this is a reference to cuckold's horns is debatable). But as in Britain, it sometimes spilled over into tragedy and violence; targets sometimes took their own lives, like Hardy's Lucetta, and in the south of France there are five recorded cases of the targets firing on their accusers, resulting in gunshot wounds and death. Given the heightened emotions around all this, it is perhaps surprising that it didn't happen more often.

The custom also migrated to the usa, borne there by British settlers but also by the French. Known in the usa as shivaree, it was essentially the same kind of thing. Quebec was host to a shivaree in 1683, after the widow of one François Vézier dit Laverdure remarried less than a month after her husband's death; this scandalously short waiting time resulted in an uprising of popular sentiment.

But there were differences between the u.s. and Canadian versions of the practice and its European and British originals. Perhaps surprisingly, given the nature of frontier society, North American shivarees do not seem to have descended into violence and some of the punishments meted out were quite jokey: having to buy candy bars for the assembled crowd. This sounds more like the 'and give us some figgy pudding' character of Wassailing than the sinister effigy drowning of *The Mayor of Casterbridge*. Historian Loretta T. Johnson quotes a participant: 'All in fun – it was just a shiveree, you know, and nobody got mad about it. At least not very mad.'[17]

As in France, the shivaree was also sometimes just a wedding custom, which is still continued today to a certain extent in the nature of playing mild practical jokes on the happy couple. It is also said to have inspired the Acadian custom in Canada of Tintamarre, the raucous celebration of National Acadian Day. Norbert Robichaud, Archbishop of Moncton in New Brunswick, suggested that his congregation follow this pattern of Tintamarre:

> Once the prayer is finished, there will be a joyful tintamarre lasting for several minutes, featuring anything, everything and everyone that can make noise, shout and ring: mill whistles, car horns, bicycle bells, squawking objects, toys, etc.[18]

Annual Tintamarres are still held across Canada today. Again, this is perceived to be a cheerful celebration of a particular heritage rather than an expression of communal disapproval.

However, while the shivaree remained relatively innocuous in the USA, one might speculate that it did so only because more extreme and violent methods of social disapproval were starting to come into play, such as whitecapping. Whitecap groups, formed of white men who were usually sharecroppers or small landowners, threatened violence to people whom they considered to have violated community standards, such as men who practised domestic violence or women who bore children out of wedlock. The custom soon became racialized and the targets became predominantly Black people, Mexicans and sometimes new white tenants coming onto land. The custom was pernicious: in some regions, such as Oklahoma, it led to segregation as threatened Black farmers moved away from white areas and grouped together for safety. It led to the migration of Black labour to the northern states, coupled with the appalling lynchings across the South. The practice was illegal and statutes were still being brought against it as late as the 1970s, as this Mississippi law from 1972 demonstrates:

> Any person or persons who shall, by placards, or other writing, or verbally, attempt by threats, direct or implied, of injury to the person or property of another, to intimidate such other person into an abandonment or change of home or employment, shall, upon conviction, be fined not exceeding five hundred dollars, or imprisoned in the county jail not exceeding six months, or in the penitentiary not exceeding five years, as the court, in its discretion may determine.[19]

There is legislation in place in various parts of the world against the charivari and other similar customs. The penal code in the Philippines mentions it by name, for example, and cites it as a form of criminal disorder invoking alarm and scandal. But with the addition of whitecapping, we are moving here from folk customs involving shaming and incidental violence to outright intimidation and threatening behaviour, which is not quite our remit, but I think it is important to put the American shivaree into a wider context and to suggest that the custom morphed back into its European character of a wedding celebration in part because there were also more aggressive mechanisms of applying social pressure coming into play.

Despite its recent – and more sedate – manifestation in Dorchester in 2022, the practices that focus on skimmity riding were banned under the Highways Act of 1882. They had an effect on their targets: it must have felt not only embarrassing but threatening to be on the receiving end of a skimmity ride, particularly one that was repeated night after night for up to a week. Some victims fled from their locality and a few took their own lives. Vigilantism is rarely popular above a community level; to the establishment and the upholders of the law, it is volatile, a little too close to an embryonic riot, and those in authority must wonder exactly where it is going to go. Could we end up with full-scale revolution, for example? With the rise of a national police force, customs like these were gradually made illegal.

These days, we still have public shaming, but it's moved onto social media – call-out and cancel cultures, for instance. The #MeToo movement came about in large part because there is no other reliable social mechanism for shaming sexual predators; many rape and assault cases do not end up in court. Parading effigies through the streets has now moved onto the Internet, with naming and shaming. Obviously, this can be weaponized and abused, but it can also provide an outlet for genuine grievances that otherwise do not have a space in which to be aired. Thus, the concept of skimmity lives on – but now it's virtual.

FOURTEEN

The Future of Folk Practice

Folk practices have, as we have seen, been subject to a constant process of change. We keep referring to traditions that have been revived in recent decades – there are a lot of them. Oak Apple Day, for instance, was discontinued as a national celebration in the 1850s; Morris dancing and May Day revels have seen dips and rises in popularity, like a mild cultural roller-coaster. Even maypoles have proved contentious, banned by the Long Parliament in 1644. But what of traditions that have died out completely?

Many of the customs and practices we've described in this book are old, at least in the sense of a hundred or more years. Some of them, like the charivari, have (thankfully) died out. Others have changed, mutated or been revived. Some have experienced a new lease of life in a slightly different way, like the women's Morris sides. But what of the future? Are there folk practices that are emerging, in response to cultural conditions or seemingly out of nowhere? Are these going to be digital, or will they take physical form?

At the time of writing, Britain is just emerging from the worst effects of the COVID-19 pandemic, although the virus itself is unfortunately still going strong; its worst effects are being mitigated by the vaccine roll-out and possibly by the changing nature of the virus itself. During the lockdowns in 2020 and

2021, a number of practices emerged, minor in form but national in character: clapping for the NHS and putting a rainbow in the front window, for example, both to show support for the beleaguered health services.

Folklorist Ceri Houlbrook notes that 'ritual deposits are placed in private spaces but for public consumption, and symbols are adopted, such as the rainbow, to express hope and support'.[1] Clapping for Carers emerged during the first lockdown for ten weeks, at 8 p.m. on Thursdays. People applauded, or banged pots and pans. This also gave rise to some public shaming – people who didn't participate in some areas found themselves frowned upon by their neighbours and criticized on social media. The practice, though short-lived, was somewhat divisive: a number of medical professionals were outspoken in their belief that they'd rather have better pay deals than clapping, and the woman who started the whole thing, Anne-Marie Plas, told *The Guardian* in May 2020 that she thought it should cease: 'To have the most impact, I think it is good to stop it at its peak. Without getting too political . . . I think the narrative is starting to change, and I don't want the clap to be negative.'[2]

The Guardian pointed out that clapping had been political from the get-go, with prominent politicians such as Rishi Sunak and Matt Hancock undertaking high-profile performances of the applause in front of the news cameras. However, there are also those who found that it put them more closely in touch with neighbours whom they did not always have the time to converse with. Writer Linda Grant told *The Guardian*: 'Ten weeks ago I drew the curtains to see if anyone but me knew anything about this clapping and the figures of strangers were standing there at the windows. Now they're familiar faces.'[3]

Nicolas Le Bigre, a folklore researcher at the Elphinstone Institute who is documenting COVID-19 customs as part of 'Lockdown Lore', says it is too early to say whether these communal acts will re-emerge in other periods of global crisis or whether they will retire, becoming symbols of this specific time. But he added, 'I can at least smile at the wealth of creativity that has come my way. And that has been a comfort to us all.'[4]

Scarecrow festivals have also emerged as a grassroots form of celebration in rural areas. Some of them are mildly subversive. I once slowed down when approaching one in our village; it was dressed in a mock policeman's hi-viz and was holding a hair-dryer like a speed gun. Some of them are more so – unflattering scarecrow images of unpopular politicians manifested during lockdowns, too, and here we are back to customs of shaming.

Roadside Shrines

Another form of grassroots commemoration is the emerging practice of roadside shrines, usually dedicated to someone who has died at or near the site of the shrine in some form of accident, or where they received fatal injuries. These usually take the form of bunches of flowers (real or artificial) tied to a nearby tree, lamppost or other vertical surface, but may include other items as well. There was a quite elaborate shrine by the side of the road in my village where a schoolboy had been knocked down and killed by a driver while he was waiting for the school bus one morning. This took the form of a small box on which was placed flowers, painted stones, small toys such as a teddy bear and so on. The shrine lasted for several years before it disappeared – I surmise when the boy's family moved away from the area.

Wayside shrines dedicated to religious figures such as local deities or, more latterly, saints or the Virgin, used to be common and are still found in Catholic countries. But they used to be found in Britain, too, in a variety of forms. Roman shrines were found across the country. Earlier Celtic monuments such as the Ogham stones also seem to have been set up to commemorate the dead, particularly in Pembrokeshire (there are more in Ireland), and there are a number of surviving Celtic crosses after the arrival of Christianity in these islands. The thirteenth-century Eleanor Crosses, set up to mark the places where Queen Eleanor of Castile's body reposed overnight in its journey back to London from Harby in Lincolnshire, where she died, can still be seen; although nine of the twelve crosses are no longer in existence, three remain at Geddington, Hardingstone and Waltham Cross. The grandest was at Charing Cross in London, which still obviously bears its name. Eleanor was buried at Westminster, or at least, bits of her were; her viscera were entombed at Lincoln and her heart was buried at Blackfriars. These are the grandest and most ornate memorial crosses in Britain, but there are others, such as a cross in the Strand erected by William II to commemorate his mother Matilda.

Now, commemorative roadside items may take forms other than crosses, such as the 'ghost bikes' that are sometimes found at the place where a cyclist has died or been fatally injured. These are old bicycles, painted white and usually with a notice bearing the dead person's name, chained to a nearby object such as a fence post. This custom possibly originated in the USA as part of an art project by San Francisco artist Jo Slota, but it seems to have been taken up in other parts of the USA not just as a memorial to the deceased cyclist, but also as a warning to motorists. (The alarming number of small white crosses placed along particularly dangerous stretches of road in Ireland has a similar function.) London Ghostcycle emerged as a movement in the early 2000s.

A similar phenomenon is 'ghost shoes' – white shoes tied to posts or branches at eye level. This began in Montreal in 2016 and has since spread; again, this is both to commemorate the dead person and to raise awareness of the danger that road traffic poses to pedestrians. It's sometimes taken up by transport activists, who place a pair of ghost shoes for each person killed in a locality to demonstrate the numbers of people who have been affected. This particular custom seems to be more prevalent in North America, but I have seen ghost shoes at some roadside shrines over here in the UK as well.

Small roadside shrines are found in Europe, too, particularly in Greece, which has a high incidence of road traffic accidents. Here, the shrines are more traditional in form: a box with a cross in which a candle can be burned, and sometimes hosting icons or images from Orthodox Christianity (some take the form of actual churches in miniature). In more secular Britain, commemorations tend to be more spontaneous and looser in form – not so religious.

These memorials seem to be growing in popularity. In Australia, one in five fatalities on the road are commemorated in this way. In the USA, mass shootings also garner their fair share of commemorative items, and readers will remember the enormous quantity of flowers placed at the gates of Buckingham Palace after the death of Princess Diana, one of the first mass outpourings of public grief for a public figure that I remember in this country. Paul Mullins, writing on roadside memorials, says:

much of what we know about these shrines as material culture is relatively impressionistic and would never satisfy an archaeologist as a rigorous material analysis. For instance, we do not have particularly systematic inventories of the sorts of things that appear in shrines; the frequency of such markers is not clearly mapped; their size and spatial arrangement remains undefined; the duration of the shrines varies widely; the geographic and cultural distinctions in patterns are unclear; and the ethnographic complexities of why particular people erect shrines remains only impressionistically documented. A narrative on roadside memorials based on such rigorously analyzed material patterns would almost certainly tell distinctive stories about society and grief.[5]

Researcher Art Jipson, who has made a study of roadside shrines dedicated to the victims of car accidents, reports that 95 per cent of these shrines are put up by the victim's family and 80 per cent of them are erected by women.[6] He says that everyone he interviewed reported that the shrine was of greater significance to them than the actual grave of the deceased person – perhaps an atavistic return to the belief that the place where the person actually died, or received fatal injuries, is of immense importance. (This is, after all, the central idea behind hauntings – the stagecoaches, headless horsemen and more modern ghosts like the spectral presences that are sometimes said to be experienced in the passenger seats of cars driving along dangerous stretches of highway.)

These memorials are commemorative, not transgressive, but they have been banned in fifteen u.s. states. They fall under violation of public property laws, and concerns have been expressed that they create a distraction for drivers, thus risking further accidents (there's no evidence of this). Some states do not go as far as banning them entirely but insist that shrines should be removed within a particular timeframe – Akron, in Ohio, insists that they must be dismantled within 45 days. However, while these dictates might be obeyed, shrines often reappear after the original has been taken down. Local governments mess with grassroots mourning rites at their peril.

> Perhaps most important is not that survivors maintain the memorial but rather that the community willingly allows it to remain in public space and implicitly respect the victims' memory and survivors' grief. Even people who may find such shrines unsettling, illegal, or unsightly seem very reluctant to remove the shrines and risk appearing to minimize those memories or grief.[7]

But it is not just in the physical realm that memorials appear; the digital world has begun to manifest them, too. The question of what to do with the social media pages of someone who has died has been well addressed by Facebook, for example. If you send proof of death, such as a death certificate, the company can either delete or memorialize a page, sometime structuring it so that the timeline is frozen but a 'tribute' page remains onto which people can post recollections or their own obituaries. These 'digital graveyards' are becoming increasingly common as the social media demographic ages.

Folk Customs of the Net

Alan Dundes holds that emerging technology would generate forms of folklore all of its own, a somewhat prescient remark given that he was writing before the rise of the Internet:

> technology isn't stamping out folklore; rather it is becoming a vital factor in the transmission of folklore and it is providing an exciting source of inspiration for the generation of new folklore. The rise of the computer symbolizes the impact of technology upon the modern world. My point is that there is folklore of and about the computer.[8]

The popularity of RPGs and online gaming do seem to bear this out to some extent. Many of those games are based on folkloric content, and on the popularity of fantasy fiction and media. *Lord of the Rings* has to be one of the most popular English-language novels of all time, but Tolkien drew much of the extensive mythology of this work from the folklore of northern Europe. The elves and dwarves that populate *Lord of the Rings* and associated books such as *The Hobbit* come from Anglo-Saxon and Norse mythology. *The Elder Scrolls V: Skyrim* (2011) also draws upon these northern European myths, relying on Scandinavian lore. It is ironic, as well as perhaps inevitable, that some of the legends that would have been familiar to our ancestors from the British Isles a thousand years ago are still fuelling some of the most successful games, novels, films and television of the twenty-first century.

Robert Glenn Howard writes:

Since the early 1990s, scholars have recognized technologically mediated folklore in the form of online traditional discourse. In forms as diverse as jokes, contemporary legends, local rumors, folk belief, music, and storytelling, this 'e-lore' is well documented and easy to assimilate into already-established genres.[9]

Dee Dee Chainey, author of the National Trust's *A Treasury of British Folklore*, comments that new folklore is constantly being generated, often through the medium of the Internet. Chainey compares Internet memes to the kind of folk superstitions passed around communities. Aliens, conspiracy theories and perhaps even contemporary fears about health and diet contribute to this new 'folklore'.

This new lore reflects modern needs. The things we dream about, and the fears that haunt us in the darkest nights today. Slenderman is an example of this. Some say he is a bogey man; tall, thin, faceless, and wearing a non-descript suit – very similar to the way the 'men in black' reputedly visit to quash rumours of aliens.[10]

The Future of Nostalgia

Part of the cultural trend that I note above – the older it is, the better it is – manifests in a fairly obvious way as nostalgia. Some people are more prone to nostalgia than others. Some are more realistic about it than others. Some, while realistic, manifest it in a toxic fashion. How might we unpack this in a useful way?

There are a lot of people who are not particularly nostalgic; they look forwards rather than back. Those are, arguably, not the sort of people to whom folk customs are likely to appeal (although, when writing this, I wondered whether this was actually true or whether I'm perpetrating a stereotype of my own). Realism is an issue: the further something recedes in actual memory, the more rose-tinted it tends to become. My father was conscripted into the Second World War, for instance; his regiment toured North Africa and he ended up at Monte Cassino, which was not, by anybody's reckoning, a picnic. I was born in 1965, relatively soon after the war had ended, and all of my adult relatives remembered the war. They'd either taken part in it directly or they'd been on the home front; my mother was in her teens and saw Coventry bombed, for example. My parents had a great deal of respect for people who had fought and they wore a poppy in November, but my father in particular was somewhat cynical about the whole Remembrance issue. He'd seen at first hand how soldiers were treated when they came back from the Front; he remembered a woman in a fur coat on the Tube drawing it ostentatiously aside and making an audible comment about 'dirty soldiers'. So his experience of Kipling's 'Tommy' was fairly direct.

As time has gone by, I have watched the Remembrance commemorations every November turn into something of a fetish. In the village in which I live, they definitely haven't been hijacked by the far-right, but they are a big deal and until the COVID-19 lockdown, we had a sort of re-enactment tea, served by ladies in 1940s dresses and with some of the military re-enactors present with old Jeeps in the car park. My mother and a couple of other older residents were the only people present who actually remembered the Second World War. We enjoyed the tea a great deal, and I do attend Remembrance commemorations, but there is a tendency now for the war to be presented in a very rosy light, by people who are the grandchildren, not even the children, of people who lived through the period itself.

This fetishization of the Second World War taps into a kind of aggressive celebration of Englishness, in particular, which I don't personally find very healthy, because it's unrealistic. Looting was rife in London, quite a lot of people ideologically supported the Nazis' anti-Jewish stance (looking at you, *Daily Mail*) and anyone reading people's diaries from the time, such as the ones published in 1946, just after the war, from the Mass-Observation Archive, will note a range of responses that definitely do not dovetail into the 'plucky little Britain' archetype with us all cheerily pulling together. That doesn't mean that everyone was at each other's throats or that people didn't help one another, but that's what nostalgia does: it tints rosily.

Nostalgia is wider than the Second World War, of course. There is a kind of nostalgia for an England that never existed. It is pastoral, cheerful, rural, in which everyone 'knew their place' and liked it. Think haymakers with wagons pulled by patient old horses, cottages with roses round the door, kindly squires – basically the kind of scenes you might find made into a certain type of jigsaw. There's absolutely nothing threatening here, and that's what tips it into a darker kind of phenomenon. This is what I mean by 'realistic but toxic': the England that appears in this form of nostalgia is almost exclusively white and is a world in which women, in particular, 'know their place'. It's not exclusively a male fantasy, but it is patriarchal, and the tradwife trend – wearing gingham and having loads of kids, not to mention obeying your husband – is perpetrated largely by young women who haven't been brought up in that kind of society. They're basically LARPing a past that never really was. This is why these kinds of images are so helpful to the far right.

Merrie Englandism is essentially nostalgic. It takes it as given that however much society has progressed materially it has lost something important on the way, and this loss is primarily in terms of 'community'. In Merrie England the social classes were held together in an interlocking web of duties and obligations. The peasants were poor but honest, strong and happy, their children were well fed and also happy, and the squire or lord of the manor cared for his people as a father would his family, while a benign parson looked after their spiritual needs. At certain points in the year, the people sang, danced and made merry – in spring, summer and autumn on the village green or in the fields, while at Christmas the squire threw open his hall, as dictated by his 'old English hospitality'. The adherents of the Merrie England school sought to recreate this golden age, and one of their key tools was to reform the pastimes of the poor that had, quite clearly in their eyes, lost both their innocence and their traditional values.[11]

In the *Oxford Dictionary of English Folklore*, Jacqueline Simpson and Steve Roud comment on the class issue, quoting the Revd Macauley writing in *The History of Claybrook* (1791):

> Before customs could be reinvented, they had to be shorn of the undesirable features which they had gathered from being in the hands of the working classes for too long. Sometimes it could be blamed on urban influences: The people of this neighbourhood are much attached to the

celebration of wakes; and on the annual return of these festivals, the cousins assemble from all quarters, fill the church on Sunday, and celebrate Monday with feasting, with musick, and with dancing. The spirit of old English hospitality is conspicuous among the farmers on these occasions; but with the lower sort of people, especially in the manufacturing villages, the return of the wake never fails to produce a week, at least, of idleness, intoxication and riot.[12]

This obviously is not to make the claim that everyone who is into Morris dancing is some kind of closet fascist. Even if you're a very traditional sort of person whose life is centred around folk music and local customs, this says nothing sub-textual about your politics; the most committed folkie I know is an equally committed Communist and has been for the past sixty years. He, like many people interested in the folklore and customs of the British Isles, is appalled at the cultural hijacking that is carried out on the part of far-right groups like Britain First and has an in-depth knowledge of British history. Those groups are usually remarkably ignorant about the actual history of this country, although I did know someone in Lewes (not a Bonfire Boy) who was into all of these customs and who was a National Front member. Was he typical, or was he an anomaly? I would have to say that he was not entirely anomalous, but he certainly wasn't typical either; everyone else I've known on the folk/folk-custom scene has been either apolitical, a sort of low-grade heart-on-sleeve type of Tory or on the actual left – a wide range that, I would argue, is fairly representative of large sections of British society whatever their hobbies. Some of my more traditionally conservative acquaintances are nonetheless supporters of Oliver Cromwell.

Cool as Folk

In 2019 the *Daily Telegraph* reported a warning by the National Trust that much of the country's folklore is dying out, a result of the impact of social media and new technology. Jessica Monaghan, the National Trust's Head of Experiences and Programming, called on the public to share its knowledge of folklore from different regions of the UK in order to keep some of these old beliefs alive:

> These tales and traditions tell us so much about our ancestors and their relationship with the world around them and help us appreciate the layers of history and symbolism in the places we live now. We're curious about the many variations of similar stories that helped shape local and regional identities. Through these tales – whether they're about white harts, mirrors, water spirits or magpies – we can explore and celebrate what makes communities around the uk unique, but also the threads that tie us together, and have done for generations.[13]

But that was before the world changed. That article was written before COVID-19, before the pandemic and lockdown. In early 2023 *The Guardian* ran an article entitled 'Cool as Folk: Why Britain's Young Rebels Are Embracing Ancient Rites'.[14] This was engendered by a new exhibition at an art gallery in Compton Verney in Warwickshire. Titled *Making Mischief*, the exhibition relates to folk costume and many of the traditions that we've been looking at in this book, such as the Padstow Obby Oss, Haxey Hood and the Jack in the Green in Hastings. The article quotes Simon Costin, a former set designer who is the current director of the Museum of Witchcraft and Magic in Boscastle and who also set up the Museum of British Folklore (we met him as one of the Gay Bogies on Acid of Hastings). Costin told *The Guardian:*

> I've been curious to watch younger people tapping into folklore. I think it started with the New Nature Writers such as Robert Macfarlane and Roger Deakin. There's also the growth of the environmental movement with groups such as Extinction Rebellion. The people engaged with folklore customs now aren't nostalgic, they're looking forward – they've realised seasonal traditions are a way to reconnect with the planet ... There's a lack of spirituality in people's lives. Organized traditional religion is abhorrent to most of them – 'thou shalt not' doesn't resonate any more – so instead they're looking at prehistoric monuments and pilgrimage routes. Folklore is pure anti-establishment chaos; in the show we look at how many traditions were suppressed because they were moments when people lost control. Many were started by communities driven to celebrate by a passion for culture. Notting Hill carnival is a good example of that.

Costin's hope was that the exhibition would demonstrate the ongoing popularity of folk customs in Britain in the twenty-first century.

I think the greater museum fraternity, in its wisdom, has undervalued vernacular culture. It's difficult for archivists to get their heads round because it's constantly mutating and growing. Museums are about things that are enshrined, and folklore resists that.[15]

The British Pilgrimage Trust is also going strong, and so is Wiltshire-based Weird Walk, which focuses on ley lines as well as pilgrimage routes. Its editors are musician Owen Tromans, designer Alex Hornsby and record-label owner James Nicholls. Hornsby says:

People are drawn to ancient sites, stories and traditions. Sacred landscapes and their lore offer respite, reconnection and an enjoyable yomp. There's usually a decent pub nearby, too. Someone recently told me that in previous years their mates used to post about going to gigs or to football on the weekend, then all of a sudden it was hikes up mountains and rituals at standing stones . . . folklore and ancient history is gaining a foothold in the era of social media.[16]

The founders of Boss Morris also subscribe to the view that folk customs have a significant role in modern times, pointing out that particularly after COVID-19 and the confines of lockdown, people are keen to get out and about and also to establish their own links with the place they live in. They describe it as 'a kind of cultural mycelium', and Lily Cheetham says:

I think traditions and things like Morris dancing really bring that back, that connectedness. The relationship these traditions have to the land – our dancing and our singing of traditional folk songs – are so closely related to identity. Maybe, having had a couple of years to think about that stuff, and being isolated, and not having those things that usually preoccupy us and keep us busy all the time, people are thinking more about the fundamental things in life.[17]

The popularity of Bridget Christie's recent sitcom *The Change* also highlights the increasing popularity of the folk vibe. Supermarket checkout clerk Linda, underappreciated by everyone around her, runs away to the Forest of Dean to find a time capsule that her ten-year-old self placed in a tree and ends up as the Eel Queen of the Forest. Although not explicitly Pagan, the series has been a big hit with Pagans and folklore enthusiasts alike, with a soundtrack supplied by folk matriarch Shirley Collins and John Renbourn.

Folk customs are, therefore, far from defunct. In fact, their popularity seems to be growing. This is, in an age of big-market corporate capitalism, an act of transgression in itself. Let's hope we can take the positive aspects of folk practice forward, leaving the charivari, the demanding money for menaces, the black-face and the violence safely behind us in the past. There is no reason why the baby should be thrown out with the cultural bathwater, and the vibrancy, fun, communitarianism and sheer eccentricity of all these practices make them well worth retaining, to leaven the increasing blandness of so much of modern mainstream culture.

References

Introduction

1 Ronald Hutton, *Stations of the Sun* (Oxford, 1996), p. 253.

ONE: What Is Folklore?

1 American Folklore Society, www.whatisfolklore.org, 3 April 2023.

2 Alan Dundes, ed., *The Study of Folklore* (Englewood Cliffs, NJ, 1965), p. 2.

3 James George Frazer, *The Golden Bough: A Study in Comparative Religion* (London, 1890).

4 Jane Ellen Harrison, *Themis: A Study of the Social Origins of Greek Religion* (Cambridge, 1912).

5 Margaret Murray, *The Witch-Cult in Western Europe* (Oxford, 1921).

6 Jacqueline Simpson, 'Margaret Murray: Who Believed Her, and Why?', *Folklore*, cv/1–2 (1994), pp. 89–96.

7 Robert Graves, *The White Goddess* (London, 1948).

TWO: Jacks in the Green

1 Julia Somerset, 'The Green Man in Church Architecture', *Folklore Journal*, L/1 (1939), pp. 45–57.

2 Stephen Winick, 'What Was the Green Man?', www.blogs.loc.gov/folklife, 2 May 2022.

3 E. K. Chambers, *The Medieval Stage* (Oxford, 1903).

4 Winick, 'What Was the Green Man?'

5 Ibid.

6 George Whetstone, *The Second Parte of the Famous Historie of Promos and Cassandra, in Heptameron of Civil Discourses* (London, 1578), Act 1, Scene 6, p. 122.

7 Winick, 'What Was the Green Man?'

8 Ibid.

9 Thomas Nashe, 'Prologue', *Summer's Last Will and Testament* (London, 1592).

10 Robert Amorye, Harl. MS. No. 2150, fol. 356; quoted in Winick, 'What Was the Green Man?'

11 Ibid.

12 Robert Withington, *English Pageantry: An Historical Outline* (Cambridge, MA, 1918).

13 Ibid., p. 74.

14 Matt Salusbury, 'The Woodwoses of Suffolk', www.mattsalusbury. blogspot.com, 1 May 2023.

15 Ibid.

16 Laurence Marcellus Larson, trans., *The King's Mirror* (*Speculum regale: Konungs skuggsjá*), Scandinavian Monographs 3 (New York, 1917), p. 110.

17 Salusbury, 'The Woodwoses of Suffolk'.

18 Ralph of Coggeshall, *Chronicon Anglicanum* [*c.* 1200] (Cambridge, 2012), p. xii.

19 Ibid., p. xvii.

20 Duncan Lunan, 'Science Fact: Children from the Sky', *Analog* (September 1996).

21 Salusbury, 'The Woodwoses of Suffolk'.

22 John Aubrey, *Remaines of Gentilisme and Judaisme* [1686/7] (London, 1881), pp. 134–5.

23 Quoted by Jacob Larwood and John Camden Hotten, *The History of Signboards* (London, 1866), p. 368.

24 Ellen E. Jones, '*The Change* review: Bridget Christie's Super-Cool Menopause Comedy Is Like Nothing Else on TV', www. theguardian.com, 21 June 2023.

25 Barbara Freitag, *Sheela-Na-Gigs: Unravelling an Enigma* (London, 2004).

26 Ibid.

27 Jenny Stevens, 'Big Vagina Energy: The Return of the Sheela-Na-Gig', www.theguardian.com, 21 June 2023.

28 Samuel Pepys, *Diary*, 1 May 1667, www.pepysdiary.com.

29 Joseph Strutt, *The Sports and Pastimes of the People of England* (London, 1801), p. 358.

30 'A History of the Jack-in-the-Green', www.thecompanyof-thegreenman.wordpress.com, quoting *Morning Chronicle and London Advertiser*, 2 May 1775.

31 Kai Bossom, 'The Legend of the Gay Bogies', www.hmag.org.uk, 29 May 2023.

32 James George Frazer, *The Golden Bough: A Study in Comparative Religion* (New York, 1925), p. 141.

33 'About Beltane Fire Festival', www.beltane.org/about-beltane, 27 January 2023.

34 'Beltane Interview with a Blue Man', www.edinburghguide.com, 27 January 2023.

35 Danya Bazaraa, 'King Charles' Coronation Invite Becomes Engulfed in "Paganism" Row', www.dailymail.co.uk, 6 April 2023.

36 Ibid.

37 Ibid.

THREE: The Mari Lwyd and Animal Figures

1 John Evans, *A Tour Through Part of North Wales* (London, 1800); Edwin Cawte, *Ritual Animal Disguise: A Historical and Geographical Study of Animal Disguise in the British Isles* (Lanham, MD, 1978).

2 Ronald Hutton, *Stations of the Sun* (Oxford, 1996), p. 81.

3 Iorwerth C. Peate, 'Mari Lwyd: A Suggested Explanation', *Royal Anthropological Institute of Great Britain and Ireland*, XLIII (May–June 1943), pp. 53–5.

4 Anon., *Black Book of Carmarthen* (Wales, prior to 1250).

5 Hutton, *Stations of the Sun*, p. 84.

6 Peate, 'Mari Lwyd: A Suggested Explanation', pp. 53–5.

7 Cawte, *Ritual Animal Disguise*, pp. 92–3.

8 Rev. William Roberts, *The Religion of the Dark Ages* (Carmarthen, 1852).

9 Hutton, *Stations of the Sun*, p. 84.

10 Phoebe Southworth, 'Mother-of-Two Dies from Neck Injuries at Obby Oss Cornish Festival', www.telegraph.co.uk, 5 May 2019.

11 Lee Trewhela, 'Padstow is "Shocked and Heartbroken" Following Obby Oss Incident', www.cornwalllive.com, 3 May 2019.

12 Ibid.

13 Ibid.

14 Andrew Cox, 'Regulation 28 Report to Prevent Future Deaths', www.judiciary.com, 7 April 2022.

15 Oliver Wright, 'Queer as Folklore: A Year of English Customs', www.bbc.co.uk, 1 January 2019.

16 Hutton, *Stations of the Sun*, p. 84.

17 Alex Merry, 'Boss Morris – The Interview', www.tradfolk.co, 24 February 2022.

18 Hutton, *Stations of the Sun*, p. 88.

19 William Barnes, 'The Dorset Ooser', www.wessexmuseums.org.uk, 25 February 2022.

20 Daniel Patrick Quinn, 'The Dorset Ooser', www.wessexmorrismen. co.uk, 2013.

21 Ibid.

22 Thomas Hardy, *The First Countess of Wessex* (London, 1890).

23 H.S.L. Dewar, 'The Dorset Ooser', *Proceedings of the Dorset Natural History and Archaeological Society*, LXXXIV (1962), p. 179.

24 Christina Hole, *English Folklore* (London, 1940), p. 161.

25 Frederick Thomas Elworthy, *Horns of Honour: And Other Studies in the By-Ways of Archaeology* (London, 1900).

26 Daniel Patrick Quinn, 'The Dorset Ooser', www.wessexmorrismen. co.uk, 2013.

27 Ibid.

28 Ibid.

29 Dewar, 'The Dorset Ooser', p. 179.

30 Henry Joseph Moule, *Letter to Somerset and Dorset Notes and Queries*, III (1892), p. 27.

31 Quinn, 'The Dorset Ooser'.

32 Susan Cooper, *The Dark Is Rising* (London, 1973), p. 174.

FOUR: Wassail, Wassail, All Over the Town

1 Geoffrey of Monmouth, *History of the Kings of Britain* (Cambridge, Ontario, 1999), p. 102.

2 William Shakespeare, *A Midsummer Night's Dream*, Act II, scene 1.

3 William Shakespeare, *Love's Labours Lost*, Act v, scene 2.

4 Robert Herrick, *Works of Robert Herrick*, ed. Alfred Pollard (London, 1891), vol. II, pp. 145–6.

5 Barbara Wells Sarudy, 'Christmas Wassailing as Social Protest in England and Her North American Colonies', www.b-womeninamericanhistory18.blogspot.com, 2018.

6 Sally-Anne Huxtable, 'Wassailing – Ritual and Revelry', www.nationaltrust.org.uk, 26 April 2022.

7 Stephen Nissenbaum, *The Battle for Christmas* (New York, 1988), p. 7.

8 Christopher Klein, 'When Massachusetts Banned Christmas', www.history.com, 2 December 2015.

9 Ibid.

10 Robert Doares, 'Wassailing through History',
www.slaveryandremembrance.org, 2006.

11 Ronald Hutton, *Stations of the Sun* (Oxford, 1996), p. 96.

12 Ibid., p. 95.

13 Carole Owens, 'Puritans Banned Christmas, Stockbridge Restored
It', www. theberkshireedge.com, 12 December 2017.

14 Governor William Bradford, *Pilgrim Roots, Of Plimoth Plantation,
1621–1650*, www.gutenberg.org.

15 Francis Phipps, 'Antiques; Vessels for Merry Holiday Wassailing',
www.nytimes.com, 24 December 1984.

16 Sarudy, 'Christmas Wassailing as Social Protest'.

17 Michael Clarke, 'Medieval Misrule and Mayhem',
www.english-heritage.org.uk, 11 July 2022.

18 Daisy Dunn, *In the Shadow of Vesuvius: A Life of Pliny* (London,
2019).

19 Lucian, *The Works of Lucian of Samosata*, vol. IV, trans. H. W. and
F. G. Fowler (London, 1908), p. 108.

20 Hutton, *Stations of the Sun*, p. 99.

21 Ibid., p. 2.

22 Nissenbaum, *The Battle for Christmas*, p. 285.

23 Doares, 'Wassailing through History'.

FIVE: Morris and Molly

1 Ronald Hutton, *Stations of the Sun* (Oxford, 1996), p. 266.

2 'Shakespeare Morris Dance from London to Norwich',
www.bbc.co.uk, 23 April 2015.

3 Hutton, *Stations of the Sun*, p. 273.

4 Joseph Strutt, *The Sports and Pastimes of the People of England*
(London, 1801), p. 223.

5 Rodney Gallop, 'The Origins of the Morris Dance', *Journal of the
English Folk and Dance Society*, 1/3 (1934), pp. 122–9.

6 '"It Was Change or Die": Why Morris Men Are Now Welcoming Morris Women', www.theguardian.com, 3 October 2022.

7 Hutton, *Stations of the Sun*, p. 276.

8 '"It Was Change or Die"'.

9 Alex Merry, 'Boss Morris – The Interview', www.tradfolk.co, 24 February 2022.

10 Rachel Adams, 'Morris is a Creature of Its Own', www.theguardian.com, 3 March 2023.

11 Merry, 'Boss Morris – The Interview'.

12 Ibid.

13 Ibid.

14 'Number of London Youth Clubs Nearly Halved since 2011'. www.theguardian.com, 22 March 2019.

15 Luke Salkeld, 'Morris Dancing to Become Extinct "Because Young People Are Too Embarrassed to Take Part"', www.dailymail.co.uk, 6 January 2009.

16 'Hammersmith Morris Men Deny Decline', www.mylondon.news, 12 January 2009.

17 '"It Was Change or Die"'.

18 Tony Forster, 'What Is Molly?', www.pigdyke.co.uk, 1 August 2022.

19 Hutton, *Stations of the Sun*, p. 127.

20 Sybil Marshall, *Fenland Chronicle* (1967), at www.pigdyke.co.uk.

21 William Arderon Papers Ms. 555 fol. 242v (1745).

22 Enid Porter, *Folklore of East Anglia* (London, 1974).

23 William Hazlitt, *Faiths and Folklore*, 2 vols (London, 1905), p. 2.

24 Jon Hooton, 'The Norwich Kitwitches', www.norwichkitwitches-mollydancers5.wordpress.com, 1 September 2022.

25 Ibid.

26 Forster, 'What Is Molly?'

27 Ibid.

28 Rictor Norton, 'Cross Dressing', https://rictornorton.co.uk, 2002.

29 Ibid.

30 More In Common, 'Britons and Gender Identity – Navigating Common Ground and Division', www.moreincommon.org.uk, June 2022.

31 Charles Kingsley, *The Water Babies* (London, 1862–3).

32 Findings from the 2020 Morris Census, www.morrisfed.org, December 2020.

33 Sophie Morris, 'The Origin of Morris Dancers Blacking Up Is Irrelevant – It Simply Needs to Stop', www.theguardian.com, 12 August 2019.

34 Nicholas Wall, Letters, www.theguardian.com, 3 May 2021.

35 'The pavan, the priest and the pseudonym: "Belle qui tiens ma vie" and Arbeau's 'Orchésographie' (1589)', www.earlymusicmuse.com, 9 March 2017.

36 Barbara Lowe, 'Early Records of the Morris in England', *Journal of the English Folk and Dance Society*, VIII/2 (1957), pp. 61–82, p. 62.

37 Nicholas Milton, 'Offensive – or Just Harmless Fun?' www.theguardian.com, 31 December 2008.

38 Pauline Greenhill, 'Folk and Academic Racism: Concepts from Morris and Folklore', *Folklore in Canada*, CXV/456 (Spring 2002), pp. 226–46, p. 232.

39 Morris, 'The Origin of Morris Dancers Blacking Up Is Irrelevant'.

40 John Ellis, 'May Day Morris Dancers Swap Black Face Paint for Blue Over Concerns of Racism', www.theguardian.com, 1 May 2021.

41 Joint Morris Organisations, 'Calling Time on Full Face Black Makeup', www.morrisfed.org.uk, 3 July 2020.

six: Mystery Plays

1 John Gassner, *Medieval and Tudor Drama* (New York, 2000), p. 35.

2 Hetta Elizabeth Howes, 'Medieval Drama and the Mystery Plays', canvas.stmarytxt.edu, 31 January 2018.

3 Ibid.

4 Barry Reay, *Popular Culture in England, c. 1500–1850* (Oxford, 1998), p. 167.

5 Anon, *The Tretise of Miraclis Pleyinge* (*c.* 1380–1425), BL: MS Add 24,202.

6 Michael Billington, '*Everyman* Review – Chiwetel Ejiofor's Rich Sinner Feels Modern Wrath of God', www.theguardian.com, 30 April 2015.

7 Abigail Sparkes, 'Away with the Faeries', www.historytoday.com, 12 December 2018.

8 John Cox, 'The Devil and Society in the English Mystery Plays', *Comparative Drama*, XXVIII/4 (Winter 1994–5), pp. 407–38, p. 407.

9 Ronald Hutton, *Stations of the Sun* (Oxford, 1996), p. 376.

10 Ian Marchant, 'The Pancester Plough Monday Mummer's Play', www.ianmarchant.com, accessed 10 July 2024.

11 William Sandys, *Christmastide, Its History, Festivities and Carols* (London, 1852), p. 152.

12 Peter Millington, 'Who Is the Guy on the Left?', *Traditional Drama Forum*, 6, www.folkplay.info, January 2003.

13 Ibid.

14 Ibid.

15 Henry Gee and William John Hardy, ed., *Documents Illustrative of English Church History, The King's Majesty's Declaration to His Subjects Concerning Lawful Sports to Be Used* [1633] (New York, 1896), pp. 528–32.

16 John Lucas, *Memoranda Book* [*c.* 1712–50] (Ann Arbor, MI, 2006), p. 164.

17 Georgina Boyes, *The Imagined Village: Culture, Ideology and the English Folk Revival* (Manchester, 1993), p. 97.

18 Robert Plot, *Natural History of Staffordshire* (Oxford, 1686), p. 434.

19 Laura Fowell, 'Abbots Bromley Horn Dance', www.facebook.com, 28 March 2023.

20 Joe Bailey, 'Abbots Bromley Horn Dance', www.facebook.com, accessed 21 October 2024.

21 Cecil Sharp, *Sword Dances of Northern Europe* (London, 1950).

22 Ronald Hutton, *Witches, Druids, and King Arthur* (London, 2003), p. 33.

23 Carl Fowell, 'Abbots Bromley Horn Dance', www.facebook.com, accessed 24 October 2024.

24 'The Hunting of the Earl of Rone', www.earl-of-rone.org.uk, accessed 10 July 2024.

25 *Illustrated London News*, 5 January 1856, p. 22.

26 J.R.W. Coxhead, *Olde Devon Customs* (Exmouth, 1957).

27 'The Hunting of the Earl of Rone'.

28 J.L.W. Page, *The Coasts of Devon and Lundy Island* (London, 1895), p. 68.

29 'The Hunting of the Earl of Rone'.

30 Ibid.

31 Ibid.

32 Ron Shuttleworth, 'Why Mummers Need Insurance', www.folkplayarchive.co.uk, 2017.

33 John Crow, www.facebook.com, 3 December 2022.

34 Ibid.

35 Jacqueline Durban, www.facebook.com, 3 December 2022.

36 Bethany North, 'I've Worked Front of House in 40 Theatres – and Audiences Behaved Terribly in All of Them', www.theguardian.com, 23 February 2023.

37 '"Worst Party in Town": Abusive Audiences Force UK Musicals to Tone Down Ads', www.theguardian.com, 14 February 2023.

38 Ibid.

SEVEN: Bonfire Night: Gunpowder, Treason and Plot

1 Antonia Fraser, *The Gunpowder Plot: Terror and Faith in 1605* (London, 1996), p. 207.

2 Francis Herring, *Pietas Pontifica* (London, 1606); John Rhodes, *A Brief Summe of the Treason Intended Against the King & State* (London, 1606); Thomas Taylor, *A Mappe of Rome* (London, 1620).

3 David Cressy, 'The Fifth of November Remembered', in *Myths of the English*, ed. Roy Porter (Cambridge, 1992), pp. 79–80.

4 David Cornforth, 'Saturnalia or Bonfire Night: How "Young Exeter" Celebrated Bonfire Night in the 19th Century', www.exetermemories.co.uk, 2024.

5 'Bonfire Night Provided Another Excuse for a Riot in City Ruled by "the Tyranny of a Mob"', www.news-archive.exeter.ac.uk, 30 October 2018.

6 Todd Grey, *Not One of Us: Individuals Set Apart By Choice, Circumstances, Crowds or the Mob in Exeter, 1451–1952* (Exeter, 2010).

7 Ibid.

8 Ibid.

9 Anita Merritt, 'The Violent and Disorderly Mobs Who Caused Chaos in Exeter on Bonfire Night Are Remembered', www.devonlive.com, 3 November 2018.

10 David Rose, 'Remember, Remember, The Guildford Guy Riots', www.guildford-dragon.com, 28 February 2012.

11 'Guildford Guy Bonfire Riots Sculpture Sparks Row', www.bbc.co.uk, 17 February 2012.

12 Ibid.

13 Ibid.

14 Helen Pidd, 'Police in Many Locations Face Violence and Anti-Social Acts on Bonfire Night', www.theguardian.com, 6 November 2022.

15 Ibid.

16 James Robinson and Dan Sales, 'Boy, 17, Who Died "When He Fell through Greenhouse While Fleeing from Police" after Bonfire Night Yobs Launched Firework Attacks on Officers', www.dailymail.co.uk, 7 November 2022.

17 Ibid.

18 Bang Out of Order Campaign, www.manchesterfire.gov.uk, 21 November 2022.

19 Robinson and Sales, 'Boy, 17, Who Died "When He Fell through Greenhouse While Fleeing from Police"'.

20 Lewes Bonfire Celebrations, www.lewesbonfirecelebrations.com, 21 November 2022.

21 Ibid.

22 Peter Bacon, *The Sussex Advertiser*, 2 November 1847.

23 Lewes Bonfire Celebrations, www.lewesbonfirecelebrations.com, 21 November 2022.

24 Patrick Barlowe and Ellie Crabbe, 'Lewes Bonfire: Liz Truss Takes Centre Stage in Parade', www.theargus.co.uk, 6 November 2022.

25 Lewes Bonfire Celebrations, www.lewesbonfirecelebrations.com.

26 Robert Booth, 'Lewes Bonfire "Blacking Up" Not Racist, Says Zulu Performer', www.theguardian.com, 30 October 2017.

27 Ibid.

28 Ibid.

29 Ibid.

30 Ibid.

31 'Lewes Bonfire Night Parade's "Racist" Costumes to Be Axed', www.bbc.co.uk, 3 November 2017.

32 Robert Booth, 'Lewes Bonfire Festival Sparks Anger with Fresh Blackface Controversy', www.theguardian.com, 1 November 2018.

33 Ibid.

34 Thomas Kuhn, *The Structure of Scientific Revolutions* (Chicago, IL, 1962).

35 'Lewes Bonfire Festival Sparks Anger with Fresh Blackface Controversy'.

36 Ibid.

37 Francesca Fairhead, 'Tradition and Cultural Appropriation in the "Bonfire Capital of the World"', www.varsity.co.uk, 4 November 2021.

38 Louise Maskill, *Sussex Dialect: A Selection of Words and Anecdotes from Around Sussex* (Bodmin, 2012), p. 44.

39 Pete Ansell, in conversation for this book.

40 'A History of Firle Bonfire Society', www.firlebonfire.co.uk.

41 Ibid.

42 Rebecca Ellinor, 'Gypsy Caravan Burned in Village Bonfire', www.theguardian.com, 31 October 2003.

43 Mark Townsend, 'A Burning Issue in the Village', www.theguardian.com, 16 November 2003.

44 Nisha Gopalan, 'Alan Moore Still Knows the Score', *Entertainment Weekly*, www.ohnotheydidn't.livejournal.com, 21 July 2008.

45 Rosie Waites, 'V for Vendetta Masks: Who's Behind Them?', www.bbc.co.uk. 20 October 2011.

46 Tom Lamont, 'Alan Moore – Meet the Man Behind the Protest Mask', www.theguardian.com, 26 November 2011.

EIGHT: All the Fun of the Fair?

1 William Blackstone, *Commentaries on the Laws of England in Four Books*, vol. ii, Book iii (Oxford, 1753), p. 31.

2 Charles Gross, *The Court of Piepowder* (Oxford, 1906), pp. 231–49.

3 '"All the fun of the Fair": A History of Chichester's Oldest Surviving Fair', www.westsussexrecordofficeblog.com, 20 October 2017.

4 Claire Violette Herbeaux, 'Everything You Need to Know about Glastonbury's Tor Fair', www.somersetlive.co.uk, 7 September 2018.

5 Tricia Lynch, comment on '"All the fun of the Fair"', 22 October 2017.

6 Darcus Howe, http://nhcarnival.org, 26 January 2023.

7 Alan Travis, 'After 44 Years Secret Papers Reveal the Truth about Five Nights of Violence in Notting Hill', www.theguardian.com, 24 August 2002.

8 Raune Laslett, http://nhcarnival.org, 26 January 2023.

9 Emma Griffiths, 'Remembering the Notting Hill Riot', www.bbc.co.uk, 25 August 2006.

10 Ibid.

11 Ibid.

12 Sami Quadri, 'Notting Hill Carnival: Questions Rise over Event Amid Safety Concerns', www.standard.co.uk, 5 September 2022.

13 'Calls for Notting Hill Carnival to Be Moved after Two Police Officers Sexually Assaulted', www.news.sky.com, 31 August 2022.

14 Evidence for Equality National Survey, www.ethnicity.ac.uk, 2023.

15 'The Future for Appleby Fair',www.travellerstimes.org.uk, 1 September 2022.

16 Ibid.

17 Sam Smedley, 'Traveller Community Stages Huge Clean-Up in Aftermath of Appleby Horse Fair', www.lancs.live, 16 June 2022.

18 'The Future for Appleby Fair'.

19 Mike Glover, 'Durham Churches Offer Fair-Bound Travellers Sanctuary on Their Land', www.theguardian.com, 29 May 2022.

20 'The Future for Appleby Fair'.

21 'Over 100 UK Festivals Commit to Tackling Sexual Violence', www.aiforg.com, 16 May 2022.

22 Nigel Ayers, 'It's 25 Years Since the Last Stonehenge Free Festival', www.andyworthington.co.uk, 20 June 2009.

23 Jake Stratton-Kent, pamphlet from the Secular Order of Druids, n.d., p. 2.

24 Ayers, 'It's 25 Years Since the Last Stonehenge Free Festival'.

25 Stratton-Kent, pamphlet from the Secular Order of Druids, p. 2.

26 Ayers, 'It's 25 Years Since the Last Stonehenge Free Festival'.

27 Stratton-Kent, pamphlet from the Secular Order of Druids.

28 Ayers, 'It's 25 Years Since the Last Stonehenge Free Festival'.

29 Emma Restall-Orr, 'A View From the Moment', www.druidry.org, 11 February 2020.

30 Mark Hudson, 'The Forgotten Festival – I Was There', www.telegraph.co.uk, 28 June 2004.

31 Ibid.

32 Ibid.

33 Convoy Steve, 'Apres Henge – Convoy to Greenham', www. ukrockfestivals.com/henge-convoy-tales.html, 3 January 2023.

34 Ibid.

35 Douglas Hurd, Hansard Hippy Convoy (New Forest), HC Deb, 3 June 1986, vol. LXLVIII, cc733-9.

36 Cathy Augustine, 'The Battle of the Beanfield: An Important Anniversary in the History of State Brutality', www.counterfire. org, 1 June 2020.

37 Ibid.

38 Richard Jinman, 'The Battle of the Beanfield: The Violent New-Age Traveller Clash With Police at Stonehenge Remembered 30 Years On', www.independent.co.uk, 31 May 2015.

39 Tony Millet, 'A Missed Anniversary: The Battle of the Beanfield and Lord Cardigan's Testimony', www.marlborough.news, 4 June 2015.

40 Alan Lodge, 'Battle of the Beanfield', www.alanlodge.co.uk, 2024.

41 Augustine, 'The Battle of the Beanfield'.

42 Jinman, 'The Battle of the Beanfield'.

43 Mark Hodkinson, 'Rose Brash, 20, Is Led Away By Police at the Battle of the Beanfield, June 1985', www.theguardian.com, 15 January 2016.

NINE: Cheese Rolling

1 '"Did I Lose Any Teeth?": Gloucester Cheese Rolling Event Returns after Pandemic', www.itv.com, 6 June 2022.

2 Ibid.

3 Steven Morris, 'Gloucestershire's Annual Cheese Rolling Cancelled Due to Health and Safety Fears', www.theguardian. com, 12 March 2010.

4 Ibid.

5 Ibid.

6 Martin Holmes, 'Cheese Rolling', www.bbc.co.uk, 13 November 2014.

7 'PETA Writes Letter to Gloucestershire Cheese-Rollers Urging Them to Use Vegan Alternative', www.itv.com, 20 May 2023.

8 Nadeem Badshaw, 'Woman Wins UK Cheese Rolling Race Despite Being Knocked Unconscious', www.theguardian.com, 19 May 2023.

TEN: Street Football

1 '"This murdering play": The Violent Origins of English Football', www.danceshistoricalmiscellany.com, 13 November 2013.

2 Philip Stubbs, *Anatomy of Abuses* (1583), www.quod.lib.umich.edu.

3 Anonymous, 16th century, translated from Old Scots. As quoted in John Fox, *The Ball: Discovering the Object of the Game* (London, 2012).

4 Charles Cotton, 'Burlesque upon the Great Frost' (1683), www.poetryexplorer.net.

5 William Fitzstephen, *Descriptio Nobilissimae Civitatis Londoniae* [*c.* 1174–83] (London, 1772), pp. 45–6.

6 'The World's Most Dangerous Game of Football', www.menshealth.com, 26 July 2016.

7 Ibid.

8 Ibid.

9 Amy Phipps and Samantha Noble, 'Royal Shrovetide Football: Up'ards Win Ancient Ashbourne Game', www.bbc.co.uk, 3 March 2022.

10 'Beginners Guide to Shrovetide Football', www.mutualshoots.com, 7 January 2023.

11 'The World's Most Dangerous Game of Football'.

12 'Beginners Guide to Shrovetide Football'.

13 'The World's Most Dangerous Game of Football'.

14 'Bruising Encounter at Historic Alnwick Ball Game', www.bbc.
    co.uk, 10 February 2016.

15 Bobby Bridge, 'The Truth behind those Atherstone Ball Game
    "Ear" Claims', www.coventrytelegraph.net, 25 February 2020.

16 Ibid.

17 Ibid.

18 Venetia Newall, 'Throwing the Hood at Haxey: A Lincolnshire
    Twelfth-Night Custom', *Folk Life*, XVII/1 (1980), pp. 7–23.

19 Jim Coulson, 'Mad Up North', www.northernlifemagazine.co.uk
    (May–June 2022).

20 'The origin of the Ba'', www.orkneyjar.com, 25 January 2022.

21 Srijandeep Das, 'From Severed Heads to the "Hex on Becks":
    Charting Football's Pagan Past', www.scroll.in, 29 January 2017.

ELEVEN: Up Helly Aa

1 Up-Helly-Aa Information Pack, www.uphellyaa.org, 2023.

2 Ibid.

3 Ronald Hutton, *Stations of the Sun* (Oxford, 1996), p. 43.

4 Up Helly Aa, public bill posted in 2022.

TWELVE: Trick or Treat

1 'Christmas is coming, the geese are getting fat', Roud Folk Song
   Index, no. 12817.

2 'Hallow Evin', *Dictionary of the Scots Language*, www.dsl.ac.uk,
   29 November 2022.

3 John A. Staples, MD, MPH, Candace Yip and Donald A. Redelmeier,
   MD, MSHSR, 'Pedestrian Fatalities Associated With Halloween
   in the United States', www.ncbi.nlm.nih.gov, 30 October 2018.

4 Chris Colin, 'Fighting Fear with Fear', www.salon.com, 21 June
   1999.

5 Rose Eveleth, 'The History of Trick-or-Treating Goes
   Back Centuries', www.smithsonianmag.com, 24 October
   2023.

6 Kevin Mason, 'October 30: The First "Beggar' Night"',
   www.notesoniowa.com, 30 October 2023.

7 Harry Ingham, 'The Unwritten Rules of Trick or Treating
   at Hallowe'en', www.hulldailymail.co.uk, 30 October 2022.

THIRTEEN: Skimmity Riding

1 Thomas Hardy, *The Mayor of Casterbridge* [1886], chapter 36,
   www.cleavebooks.co.uk.

2 Ibid.

3 Ibid.

4 Diana Gardner, 'Skimmity-Riding', www.steepleastonarchive.
   org.uk, 28 August 2022.

5 Ibid.

6 Ibid.

7 Ibid.

8 George Roberts, *History of Lyme Regis* (Lyme Regis, 1834),
   p. 258.

9 Stephen Banks, *Informal Justice in England and Wales, 1760–1914*
   (Martlesham, 2014).

10 Leonard Baker, '"West Country Scum": National Politics, Local
   Ritual and Space in the English South West, *c.* 1820–1832',
   Romance, Revolution and Reform, 1 (April 2019), www.rrjournal.
   com.

11 Ibid.

12 Ibid.

13 Ibid.

14 'The Nominy while Riding the Stang', www.allpoetry.com.

15 Christine Bloxham, *Folklore of Oxfordshire* (Stroud, 2005),
   pp. 60–61.

16 South Wales Police Museum, 'The Rebecca Riots', www.swplive. blob.core.windows.net/wordpress-uploads/10-HN-Rebecca-Riots. pdf, 24 December 2012.

17 Loretta T. Johnson, 'Charivari/Shivaree: A European Folk Ritual on American Plains', *Journal of Interdisciplinary History*, xx/3 (1990), pp. 371–87, p. 379.

18 Le Tintamarre, Cyber Acadie, www.webarchive.org, 15 August 2010.

19 2020 Mississippi Code, Title 97 – Crime, Chapter 3 – Crimes Against the Person §§97-3-87. Threats and intimidation; whitecapping.

FOURTEEN: The Future of Folk Practice

1 Quoted in Andrew Robinson, 'Five COVID Customs Which Emerged During Lockdown', www.theconversation.com, 30 September 2020.

2 Esther Addley, 'Clap for Our Carers', www.theguardian.com, 28 May 2020.

3 Ibid.

4 Robinson, 'Five COVID Customs Which Emerged During Lockdown'.

5 Paul Mullins, 'Spontaneous Mourning and Material Culture: The Archaeology of Roadside Memorials', www.wordpress.com, 24 July 2012.

6 Art Jipson, 'Roadside Memorials in the Community', www.graphics8.nytimes.com

7 Ibid.

8 Alan Dundes, *Interpreting Folklore* (Bloomington, IN, 1980), p. 17.

9 Robert Glenn Howard, 'Electronic Hybridity: The Persistent Processes of the Vernacular Web', *Journal of American Folklore*, CXXI/480 (Spring 2008), pp. 192–218, p. 193.

10 Quoted in Victoria Ward, 'Folklore Is Dying Out Due to Rise of Social Media, National Trust Warns', www.telegraph.co.uk, 7 October 2019.

11 Jacqueline Simpson and Steve Roud, *The Oxford Dictinary of English Folklore* (Oxford, 2000), p. 235.

12 Ibid.

13 Ward, 'Folklore Is Dying Out Due to Rise of Social Media'.

14 Alice Fisher, 'Cool as Folk: Why Britain's Young Rebels Are Embracing Ancient Rites', www.theguardian.com, 12 February 2023.

15 Ibid.

16 Ibid.

17 Alex Merry, 'Boss Morris: The Interview', www.tradfolk.co, 24 February 2022.

Bibliography

Cawte, Edwin, *Ritual Animal Disguise: A Historical and Geographical Study of Animal Disguise in the British Isles*, Folklore Society (Lanham, MD, 1978)

Chambers, E. K., *The Medieval Stage* (Oxford, 1903)

Cooper, Susan, *The Dark Is Rising* (London, 1973)

Dundes, Alan, ed., *The Study of Folklore* (Englewood Cliffs, NJ, 1965)

Elworthy, Frederick Thomas, *Horns of Honour: And Other Studies in the By-Ways of Archaeology* (London, 1900)

Evans, John, *A Tour Through Part of North Wales* (London, 1800)

Frazer, James George, *The Golden Bough: A Study in Comparative Religion* (London, 1890)

Gassner, John, *Medieval and Tudor Drama* (New York, 2000)

Graves, Robert, *The White Goddess* (London, 1948)

Grey, Todd, *Not One of Us: Individuals Set Apart by Choice, Circumstances, Crowds or the Mob in Exeter, 1451–1952* (Exeter, 2010)

Gross, Charles, *The Court of Piepowder* (Oxford, 1906)

Hardy, Thomas, *The Return of the Native* (London, 1878)

—, *The Mayor of Casterbridge* (London, 1886)

—, *The First Countess of Wessex* (London, 1890)

Harrison, Jane Ellen, *Themis: A Study of the Social Origins of Greek Religion* (Cambridge, 1912)

Hutton, Ronald, *Stations of the Sun* (Oxford, 1996)

Murray, Margaret, *The Witch-Cult in Western Europe* (Oxford, 1921)

Nissenbaum, Stephen, *The Battle for Christmas* (New York, 1988)

Sharp, Cecil, *Sword Dances of Northern Europe* (London, 1950)

Strutt, Joseph, *The Sports and Pastimes of the People of England* (London, 1801)

Acknowledgements

The author would like to thank Ronald Hutton, Trevor Jones and
Kari Maund.

Permissions

The author is grateful for permission to quote from interviews held with
Pete Ansell, Nimue Brown, Elizabeth Cruse, Ben Delabane, Jacqueline
Durban, Julia Hawkes-Moore, Ben Jeapes, Daniel McKenzie, Nick
Ford, Marion Pitman, Lynne Tan-Watson.

Index